Family and Succession Law in the Czech Republic

Milana Hrušáková
Lenka Westphalová
Renáta Šínová
Zdeňka Králíčková
Lenka Dobešová

This book was originally published as a monograph in the International Encyclopaedia of Laws/Family and Succession Law.

Founding Editor: Roger Blanpain†
General Editor: Frank Hendrickx
Volume Editor: Walter Pintens

Wolters Kluwer

Published by:
Kluwer Law International B.V.
PO Box 316
2400 AH Alphen aan den Rijn
The Netherlands
E-mail: lrs-sales@wolterskluwer.com
Website: www.wolterskluwer.com/en/solutions/kluwerlawinternational

Sold and distributed by:
Wolters Kluwer Legal & Regulatory U.S.
920 Links Avenue
Landisville, PA 17538
United States of America
E-mail: customer.service@wolterskluwer.com

ISBN 978-94-035-3266-0

e-Book: ISBN 978-94-035-3336-0
web-PDF: ISBN 978-94-035-3376-6

This title is available on www.kluwerlawonline.com

Family and Succession Law in the Czech Republic

The Authors

Prof. JUDr Milana Hrušáková, CSc., after graduating from the Faculty of Law of Masaryk University in Brno and working for many years at the Department of Civil Law there, served as Dean of the Faculty of Law of Palacký University in Olomouc. Currently, she teaches there as a professor of the Department of Private Law and Civil Procedure, especially Family Law. She has significantly contributed to the recodification of family law within the civil code, both in the beginning and in the final part of her work. She is the author of numerous monographs, commentaries, textbooks, essays and national reports.

JUDr Lenka Westphalová, PhD, graduated from the Faculty of Law of Palacký University in Olomouc, where she has been working since her graduation at the Department of Private Law and Civil Procedure. She is currently working as an assistant professor focusing on family law and alternative ways of solving family conflicts. She is the author and co-author of a number of professional studies and monographs. She regularly participates in the European Family Law Symposia held in Regensburg. She is a member of the international editorial board of FamRZ.

JUDr Renáta Šínová, PhD, graduated from the Faculty of Law of Palacký University in Olomouc. She focuses on civil procedural and family law. She works as an assistant professor at the Faculty of Law of UP and as a legal expert at Havel and Partners, s.r.o. She is a co-author of commentaries, textbooks and articles.

The Authors

Prof. JUDr Zdeňka Králíčková, PhD, is a graduate of the Faculty of Law of Masaryk University in Brno. At the Department of Civil Law, she teaches mainly Family Law and runs a course on law against domestic violence. She has also worked as an assistant to a Supreme Court judge and as an advocate. She was a member of the mini-team for family law within the framework of the recodification work on the new Civil Code. Her publications focus mainly on the human rights dimension of family law, issues of parenting, foster care and maintenance. She is the author of several commentaries and textbooks. She is actively involved in a number of international projects, particularly in connection with her membership of the International Society for Family Law (ISFL), the International Academy for the Study of Jurisprudence on the Family (IASJF) and the Turin Common Core of European Private Law.

JUDr Lenka Dobešová, PhD, was born in Brno, the Czech Republic, in 1972 and graduated from the Faculty of Law of Masaryk University in 1995, where she has been working as an assistant and then as a full-time lecturer since 1996. In addition to giving lectures, doing research, and involving herself in publication activities (as an author or a co-author, she has published five books and more than ten articles and papers in journals and specialized publications), she has been engaged in a number of other activities related to legal practice. She was a member of the Civil Code recodification committee of the Ministry of Justice and also worked as an assistant to a Justice of the Constitutional Court (2003–2004). In 2016, she was awarded by the president of Masaryk University as the best teacher of MU. She obtained her PhD for her dissertation entitled ‘Liability for Injury to Health’. Currently, she is a member of the Civil Law Department of the Faculty of Law, MU Brno.

Table of Contents

List of Abbreviations

ABGB	Austrian Civil Code, Allgemeines Bürgerliches Gesetzbuch 1811
CC 1964	Act No. 40/1964 Coll., former Civil Code, effective from 1 April 1964 to 1 December 2013
CC	Act No. 89/2012 Coll., Civil Code, Effective as of 1 January 2014
CCP	Act No. 99/1963 Coll., Civil Procedure Code
CJEU	Court of Justice of the EU
Coll.	Collection of Statutes
CRA	Act No. 301/2000 Coll., Civil Registry Act
ECHR	European Convention on Human Rights
EU	European Union
FC	Act No. 94/1963 Coll., Family Code, Effective from 1 April 1964 to 31 December 2023
I.T.Coll.	Collection of International Treaties
RP	Act No. 115/2006 Coll., on Registered Partnership
SCP	Act No. 292/2013 Coll., Act on Special Court Proceedings

List of Abbreviations

Preface

Fortunae suae unus quique faber – We all make our own fates

Treatment of relations in marriage and family is of great interest for both laymen and specialists. No wonder, as each of us lives in a family, we marry, bring up children, look after them, take care of our parents and have our own visions on what family is and how it should work. As everybody lives in a different family, his/her visions of family, its functioning, way of bringing up children – both his/her own and those 'acquired' by marriage – differ as a result of the person's previous good and bad experiences. Thus, family and marriage are obscured by a number of myths, being a source of a number of more or less militant prejudices. All this is reflected in the respective legislation.

The fact that the Family Law Act was in force for over thirty years (including eight years after the fall of communism) with no substantial amendments proved its relative vitality and practicability due greatly to its provisions drawn up in a very general manner, as well as the difficulty of finding an appropriate expression of necessary (and also not so very necessary, as viewed in the whole context) changes that would be widely and generally supported by specialists as well as laymen.

After numerous reversals involving also the concepts of the new legislation, the substantial and extensive reform was eventually concluded to be operative on 1 August 1998. A number of provisions are marked by pervading changes concerning not only the subject matter itself but also conceptual and theoretical novelties which considerably affect our habitual manners in interpreting the particular provisions, as well as the common ideas and myths on family, marriage and children. A number of new provisions will prove to be efficient and long-lasting only after a time.

However, family and its inner relations seem to be rather resistant to the attempts of legislators. Namely, Czech family law withstood the many transformation efforts of socialist legislators. Nevertheless, even today, we can encounter undesirable consequences of originally well-meant stipulations.

The system of socialist law was based on the concept of single, rather independent, branches of law. The traditional division of law into private law and public law had been rejected. In this view, family law was deemed an independent branch of law, closely linked with civil law and administrative law.

The extinction of communism brought an end to the concept of separate legal branches, and the jurisprudence returned to a precise distinction of private and public law. Family law is commonly considered a part of private law, and within the legislative activities involving the new civil law under preparation, it is deemed a part of the prospective Civil Code.

However, it is not possible to disregard a number of specific features distinguishing relations among family members from other private law relations.

The essence of family law relations implies one of its most significant characteristics, serving to support their substance and efficiency, that is, the existence of a certain personal or emotional bond. This personal bond is of such significance that, in some cases, it is a prerequisite of the existence of a legal relation itself. No one will marry (except if the reason to marry is evading the law or acquiring a status of permanent residence in the country) without a positive emotional bond towards the other partner (or to his/her property at least).

In some legal relations among family members, such emotional bond arises, regardless of any legal regulation, first of all, based on kinship, while with other 'artificial' family relations (relations in substitute family care), these emotional bonds are created only in the course of existence of such relation and they are prerequisites of their proper functioning. (For this reason, for example, adopters must have a child in their care for three months prior to adoption itself to be able to test whether the emotional bonds commonly arising between natural parents and children may arise here too.)

However, the non-existence of mutual emotional links between subjects does not necessarily mean an extinction of the resulting respective legal relation. The fact that an emotional bond between married spouses no longer exists does not mean that the marriage becomes extinct as well or that the court would be bound to dissolve such marriage by divorce.

In some cases, non-existence of emotional bonds between subjects results in the necessity of interference by the state, that is, when the respective legal relation ceases to fulfil its purpose as a result of impaired or non-existing personal emotional bonds.

Of course, no emotional bond is required to conceive a child – a simple ability to do so is sufficient here – but what legal consequences it brings! If the relations of a parent (parents) towards the child are expressly negative, they reflect, as a rule, insufficient child care and instigate necessary intervention by the state.

Emotional bonds are evidently of no importance in civil law relations; tenancy may and will normally work without the landlord having an emotional bond with the tenant; a contract of sale is not made among subjects because of affection between them, but because they each want to satisfy certain needs.

Family law, in its essence, is aimed first of all to protect a weaker counterpart, namely, a child. Child protection is a matter not only of family law in a traditional, narrower sense, but also of a child being granted protection by courts and also by other state authorities that are bound to safeguard the child and protect him/her not only from adverse influences but also from their own unworthy parents.

In the Czech Republic, the law of succession is traditionally deemed an integral part of civil law, thus making it a part of the Civil Code. Contrary to family law, it is not really favoured by students, who tend to find succession law not very interesting and a rather marginal matter. (Traditionally, it is placed at the very end of a large volume of civil law textbooks too.) They feel young and immortal, considering succession law an issue for notaries and very old people (over 45 years of age).

When, after graduating from the Faculty of Law in Brno in the autumn of 1975, I started to work in the Faculty as a junior teacher, I supposed I would concentrate on commercial law for some years and become a legal practitioner later. I had no idea everything would prove otherwise, and I would remain the Faculty teacher involved in family law, that would become not only my beloved specialization but also my great hobby. It is a great honour for me to give readers from all over the world essential and overall information on Czech family and succession law.

Hopefully, this book will help in understanding the essential principles of law and subsequent amendments, existing and applied in a small country in the centre of Europe upon its 'comeback' into European civilization.

I would like to express my gratitude to Dr Anna Lysa from the Faculty of Law, Comenius University, Bratislava, for translating this book into intelligible English, and to my secretary, Ms Gabriela Uhlirova, for her indispensable help in the preparation and typing of this book.

The contents of the books are based on the legal situation in the country on 1 January 2002, as reflected in the book.

Milana Hrušáková
Brno
February 2002

Since 2002, a lot has happened in Czech Family Law. The main questionable domain that has been changed is the new Act on Registered Partnerships (RP). This was discussed for a long time, and there were several proposals in the last ten years that did not pass through parliament. However, in 2006, parliament adopted the act, which was not perfect, but at least regulates the status consequences of the relationship of same-sex couples.

Since 9 January 2004, the child's delivery with the withheld identity of the mother was made possible. This regulation, placed in administrative law, is very problematic and involves a lot of complications, especially with respect to the conception of status rights.

The next problematic area is the regulation about domestic violence. This happened slowly and in steps. First, this social phenomenon was fought by criminal law, and lately, the private law has reacted.

A few revisions were made in the regulation of artificial insemination, paternity and adoption. With respect to international parental child abduction in the Czech Republic, we have been a Member State since 3 January 1998, but the enforcement of the right of one parent was very slow. That is why we made new provisions in this area.

The content of the changes is based on the legal situation in the country on 1 January 2011.

Lenka Westphalová
Olomouc
January 2011

Much has changed in Czech family law since 2011. A major change is the adoption of the new Civil Code. The Civil Code (also known as the New Civil Code to distinguish it from the previous Civil Code) is a law that was adopted by the Parliament of the Czech Republic and published in the Collection of Laws under the number 89/2012 Coll. This Civil Code recodified Czech private law and replaced the previous Czechoslovak Civil Code of 1964 and other laws, including the Family Act and the Act on Ownership of Flats. It became effective on 1 January 2014.

There have been several attempts over the years to fundamentally change family law as part of the recodification of civil law. The beginnings of the recodification work on the current Civil Code were linked to the Ministry of Justice's Substantive Plan (No. 2623/00-L of 29 January 2001), which implied an attempt to create a European continental civilist concept of family law. The family law rules have been incorporated into the second part of the paragraphed working version of the draft recodified private law code (cf. Eliáš, K., Zuklínová, M. Principles and foundations of the new private law code. Prague: Linde Praha, 2001). However, a relatively long time has passed since the substantive plan of the new Civil Code was approved. The original version of the paragraphed text of the second part of the forthcoming Civil Code has gone through many peripeties and an extensive commenting procedure. In particular, there was a heated debate on religious marriage, registered same-sex partnerships, the reconsideration of paternity arrangements, the concept of adoption and surrogacy in general, and last but not least, the controversial issue of surrogacy. The collapse of the government in 2009 prevented the adoption of the new draft Civil Code.

Under the new government that emerged from the 2010 elections, the work of the previous recodification commission was built upon. It was approved by the Chamber of Deputies on 9 November 2011. The Senate debated the proposal in plenary on 25 January 2012. On 20 February 2012, the President of the Republic signed the law and the new Civil Code was subsequently published in the Collection of Laws (Act No. 89/2012 Coll.).[1] This completed the legislator's efforts to recodify family law, represented in particular by the Family Act and the Civil Code dating back to the 1960s. These codes were repealed with effect from 1 January 2014.[2]

The Explanatory Memorandum to the Civil Code speaks of the need for discontinuity with the regulation, which has its roots in the law of the 1950s or even the late 1940s and which has gradually replaced many traditional institutions. For family law, however, the new Civil Code represents more of a continuity. This is mainly due to the fact that substantial changes in family law have already been made by the significant amendment of its predecessor, the Family Law Act, in 1998. Much has also changed due to the new view of family law by the Constitutional Court, not only in terms of the actual text of the law but especially in terms of its interpretation and application. However, it cannot be overlooked that there are also changes in family law, as enshrined in the second part of the Civil Code. First of all, it should be stressed that the reintroduction of family law into the Civil Code entails the need to work with the entire Code. This presupposes not only knowledge of the very important general part, referring in particular to the foundations, values and rules of interpretation, but also an understanding of the new concept and content of many of the institutes incorporated into other parts of the Civil Code.

1. For this, *see* Eliáš, K., *The New Civil Code in the Collection of Laws*, Právní rozhledy 2012, No. 7, pp. 229 ff.
2. English version available: chrome-extension://efaidnbmnnnibpcajpcglclefindmkaj/http://obcanskyzakonik.justice.cz/images/pdf/Civil-Code.pdf.

We consider the incorporation of matrimonial property law and matrimonial housing law, including special provisions for protection against domestic violence, into matrimonial law and the new content of a number of provisions to be very significant. In particular, the issue of the protection of the family home and the usual furnishings of the family household reflects the desire of the main drafters of the new Code to achieve comprehensiveness and to follow European standards. As regards other innovations, especially in terms of content, let us mention the new concept of parental responsibility inspired by the Principles of European Family Law and the new concept of the institution of adoption of a minor incompetent child, reflecting international conventions. A completely new institution is the adoption of an adult, which follows traditions.

In general, the legislator was faced with the difficult legal and political task of reconciling civilist traditions, conservative approaches to the family and, on the contrary, completely liberal views and attitudes. The result of the new legislation is thus more of a compromise.

Since 2014, the Civil Code has undergone partial changes, only some of which have affected family law, such as Act No. 460/2016 Coll., which affects dependent work of minor children, Act No. 192/2021 Coll., which attempts to mitigate the impact of debt payment on so-called child debtors, Act No. 414/2023 Coll., which amended in particular the Act on registry offices and, in this context, some institutes of family law.

The present monograph, Family Law, takes into account the state of family law and succession law in the Czech Republic as of 1 January 2024.

Lenka Westphalová
Olomouc
January 2024

As of 1 January 2025, one change has taken place in Czech family law that fundamentally alters the status of same-sex unions. Although there was an initial push for marriage for all, this change was not accepted, and a compromise solution was passed in Parliament, which introduces another union alongside marriage and registered partnerships, the Civil Code partnership. In particular, it has a different name, which was important to certain groups of Members of Parliament. Furthermore, joint adoption of children is excluded, but successive adoption is allowed. So there has been some equalisation of obligations and rights, but some exceptions remain.

The publication has been updated to 1 April 2025.

Lenka Westphalová
Olomouc April 2025

General Introduction

§1. General Background of the Country (Demographic Data)

I. Introduction

1. The origin of the Czech State should be dated to the rise of the first state-like formation in the territory – the Great Moravian Empire (833–906). The rise of the Czech State, originating from a long-term uniting process of tribes under the rule of the House of Premysl, has been dated to the year 995 AD, and in a short time, the Czech State had extended to the Moravian territory.

The Czech State lost its independence with the succession of the House of Habsburg to the Czech throne in 1526.

2. As a result of World War I, the conflicts within the Habsburg monarchy became acute. In its course, the visions of an essential change of the Czech State within the Habsburg monarchy were outlined, resulting eventually in a demand for an independent Czech State. It was the Czechoslovak National Council, founded in Paris in 1916, headed by T.G. Masaryk, E. Benes and M.R. Stefanik, that became the bearer of this idea. By the end of the same year, the National Committee was founded as a representative body of the domestic political scene. The National Committee was purposefully preparing to take over the power in the Czech lands the instant the Austrian-Hungarian Empire fell.

During the Pittsburgh (Pennsylvania, USA) negotiations in May 1918, attended by T.G. Masaryk, an agreement among the representatives of Czech and Slovak immigrants was arrived at, implying an approval of the political programme of the Czechoslovak National Council residing in Paris and striving for the creation of an independent state of Czechoslovakia. The newly arising state was to adopt a republican and a democratic constitution.

Under the Pittsburgh Treaty, Slovakia was promised an administration, an Assembly and a judiciary of its own; the Slovak language was to become an official language in schools and public life within the territory of Slovakia.

Reacting to the general strike of 14 October 1918, T.G. Masaryk delivered President Wilson a so-called Washington Declaration (prepared in Paris) on 18 October 1918, containing a declaration of the independence of Czechoslovakia.

The rise of Czechoslovakia itself as an independent state was declared on 28 October 1918. Tomas Garrigue Masaryk was elected the first president of the Czechoslovak Republic.

Based on the Saint Germain Peace Treaty of 10 September 1919, Austria, in addition to others, acknowledged the state independence of Czechoslovakia. With some exceptions, Czechoslovakia was confirmed to be constituted by the Czech and Moravian historical lands with a part of Silesia, as well as by the territory of Slovakia. Under this peace treaty, Sub-Carpathian Russia was made part of Czechoslovakia too.

3. The Munich 'Treaty' among Germany, Italy, France and Great Britain, leaving out Czechoslovakia as a party, signed on the night of 29–30 September 1938, brought about an actual end to the independence (sovereignty) of Czechoslovakia, as on its basis, the regions bordering the Czechoslovak frontiers (altogether over 41,000 km^2) were broken away and annexed by Germany, Hungary and Poland. On 14 March 1939, an independent Slovak state was declared, the rest of the historical Czech lands were occupied by Nazi Germany on 15 March 1939, and the Protectorate of Bohemia and Moravia was declared on 16 March 1939.

4. The Yalta Conference in February 1945 left Czechoslovakia in the Soviet Union's sphere of interest. Under the military pressure of the Red Army in November 1944, Sub-Carpathian Russia (subsequently called Transcarpathian Ukraine) seceded from the state unit of the Czechoslovak Republic and applied to be part of the Union of the Soviet Socialist Republics (USSR). After difficult negotiations, this became a reality based on a treaty between the Czechoslovak Republic and the Soviet Union.

The post-war enthusiastic restoration of the economy destroyed by war was reflected in the 1946 elections, in which the Communist Party of Czechoslovakia proved a winner. A constitutional crisis in February 1948 (resignation of ministers appointed by other parties) culminated in the taking over of state powers by the communists.

Upon adopting the new Constitution of 1960, declaring socialism to be built up and established in Czechoslovakia, the name of the country was changed to the Czechoslovak Socialistic Republic.

Gradual easement in the political climate led to an effort to reform the rigid Communist Party in the spring of 1968 (the Prague Spring 1968). This democratic process was held up during the occupation of Czechoslovakia by the Soviet Union on 21 August 1968.

5. One of the outcomes of the Prague Spring was that a new federative system of the state was established.[3] The previous Unitarian state was changed into a 'federative state of two equal brotherly nations, the Czechs and the Slovaks'; thus, the Czechoslovak Socialist Republic was further constituted by the Czech Socialist Republic and the Slovak Socialist Republic based on the principle of equality. The legislature was either exclusively federal (e.g., currency, foreign policy, national defence) or that of the republics, and family law and civil law fell within the powers of federal authorities.

3. Constitutional Act No. 143/1968 Coll., on the Czechoslovak Federation.

6. 17 October 1989 (the so-called Velvet Revolution) has become a symbol of the fall of the communist system in Czechoslovakia as well as the rise of the changes to come, of the political system based on free competing of political parties within political pluralism, gradual creation of an economic system arising from the same legal content and protection of property ownership, free entrepreneuring and market economy values, and gradual approximation to the West-European structures.

In addition to a rather simple change of an official name of both republics (the word 'socialist' was omitted) after difficult disputes in 1990, the names of the states were changed into the Czech and Slovak Federative Republics.

As a result of the June 1992 election outcome and negotiations between the Czech and Slovak counterparts in the Federation, an agreement on the extinction of the common state was arrived at, and on 1 January 1993, two independent republics were created, the Czech Republic and the Slovak Republic. Constitutional and other acts of law and other provisions effective on the day of the extinction of the Czech and Slovak Federative Republic in the territory of the Czech Republic remained in force.[4]

II. Demography

7. The Czech Republic is an inland country, lying in the central part of Europe, in the middle of the temperate zone of the northern hemisphere. It has an area of 78,866 square km, with a population in the year 2023 of 10,880,000 people and a population density of 133 inhabitants per square km. The country borders Poland (761 km), Germany (810 km), Austria (466 km) and Slovakia (251 km).

The Czech Republic is divided into ninety-one administrative districts. Before 1 January 2000, there were eight regions – higher territorial administrative units in the country, including the region of the capital city of Prague. Since 1 January 2000, a new territorial set-up has been in force, with the existing districts grouped to make up fourteen new regions.

The capital city of Prague had in the year 2023 1,357,000 inhabitants.

8. The nature of a contemporary Czech family and the related demographic data have been significantly influenced by the family policy developing since the early fifties and linked with the basic aims and ideals of socialism. However, these ideals were realized in practice in a distorted way, as their bringing into existence was limited, besides others, by the country's economic potential and its 'directively' managed economy.

9. The main aim of family policy in the fifties was the liberation of women, intending to make them fully equal – politically, socially and economically.

This emancipation was formally realized at the level of the law, not, however, in practice. For women, it brought about new problems, failing to be accompanied by

4. Constitutional Act No. 4/1993 Coll., on Measures Related to the Extinction of the Czech and Slovak Federative Republic.

an appropriate development of service industry and other prerequisites. Emancipation of women through their full employment, including mothers with young children, appeared to be an ideal solution to resolve emancipation problems not merely for the state and party authorities but also for the women themselves.

The social function of the family was transferred to state institutions. In this respect, 'success' came rather soon, namely, in introducing institutional facilities providing children's care, their upbringing and leisure time activities. However, no institution may fully make up for the roles of mother and family in having a child at a very young age. The slogan that 'institutional care is always better than a failing family' was slowly given up only in the early seventies, along with the discovery of the so-called deprivation syndrome of children brought up, from birth, in children's homes. The growth of the demands upon children of older age groups, namely, in school education, has caused the family to take over more and more social functions; however, under the conditions in which it was no longer able to carry them out. Still, the families were blamed for the defective phenomena in children's and young people's behaviour, with respect to this situation.

10. In spite of realizing a rather extensive housing policy, families' problems regarding somewhere to live remained. Since 1990, insufficient policy in this respect has caused the housing situation to remain a decisive factor of natality behaviour, and, however, it has restricted the possibilities of children living with parents and being taken care of by them.

11. In spite of formally promoted education and upbringing leading to a responsible marriage and parenthood, regarding rather liberal provisions concerning abortions, the number was growing dangerously. In comparison to other European countries, an extremely high number of births given by women around 18 years of age was typical for Czechoslovakia. Along with all the above-mentioned circumstances and an overall climate in the society, that is, impossibility to select a different lifestyle from a family one, this fact led to so-called cumulation of life starts, that is, concurrent starting of economic activity, marital and parental lives, with all the problems related arising (including economic dependence on parents, housing problems, insufficient social maturity and a resulting high divorce rate in the first three years of marriage).

The decision to get married immediately following the completion of education and a compulsory start of first employment (for men, after finishing their compulsory basic army service) was essentially the first and often the only free life decision for a long time to come. An insufficient economic security of the new family was made up for by an indisputable belief that the paternalistic state (and the parents) would look after the new family. Preferring marriage, at a young age, to any other form of cohabitation led to a high marriage rate and a very low average age of marrying (20–23 years for women).

The relationship between marrying and the birth of the first child was quite apparent. Referring to sociologists' surveys, about 51% of married women were already pregnant. The number of these women decreased with age growth approximately from 80% in marriages up to 17 years of age to 43% for women getting married after 24–25 years of age. For women marrying after their 26th year, the percentage increased a little (40%). Since the seventies, pregnancy of brides was no longer considered a violation of societal standards, being often 'included' in the life plans of single women.

12. The number of divorces between 1919 and 1939 ranged around 4,500 divorces a year. After the Family Law Act was adopted in 1949, the divorce rate was expected to grow rapidly, and in this way, the problem of marriages being dead or non-functioning for many years, based entirely on property interests, was expected to be resolved, with the divorce rate decreasing afterwards. Only the first expectation came true, and the number of divorces following the Family Law Act adoption almost doubled. For the years 1920–1924, the statistics yearbook stated the yearly average of 4,658 divorces (legal termination of marriage); the average for the years 1950–1954 was as many as 10,535 divorces a year. The divorce rate thus grew rapidly not to drop any more, and by the early nineties, it was growing almost linearly.

The divorce rate curve stopped increasing only in 1990, after reaching a historical peak of 32,055 divorces a year. In 1991 and 1992, a slight decrease in divorce rate was noted (29,366 divorces in 1991 and 28,572 divorces in 1992), and then the number of divorces started to grow slightly, arriving at a peak in 1998.

The decrease of the divorce rate in the early nineties might be a result of feelings of uncertainty related to fundamental social changes, but it was also a result of growing numbers of lawsuits in this period (namely a great impact of restitution disputes and many experienced judges leaving the court practice), causing a considerably longer time-period needed for court proceedings.

The almost incredible number of divorces following 1998 (in 1999, a 'mere' 23,657 married couples were divorced) did not mean that married spouses did not wish to get divorced anymore; rather, it was a result of a substantial change in divorce rules, accompanied by an overall extension of divorce proceedings in cases of spouses with minor children.

13. Statistics and various sociological surveys have proved that the divorce rate differs in various regions. It is not surprising that the lowest divorce rate in the long term has been found in agricultural regions and in typical religious regions (e.g., South Moravia). However, large cities with a considerable population migration (and a number of tempting opportunities) are, in the long term, typical of their high divorce rate.

It often happens that even having several minor children does not prevent people from getting divorced. Divorce judges face very nasty disputes on placing children into the custody of one of the parents, but all the more, they encounter a strange phenomenon when neither parent is genuinely interested in the child being placed in his/her custody.

14. Unlike the divorce rate, the marriage rate began to decrease significantly since the early nineties. Along with it, the number of children that have been born decreased in spite of the fact that the persons born in the populous years have attained their fertile age. More optimistic prognoses explain this fact by putting off marriage and the birth of the first child to a later age, as nowadays, young people have the chance to travel, study abroad, etc. At the same time, the number of non-marital spouses cohabiting as well as the number of children born out of wedlock have been growing significantly. If in the era of socialism, no more than 7%–10% of children were born out of wedlock, in 1996, over 15% of the children born were born out of wedlock and at present this number ranges around 50%.

§2. Historical Background of Family and Succession Law

I. Family Law

15. After the rise of an independent Czechoslovak Republic on 28 October 1918, by means of the so-called reception rule,[5] the previous civil law effective in the territory of the former Austrian-Hungarian Empire was taken over. Marital and family relations in the territory of the contemporary Czech Republic were stipulated by the Austrian Civil Code, adopted Allgemeines Bürgerliches Gesetzbuch (ABGB) of 1811, as later amended.

Family law was stipulated under considerable influence of canon law, as by the sixteenth century, the Roman Catholic Church had enjoyed exclusive power and legislation in marital and family matters. The Civil Code was generally based on a religious principle, and thus, marriage dissolution was possible only for non-Catholic marriages.

16. From the very beginning, the new state legislature had to face the serious problem of reform in marital and family relations, shaken by war events. How urgent the need to reform these relations was is apparent from the fact that the very first bill introduced on the proposal of Dr Boucek in the so-called Revolutionary National Assembly in its first session on 14 November 1918 concerned a marital law reform.

Shortly after the rise of the CSR, a new regulation of marital relations was under preparation. As compared to the initial enthusiastic approaches, the so-called Marriage Amendment of 1919[6] was considerably compromising. It stipulated newly made marriages, legal obstacles to marriage, and divorce.

The Marriage Amendment had introduced, in addition to a church wedding, an option of a civil wedding as well as the possibility of divorce as a legal termination of marriage, regardless of the religion of the spouses, and retained the earlier institute of marriage separation (*separatio a mensa et thora*) which, however, did not have the effects of legal termination of marriage, as through granting marriage separation only did the duty of spouses to cohabit became extinct.

Legal rules for divorce were rather complex. So-called absolute grounds for divorce were given under the Amendment; however, they also recognized so-called relative grounds (irresistible aversion and breakdown of marital relations). The proceedings were complex, and in some cases, a separation suit had to be filed prior to petitioning for divorce.

5. Act No. 11/1918 Coll.
6. Act No. 320/1919 Coll.

Relations between spouses and between parents and children were based on the principle of the superior position of the man in matrimony and family. The marital father was granted so-called parental power. If a marital father was not alive or deprived of his paternal power, a guardian had to be appointed for the children. The AGBG principally distinguished between children born in and out of wedlock in questions like parental power, performance, duty to maintain, succession law, etc.

17. In 1928, a new regulation of adoption was passed.[7] It was based on a contractual principle, and its main purpose was not to provide for childcare but rather to secure property transfer. Therefore, it was possible to adopt an adult person, even a married woman (with her husband's consent). Property interests of the adoptive parent's other children might not be challenged by adoption.

18. State power taken over by the Communist Party in February 1948 resulted not only in adopting a new constitution but also a new regulation of family law. The Family Law Act[8] separated stipulating family relations from the Civil Code for a long time. At the same time, new legislation on registries and on using and changing names and surnames was adopted.[9] A year later, the new Civil Code and Civil Procedure Code became operative.[10]

19. Separating legal regulations of family law relations from civil law relations was a technical measure influenced mainly by the Soviet law of the time. Also, an effort to regulate family relations in a new manner, as relations of a typically personal nature, separate from proprietary civil law relations, and thus to emphasize their socialist character, free from property aspects important in the previous legislation, played an important role.

20. The Family Law Act arose from the ideals embedded in the Constitution of 9 May 1948. It stipulated equality of men and women in marriage and family, with the children born in and also out of wedlock made equal. The concept of marriage as a contractual relationship was disregarded, and marriage was made upon an affirmation of spouses on marrying before a national committee. Thus, the form of obligatory civil marriage was stipulated. The terms for a rise in valid marriages were essentially simplified.

Also, marriage dissolution was considerably simplified. The old institute of separation was repealed, as well as the old concept of the divorce institute. Marriage was terminated by divorce based on an objective principle – the breakdown of relations between the spouses. This objective principle was modified by the principle of a breakdown caused by one of the spouses' fault, namely in case of granting a divorce and its legal consequences. Married spouses could not be divorced without consent

7. Act No. 52/1928 Coll.
8. Act No. 265/1949 Coll., Family Law Act operative on 1 Jan. 1950.
9. Act No. 268/1949 Coll., on Registries, operative on 1 Jan. 1950, Act No. 55/1950 Coll., on Using and Changing Names and Surnames operative on 7 Jul. 1950.
10. Act No. 141/1950 Coll., Civil Code operative on 1 Jan. 1951, Act No. 142/1950 Coll., Civil Procedure Code operative on 7 Jan. 1951.

granted by the so-called exclusively faultless spouse. If so petitioned by both spouses, the court could omit the fault to be rendered in the verdict.

Newly stipulated were also property relations between spouses on the principle of the so-called legal property community with an option of contractual modifications.

An institute of parental power was revoked in relations between children and parents, and for the parents, the parental power was introduced instead. Parents were also bound to administer the child's property with due care.

21. Shortly after adopting the Family Law Act, a discriminatory law stipulating marriages with aliens was passed.[11] Under this law, to marry a person other than a Czechoslovak citizen was possible only on approval of the Ministry of Home Affairs or an authority empowered by it, without which no such marriage might arise. This law was revoked only by a new family law in 1964.

22. The Family Law Act was amended twice in the course of its operation. The impossibility of a married couple to divorce against the will of the exclusively faultless spouse led, in practice, to a number of so-called dead marriages failing to fulfil their social functions. Therefore, this provision was modified in the sense that divorce could be exceptionally granted even against the will of the exclusively faultless spouse if the marriage, which had entirely and irrevocably broken down, had not been fulfilling its social functions for a long time.[12]

An essential change in adoption legislation was brought about by the Second Amendment to the Act.[13] So-called irrevocable adoption was provided for here, along with the adopters to be recorded in the birth register instead of the natural parents.

23. Following the rise of the Czechoslovak Republic, the protection of minor children under public law was stipulated in the legislation on protection of children placed in strangers' care, and of illegitimate children.[14] The protection was provided to all children below 14 who could be admitted by strangers into their care only upon the approval of a relevant state authority. Special attention was paid to Gypsy children.[15]

During the operation of the Family Law Act, the protection of minor children under public law was stipulated by separate legislation.[16]

24. In relation to the adoption of the new Constitution in 1960, proclaiming the victory of socialism in Czechoslovakia, all previous essential codes of law underwent substantial changes. Thus, a new legislation on family matters (the Family

11. Act No. 59/1952 Coll., on Marrying Aliens.
12. Legal Measure of the National Assembly Board No. 61/1955 Coll., imposing modified divorce rules. Lawfulness of this regulation is very dubious.
13. Act No. 15/1958 Coll., on Modified Adoption Rules.
14. Act No. 256/1921 Coll., on Protection of Children in Strangers' Care and of Illegitimate Children.
15. Act No. 117/1927 Coll., on Gypsy Children.
16. In this respect, namely Act No. 69/1952 Coll., on Social and Legal Protection of Children must be mentioned.

Code), the Civil Code, as well as the Civil Procedure Code were adopted. All these regulations became operative on 1 April 1964, and as subsequently and essentially amended mainly in the nineties, they are operative even now.[17]

25. A substantial change was brought about by the newly stipulated family law, which transferred property rights between spouses back to the new Civil Code. The previous legal property community was replaced by rather fragmented stipulations on property relations between spouses, with a newly introduced provision regarding the undivided co-ownership of spouses as the basis.

Socialist jurisprudence gave up distinguishing private and public law. This was also reflected in the Family Code in a part, named 'Participation of the society in performing parental rights and obligations', which contained the possible interventions of the state in family relations, promoting the child's interests and welfare, that is, protection of children under public law.

Shortly after November 1989, voices began to be heard calling for an immediate amendment of the Family Code, which was considered outdated and out of date. In June 1992, the principles for the amendment of the Family Law were submitted to the then Federal Government. In the meantime, however, at the last session of the Federal Assembly before the elections, an initiative proposal of the deputies (originally a proposal of the Slovak National Council, which the Federal Government, after discussion, refused to submit to the Federal Assembly because of factual errors) was adopted very quickly, without much discussion and deliberation, which regulated only the ecclesiastical form of marriage without touching the regulation of other family law relations (Act No. 234/1992 Coll.).

The new government resulting from the 1996 elections changed the concept of regulation, and it was decided to amend the Family Code. Before the Government's draft amendment to the Family Code was submitted to Parliament, early elections were on the horizon. Eventually, an initiative proposal by MPs was adopted in 1998 as a so-called major amendment to the Family Code, the basis of which was all previous government proposals (Act No. 91/1998 Coll.).[18] This important amendment to the Family Code explicitly established non-existent marriages (§17a of the Family Code); significantly affected the legal regulation of divorce, allowing in particular so-called uncontested divorce (§24a of the Family Code) and divorce with a so-called hardness clause (§24b of the Family Code), newly regulated parental responsibility, including the possibility of its partial granting to the minor parent of the child (§§31 et seq. of the Family Code), institution of guardianship (§78 of the Family Code), expressly regulated maternity (§50a of the Family Code) and the protection of the so-called potential father (§54(1), §70a of the Family Code); brought the institution of adoption closer to international conventions (cf. in particular §68 and 68a of the Family Code), improved the regulation of maintenance, in particular

17. Act No. 94/1963 Coll., Family Code was significantly changed by Act No. 91/1998 Coll. Act No. 40/1964 Coll., Civil Code was significantly changed by Act No. 509/1991 Coll. Act No. 99/1963 Coll., Civil Procedure Code was significantly changed by Act No. 30/2000 Coll.
18. Haderka, J., *On the Origin and Basic Problems of the 1998 Amendment to the Family Act*, Právní praxe 1998, No. 5.

by replacing the consumer character of maintenance with the right to an equal standard of living among many subjects (cf. §86 and 86a, §§92 and 93 of the Family Code), by extending the property rights of the unwed mother or her right to maintenance for two years (§95 of the Family Code), etc.

Subsequently, the long-prepared and much-awaited Act on Social and Legal Protection of Children was adopted (Act No. 359/1999 Coll., with effect from 1 April 2000). Furthermore, certain laws were amended in connection with the adoption of the Act on Social and Legal Protection of Children (Act No. 360/1999 Coll.). Those provisions of the Family Code which are of a public law nature and regulate the activities of child social protection bodies were removed from the Family Act and incorporated into the new Act on Child Social Protection. The Family Code was limited to regulating the intervention of the court in family law relations. In this context, the Act on Foster Care (Act No. 50/1973 Coll.) was also repealed, and the basic regulation of the institution of foster care was incorporated into the Family Act (§45a to 45d of the Family Code). Subsequently, a new registry law was adopted (Act No. 301/2000 Coll., on registers, names and surnames and amending certain related acts, which entered into force on 1 July 2001). This amended partly the Family Code in the provisions governing marriage in the form of a civil marriage.

There were also other partial changes. A controversial law on so-called clandestine births (Act No. 422/2004 Coll.) was adopted on the proposal of a group of MPs. The explanatory memorandum to the Act shows an attempt to create conditions to reduce the number of induced abortions, prevent the murder of a newborn child by the mother and prevent cases of child abandonment. It is scandalous that such a serious interference with status rights, which have their basis in private law, has been carried out by amending public law norms, without careful consideration of the legal consequences of such an amendment. The Act cited did not amend the Family Law, which regulated the creation of maternity by dicta: The mother of the child is the woman who gave birth to the child (§50a of the Family Code).[19] Another law, resulting from a parliamentary initiative, is the Registered Partnership Act (Act No. 115/2006 Coll.) (RP).

This was followed by the adoption of new health regulations, regulating, for example, clandestine births or artificial insemination (Act No. 372/2011 Coll., on health services and conditions of their provision, and Act No. 373/2011 Coll., on specific health services).

The ruling of Constitutional Court No. 405/2009 on the repeal of §57(1) of the Family Code in its original wording, which established a six-month denial period for denying the paternity of the mother's husband, was followed by a significant amendment to the Family Code, which regulated the denial period in a new way and also specified the right of denial of the Supreme State Prosecutor (Act No. 84/2012 Coll.).

In 2012, a very significant amendment to the Act on Social and Legal Protection of Children (Act No. 401/2012 Coll.) was also adopted, which amended the Family Act, in particular with regard to the entrustment of the custody of a child by a person other than a parent, foster care, institutional care and adoption.

---

19. For criticism *see* Hrušáková, M. & Králíčková, Z., *Anonymous and Clandestine Motherhood in the Czech Republic – Utopia or Reality?*, PR 2005, No. 2, pp. 53 ff.

II. Succession Law

26. The ABGB 1811 stipulated succession law in detail based on traditional principles contained in all great civil codes of the eighteenth and nineteenth centuries.

Among basic principles of succession law provisions, the institutes of *hereditas iacens*, secession application, disinheritance, legacy and substitutional trust (*fideikomis*) must be mentioned. The titles to succession as provided for by the ABGB were the succession deed between married spouses, the last will and the law. An orally expressed last will was admissible.

Intestate heirs were ordered in four rather complex succession groups, distinguishing succession rights of children born in or out of wedlock. The range of intestate heirs, in addition to relatives in direct line, included also uncles, aunts, nephews and nieces, and even cousins.

27. While the ABGB regulated succession law in about 300 sections, by adopting the Civil Code in 1950, the respective regulations were simplified into about fifty sections.

The main change was revocation of the institute of *hereditas iacens* as inheritance was acquired upon the death of the testator.

The law proclaimed preferring intestate succession to testamentary succession. Intestate heirs were ordered in three groups, while intestate succession was limited to the marital spouse, children (regardless of their legitimacy), parents, siblings and persons sharing a common household (so-called co-living persons).

The institute of succession deed among married spouses was repealed, similarly to *donatio mortis causa* and substitutional trust.

The law substantially restricted testing the discretion of the testator by banning any testamentary conditions. A joint will made by marital spouses was not admissible, some forms of wills were repealed, etc.

Moreover, due to extensive nationalization of property and other means of property removal, only the so-called testator's personal property of small scope constituted the estate, the acquiring and administration of which did not require, in the view of legislators, any profound legislation.

28. Operative on 1 January 1955, probate proceedings were withdrawn from the jurisdiction of courts and probates were carried out by state notary offices within every court district.[20] On 1 July 1957, the jurisdiction of state notary offices was introduced in levying succession tax, by that time vested in state finance authorities.[21]

29. The Civil Code of 1964 simplified this very brief legal rule by repealing the institute of disinheritance and further restricting the types of last wills. Disinheritance was provided for again only under the amendment of 1982 to the Civil Code.

20. Act No. 52/1954 Coll.
21. Act No. 26/1957 Coll.

Substantial changes in legal regulation of succession law, restoring some of the well-established institutes, were adopted only in the Civil Code Amendment of 1991.[22]

30. To start with the year 1993, substantial changes were adopted concerning probate provisions.[23] State notary offices were repealed, and probate proceedings returned to court jurisdiction. A notary, based on the empowering court (as a court commissioner), now performs all acts in probates.

The Civil Code has brought huge changes to the legal regulation of inheritance law. They have manifested themselves in particular by extending the autonomy of the will on the part of both the testator and the heir. Since 1 January 2014, it has been possible to include a condition in the last acquisition, a command, to prove time and also to establish a legacy or a trust succession. The heir, in turn, can now reserve an inventory of the estate, renounce the inheritance or disinherit. As of 1 January 2014, a succession contract (which was not in the legislation from 1950 to 2014) was again included among the succession titles. Instead of four inheritance classes, there are now six inheritance classes in the Czech legal system as of 1 January 2014, which strengthens the transfer of property to individuals.

§3. Sources of Family and Succession Law

I. Constitution

31. A basic source of family law legislation is the Charter on Fundamental Rights and Freedoms, which is a part of the Czech Constitution.[24]

In Article 32 of the Charter, the framework of constitutional protection of family and parenthood is defined. Under this Article, parenthood and family are protected by law. Special protection of children and young persons is guaranteed. Special care is also guaranteed to women during pregnancy. Equality of children born either in or out of wedlock is specifically emphasized.

The Charter also explicitly specifies that children's care and upbringing is deemed the right of parents. Children have a right to parental care and upbringing. The parental rights may be restricted, and minor children may be taken away from their parents against their will, only based on court decisions and under the law. Parents, taking care of children, are entitled to state support.

22. Act No. 509/1991 Coll., operative on 1 Jan. 1992.
23. Act No. 264/1992 Coll., amending the Civil Code. Act No. 358/1992 Coll., on Notaries and their Activities (Notary Code).
24. Constitutional Act No. 23/1991 Coll., bringing into operation the Charter of Fundamental Rights and Freedoms as a constitutional law adopted by the Federal Assembly of the Czech and Slovak Federal Republic, implemented in constitutional law of the Czech Republic by ruling of the Board of the Czech National Council No. 2/1993 Coll.

II. Legislation

32. Another basic source of Czech family law is the UN Convention on the Rights of the Child 1989.[25] With regard to the provisions of Article 10 of the Constitution under which the ratified and declared international agreements on human rights and fundamental freedoms are binding for the Czech Republic, and prevail over domestic law, it should be assumed that the UN Convention on the Rights of the Child (a child's rights, of course, are part of human rights) which is a part of the Czech law prevails over domestic family law provisions.

Civil Code

33. The key source of family law is the Civil Code (Act No. 89/2012 Coll.), which was adopted after long preparations in an effort to return family law to the 'womb of civil law' and thus to build on the traditions of Czech and international civil law and science of family law. The Civil Code came into force on 1 January 2014 and abolished, among other things, not only the previous Civil Code of 1964 but also the Family Act of 1963, in which the material on family law was concentrated (except for community property and family housing, or joint tenancy of a flat by spouses). Family law now once again forms an integral part of general private law, i.e., civil law.

Part Two of the Civil Code, entitled Family Law, is divided into three titles dealing with marriage (Title I), kinship and filiation (Title II) and guardianship and other forms of child custody (Title III). Not only Part II Family Law of the Civil Code but also Part I General Part is important for family law, which regulates key institutions relevant to the human being, his/her family and family life (e.g., legal capacity, close persons), principles, rules of interpretation and application, etc.

Act on Registered Same-Sex Partnerships

34. Another source of family law is the RP (Act No. 115/2006 Coll., as amended, and in particular the judgment of Constitutional Court 7/15, which repealed §13(2) of the RegP). The Civil Code contains an injunction to apply the provisions of Parts One, Three and Four, which deal with marriage and the obligations and rights of spouses, to same-sex couples living in a registered partnership (§3020 of the Civil Code). This is also to say that the provisions of Part Two no longer apply by analogy, which is significant, especially when it comes to housing, a derivative legal ground. However, the provisions on protection against domestic violence can be applied (e.g., the diction of §3021 of the Civil Code), as can the provisions governing the right to provision from the estate (§1666 of the Civil Code) and the right to movable property constituting the basic equipment of the family household (§1667 of the Civil Code).

On 1 January 2025, Act No. 123/2024 Coll. came into force, which fundamentally changes the Civil Code regarding unions of same-sex couples. Although the original proposal wanted marriage for all without distinction, the current situation is unclear; a new union, called a partnership, has been created. Act No. 123/2024 Coll.

25. Notice of the Federal Ministry of Foreign Affairs No. 104/1991 Coll.

does not abolish the law on registered partnership; this union will continue to give rise to the rights and obligations of registered partners. However, as of 1 January 2025, it is no longer possible to enter into a registered partnership in the Czech Republic. Same-sex couples can enter into a civil partnership under the Civil Code.

Act on Social and Legal Protection of Children

35. The key law that guarantees the protection of the rights and legitimate interests of the child by the state and sets rules and limits for the state authorities is the Act on Social and Legal Protection of Children (Act No. 359/1999 Coll., as amended). This is a public law provision, which has already been said to be subject to the principle that 'only what the law provides for, within its limits and in the ways specified' (Article 2(2) of the Charter of Fundamental Rights and Freedoms), is permitted in its interpretation and application.

This Act defines, in particular, the range of children who must be given special care and protection or special attention, as they are children in danger, abused or at risk, the rights and obligations of social protection authorities in the context of preventive and advisory activities or decision-making, e.g., on child protection measures, in mediating foster care and adoption, and the rules relating to cooperation in ordering institutional or protective education, etc. The basic aim of social and legal protection of children is to speak, prevent and protect, and especially to make them responsible. The benefits of foster care are newly established in this law.

This act also regulates the social and legal protection of children in relation to foreign countries, in particular by the Office for the International Protection of Children, which also acts as a central authority in the sense of some of the abovementioned international treaties.

Private International Law Act

36. Family law relationships with an international element must be assessed in accordance with the Private International Law Act (Act No. 91/2012 Coll.), unless otherwise provided by an international treaty or a directly applicable European Union (EU) regulation. The Act contains rules on international jurisdiction, applicable law and recognition and enforcement for spousal relationships (§§47 et seq. Private International Law Act), parent-child relationships (§§53 et seq. Private International Law Act), rights of unwed mothers (§59 Private International Law Act), adoption (§§60 et seq. Private International Law Act), guardianship and custody of minors (§§64 et seq. Private International Law Act) and registered partnerships (§67 Private International Law Act).

Civil Procedure Code

37. This is a general procedural rule which establishes the procedure of the court and the parties in civil court proceedings in order to ensure fair protection of the private rights and legitimate interests of the parties, as well as to educate them to respect contracts and thc law, to perform their duties honestly and to respect the rights of others, and to guarantee justice and the law, serving to consolidate and develop the principles of private law (Act No. 99/1963 Coll., Code of Civil Procedure, as amended, in particular §§1 and 3 of the Civil Procedure Code). This Code is followed in particular in disputed matters, e.g., in proceedings for maintenance between spouses, division of the matrimonial property.

Act on Special Court Proceedings

38. This Act (Act No. 292/2013 Coll. on Special Court Proceedings) regulates primarily the hearing and determination of uncontested legal matters, particularly in the context of proceedings in family law cases (Title V, §§367 et seq. of the Special Court Proceedings). Under the Special Court Proceedings Act, proceedings for the authorization of marriage, proceedings for the establishment and denial of parenthood, proceedings for adoption and, in particular, proceedings for the care of minors (e.g., name and surname, custody, maintenance, contact, parental responsibility, representation and administration of property, guardianship and custody, foster care, institutional care and protective measures) and for the granting of legal capacity are dealt with.

Mediation Act

39. The Act has only recently been adopted (Act No. 202/2012 Coll., on Mediation), in particular in relation to the Council of Europe Recommendation Rec(98)1E/21 January 1998 and the Council of Europe Recommendation on Civil Mediation Rec(2002)10E/18 September 2002.

Civil Registry Act

40. The Civil Registry Act (Act No. 301/2000 Coll.) is also important for family law, as it defines, for example, the public authorities before which a marriage may be contracted, determines what is entered in the registry books and regulates the rules for determining or changing names and surnames.

Succession Law: Legislation

41. Succession law is provided in Part III. Absolute Property Rights, Title III of the Civil Code. In the Czech Republic, the death of every person is obligatorily connected with the probate proceedings. The legal regulation of survivorship proceedings is implemented in Act No. 292/2013 Coll., on Special Court Proceedings. Probate proceedings are initiated without a petition after each deceased person when the court learns of the death of a deceased. The heirs tend to take their position as heirs already at the moment of death but can dispose of the property as heirs only when there is a confirmation of the acquisition of the inheritance by the court, which has retroactive effects to the date of death. In the course of the succession proceedings, situations may arise, such as the rejection of the succession, the renunciation of the succession, AND the reservation of the inventory of the estate, which may result in the circle of heirs, or the liability for the debts of the heirs, looking different by the end of the proceedings than if these acts had not taken place.

The court has jurisdiction over the proceedings, but it authorizes the notary in its district to carry out the acts in the succession proceedings (§100(1) of the Special Court Proceedings Act). Most parties to the succession proceedings thus only come into contact with the notary. He summons the heirs, ascertains the scope of the estate, secures the property, ascertains the existence and content of the last acquisitions, etc.

In the first instance, the district courts (in Prague, the district courts and in Brno, the Municipal Court – §3(1) of the Act on Special Court Proceedings) have jurisdiction over the estate. The court in whose district the estate is located has local jurisdiction under §98 of the Act on Special Court Proceedings:

a. the deceased had a registered place of permanent residence at the time of death;
b. the deceased had a domicile or a place where he/she last resided;
c. if jurisdiction is not available under (a) or (b) then the place where the real estate of the deceased is located;
d. if jurisdiction is not available under any of the above points, then the place where the testator died.

The principles on which probate proceedings are based are as follows:

- The principle of the independence of courts, judges and notaries.
- The principle of equality and adversarial procedure – no party to the proceedings may be discriminated against, and everyone has the right to be heard on all facts and evidence.
- Principle of non-publicity – this is an exception; most civil proceedings are public, but in the case of inheritance proceedings, the proceedings are not public (§182(1), second sentence of the Special Court Proceedings Act).
- Principle of orality and directness – oral contact of the parties with the notary or the court prevails. However, written submissions are also taken into account and are not excluded.
- Principle of legal order – certain acts need only be carried out at certain stages of the process.

The two main objectives pursued by the probate procedure are to establish the person or persons of the heir or heirs of the deceased and to establish the assets and liabilities of the estate. In order to identify the heirs, the Register of Legal Transactions on Death is used to check whether there is a contract of succession, a will, a deed of disinheritance, a contract of renunciation or a deed of revocation of these legal transactions. In addition, as part of the so-called preliminary investigation, information on heirs is obtained from lists or systems maintained under special legislation, most often from the central death register. In addition, unknown heirs are notified of their right to inherit by decree or heirs of unknown residence.

In order to determine assets and liabilities, an enquiry is made, for example, in the Register of Documents on the matrimonial property regime maintained by the Chamber of Notaries of the Czech Republic, the status of these documents is ascertained, the data necessary to determine the deceased's assets and debts are obtained, data are obtained, for example, from the Land Registry or the Commercial Register, from the motor vehicle register or from banks. The heirs must be informed of the right to reserve the inventory of the estate, which has a consequent effect on the extent of the heirs' liability for the debts of the deceased towards creditors.

Other ancillary tasks of the succession proceedings include ensuring the administration of the estate during the proceedings if it is not sufficiently secured, and also ensuring that the testator's will is carried out if one was annexed in the last acquisition.

A special type of proceeding is the eventual liquidation of the estate, the function of which is, in particular, the payment of the debts of the testator to creditors and the eventual payment of the balance to the heirs.

At the end of the succession proceedings, which may involve, for example, a dispute as to the validity of the will or the disinheritance deed, where the proceedings are transferred in the form of a dispute to a court hearing and the result is subsequently returned to the notary, an order confirming the acquisition of the succession is issued.

III. Treaties

42. The Czech Republic is bound by a number of multilateral international treaties. In addition to the aforementioned UN Convention on the Rights of the Child, the most important are as follows:

- Convention on Collecting Maintenance in Foreign Countries, New York 1956 (Reg. No. 33/1959 Coll.).
- Convention on Recognition and Enforcement of Rulings Concerning Maintenance Duty to Children, the Hague 1958 (Reg. No. 14/1974 Coll.).
- Convention on Recognizing Divorces and Termination of Marital Cohabitation, the Hague 1970 (Reg. No. 132/1976 Coll.).
- Convention on Granting Consent to Marriages, the Lowest Age to Marry and Marriage Registrations, New York 1962 (Reg. No. 124/1968 Coll.).
- Convention on Civil Law Aspects of International Kidnapping of Children (Notice of the Ministry of Foreign Affairs No. 43/2000 Coll.).
- Convention on Children's Protection and Cooperation in International Adoptions (Notice of the Ministry of Foreign Affairs No. 43/2000 I.T.Coll.).
- European Convention on Recognition and Enforcement of Decisions Concerning Custody of Children and Restoration of Custody of Children, Luxembourg 1980 (Notice of the Ministry of Foreign Affairs No. 66/2000 I.T.Coll.).
- European Convention on the Adoption of Children, Strasbourg 1967 (Notice of the Ministry of Foreign Affairs No. 132/2000 I.T.Coll.).
- European Convention on the Legal Status of Children Born out of Wedlock, Strasbourg 1975 (Notice of the Ministry of Foreign Affairs No. 47/2001 I.T.Coll.).
- European Convention on the Exercise of Children's Rights, Strasbourg 1996 (Notice of the Ministry of Foreign Affairs No. 54/2001 I.T.Coll.).
- Convention on Human Rights and Bio-medicine, Oviedo 1997 (Notice of the Ministry of Foreign Affairs No. 96/2001 I.T.Coll.).
- The Convention on the International Recovery of Child Support and Other Forms of Maintenance Arising out of Family Relations was signed in 2007 in The Hague.

- The Protocol on the Law Applicable to Maintenance Obligations was signed in 2007 in The Hague.
- The European Convention on the Status of Children born out of wedlock was adopted in 1975 in Strasbourg (Notice of the Ministry of Foreign Affairs No. 47/2001 I.T.Coll.).
- The European Convention on the Exercise of the Rights of the Child was adopted in 1996 in Strasbourg (Notice of the Ministry of Foreign Affairs No. 54/2001 I.T.Coll.).
- The Convention on the Prohibition and Immediate Action for the Elimination of the Worst Forms of Child Labour was adopted in 1999 in Geneva (Notice of the Ministry of Foreign Affairs No. 90/2002 I.T.Coll.).
- The Council of Europe Convention for the Protection of Children against Sexual Exploitation and Sexual Abuse was adopted in Lanzarote in 2007 (Notice of the Ministry of Foreign Affairs No. 59/2016 I.T.Coll.).
- The Convention on Contact with Children was adopted in Strasbourg in 2003 (Notice of the Ministry of Foreign Affairs No. 91/2005 I.T.Coll.).
- The Convention on the Civil Aspects of International Child Abduction was adopted in 1980 in The Hague (Notice of the Ministry of Foreign Affairs No. 34/1998 I.T.Coll.).
- The Convention on Protection of Children and Cooperation in respect of Inter-country Adoption was signed in 1993 in The Hague (Notice of the Ministry of Foreign Affairs No. 43/2000 I.T.Coll.).
- The European Convention on the Adoption of Children was signed in 1967 in Strasbourg (Notice of the Ministry of Foreign Affairs No. 132/2000 I.T.Coll.; its revised version of 2008 has not yet entered into force).
- The Convention on the Recognition and Enforcement of Decisions on the Education of Children and on the Restitution of Children was adopted in 1980 in Luxembourg (Notice of the Ministry of Foreign Affairs No. 66/2000 I.T.Coll.).
- The Convention on Jurisdiction, Applicable Law, Recognition, Enforcement and Cooperation in respect of Parental Responsibility and Measures for the Protection of Children was adopted in 1996 in The Hague (Notice of the Ministry of Foreign Affairs No. 141/2001 I.T.Coll.).

EU Law

43. Since the Czech Republic's accession to the EU, the sources of EU law, which are directly applicable and generally take precedence over laws, are also binding. The relationship of regulations to international treaties is regulated separately by individual regulations. Aspects of family law concern in particular:

a. Council Regulation (EU) No. 2019/1111 of 25 June 2019 on jurisdiction and the recognition and enforcement of judgments in matrimonial matters and the matters of parental responsibility, and on international child abduction (i.e., the Brussels II ter Regulation).
b. Council Regulation (EC) No. 4/2009 of 18 December 2008 on jurisdiction, applicable law, recognition and enforcement of decisions and cooperation in matters relating to maintenance obligations.

IV. Court Decisions

44. Czech law is a continental-type law. The judge is bound by law in his/her decision-making. He/she is entitled to consider consistency of another legal rule with the law.[26] Judges are independent in exercising their functions and bound by law only. They are bound to interpret rules of law in accordance with their best knowledge and conscience and are obliged to decide impartially, fairly and with no delay, based on the facts found, consistent with the law only.[27]

45. Supreme Court rulings, which also generally and significantly interpret particular legal provisions, are published in a separate Collection of the Supreme Court Decisions. At present, important judgments of the High Courts and Regional Courts are published in specialist magazines. All published decisions serve only to unify court practice and to provide detailed information not only to judges but also to lawyers in general as well as to laymen. However, an opinion of a superior court is not legally binding for a judge, with the exception of an appellate court opinion in a particular matter remanded to the court of the first degree for a new hearing and ruling.

§4. The Courts Administering Family and Succession Law

46. The Czech Republic has a uniform system of courts, thus having no specialized family courts.

Within an internal court organization of the particular court levels, there exist only departments specializing in criminal matters and in civil matters that include sub-departments for so-called non-contentious matters. These judges specialize in deciding all non-contentious family law matters as specified under the Act on Special Court Proceedings. These are matters concerning a minor's care (namely, custody, determining duty to maintain a minor, adoption, foster care, proceedings considering court consent to be granted to a minor in order to marry, affiliation proceedings, etc.). Other proceedings in family law matters commenced only upon petitioning are held as any other contentious matters and judges do not specialize in hearing such matters. An example of a contentious proceeding in family law matters is a proceeding for maintenance between adults or the settlement of matrimonial property.

A single judge always decides first instance family and succession matters.

47. Probates are also heard in first instance courts with a notary as a court commissioner co-operating. Probates are conducted by a judge of a specialized sub-department for non-contentious matters, who handles succession matters only.

48. Appeals against first instance court decisions are always heard by regional court sitting as an appellate court. There are seven regional courts (Prague, Usti nad Labem, Pilsen, Ceske Budejovice, Hradec Kralove, Ostrava and Brno). The court

26. The Constitution of the Czech Republic 1993.
27. Act No. 6/2002 Coll., on Courts and Judges, §79.

system at present disregards the new regional administration (comprising fourteen regions). For now, a discussion is held on establishing courts in the new regional centres.

Decisions in regional courts are rendered by a panel of three judges.

49. In consistency with the law, some matters of family law may eventually be decided by the Supreme Court of the Czech Republic residing in Brno. The Supreme Court hears re-appeals (an extraordinary remedy) against appellate courts' decisions.

50. There is also a Constitutional Court established in the Czech Republic, residing in Brno, which is a judicial authority for constitutionality protection and in addition to determining revocation of acts of law or single legal provisions if they are conflicting with a constitutional law or an international treaty related to human rights. The Constitutional Court also hears constitutional complaints against effective decisions and other public authorities interfering in the rights and freedoms guaranteed by the Constitution.[28]

51. Since appeals are not always possible in family law, complainants often turn to the Constitutional Court when they feel their fundamental rights have been affected. When the Constitutional Court rules in these individual cases, its rulings are binding only in the cassation sense but not in the precedential sense. In such cases, therefore, the general binding force of the Constitutional Court's decisions is not given, although indirectly – through its sophistication and the nature of its reasoning – the case law of the Constitutional Court should guide the decision-making practice of the general courts in the area of constitutionality.[29] Thus, from this perspective, the decisions of the Constitutional Court in individual cases are not generally binding but are binding only in a given individual case, although in practice the legal opinion stated therein is undoubtedly of considerable importance in the decision-making activities of general courts in similar cases.

52. Criminal matters concerning minors[30] (young persons between the ages of 15 and 18 years) are heard by a special senate in an appropriate district or regional court. There are several variations against normal criminal proceedings as well as in punishment. Concerning children under 15 years of age who committed such an act that otherwise would be a criminal offence, the special senate decides upon the Civil Procedure Code. Depending on the particular criminal offence, the matter is decided by the particular district or regional court as a first instance court.

---

28. Constitution, Art. 87. Act No. 182/1993 Coll., on Constitutional Court.
29. Šimíček, V., *Constitutional Complaint*, Linde Praha, a. s. 2001, p. 267.
30. Act No. 218/2003 Coll., on Responsibility of Juveniles for Crimes and on Jurisdiction in these Cases, operative on 1 Jan. 2004.

Part I. Persons

Chapter 1. The Status of a Person

§1. Definition of a Person

53. Under Czech law, personality may be attached to either a human being (a natural person, an individual) or to a corporation (legal entity, legal person, juridical person).

Any person, not otherwise specified (e.g., by citizenship, gender, nationality, social status, political appurtenance, etc.), is deemed a natural person under family law and civil law.

If the state is a party to a private law relationship, it is deemed to be a legal entity.[31]

54. A natural person (an individual) acquires the capacity to have rights and obligations at birth. For his/her entire life, each human being possesses the capacity to have rights and obligations. A natural person may not be deprived of or restricted in this capacity. It is an expression of the equality principle of all citizens before law.[32] Capacity to have rights and duties is an unalienable right that no citizen may effectively waive or be deprived of.

Still, we cannot speak about an absolute capacity, free from any restraints, of natural persons to have rights and duties. The conditions of such restraints, likewise as in restraining all fundamental rights and freedoms, may only be given by law.[33]

55. Such capacity is also possessed by a conceived baby if it is born alive.[34] Acknowledging the conditional status of juridical person to a child conceived has had a long tradition in the Czech legal history. ABGB 1811 considered a *nasciturus* a being enjoying special legal protection, namely, in obtaining certain advantages. Thus, a *nasciturus* might acquire rights with a suspensive condition, but not duties. However, in the view of third persons, a human being became legally relevant only after birth, not by conception. *Nasciturus* could also be appointed a custodian for securing his/her rights. The custodian was not called to act in legal matters on his/

31. Civil Code §21.
32. The Charter of Fundamental Rights and Freedoms, Arts 1 and 5.
33. *Ibid.*, Art. 4.
34. Civil Code §25.

her behalf, not even in those aimed exclusively at promoting the *nasciturus*' interests and welfare; he/she could not accept a gift, assume a possession on the *nasciturus*' behalf, nor could he/she act and decide in legal matters on his/her behalf with a suspensive condition that the child will be born alive. Securing the *nasciturus*' rights arising from a last will, a foundation, or a contract in favour of the third person was the main sphere of custodian's activities.

Also, the Civil Code 1950 arose from a fictitious presumption acknowledging to a conceived, but not yet born, child a capacity to have rights under the condition that the child will be born alive.

In case of doubt, a refutable presumption that the child would have been born alive was stated. During the whole period of operation of the Civil Code 1950, it remained questionable whether a *nasciturus* had the capacity to have not only rights but also obligations. Gradually, the opinion prevailed that the provisions mentioned should be understood so that a *nasciturus* may be subject only to such legal terms in which his/her rights promoting his/her welfare prevail. It was also possible to appoint a custodian for an unborn child if it was necessary for the sake of his/her rights' protection.

The Civil Code 1964 removed this questionable issue by explicitly stating that a *nasciturus* enjoys capacity to have not only rights but also obligations, including the same condition as the two previous rules, that is, that the child will be born alive. In contrast to the Civil Code 1950, it did not take over the presumption that the child has been born alive, leaving this issue to medical rules.

Contemporary law arises from a traditional concept deeming *nasciturus* a person '*in fieri*'. Thus, *nasciturus* may acquire rights and obligations with a suspensive condition effective *ex tunc*. The acquisition becomes non-conditional if the child is born alive, even though unable to live and survive only for a short time. If a child was not born as, for example, a result of a miscarriage or abortion, or the child was stillborn, the *nasciturus* is deemed as never having become the subject of rights and duties.

Medical examination carried out by a medical doctor is decisive in considering whether a child was indeed born and whether it was born alive. A live-born child is a child who shows a sign of life (respiration, heartbeat, active movement of muscles, umbilicus pulsation) and whose birth weight is 500 g or more, or whose birth weight is below 500 g if he/she survives twenty-four hours after delivery. A stillborn child is a child not showing any signs of life whose birth weight is 1,000 g or more.[35]

56. The capacity to have rights and duties ceases on death. If death cannot be proved in the prescribed manner, the court will proclaim such individual dead if establishing his/her death in another manner.[36]

57. Also, legal entities (corporations) possess capacity to have rights and obligations. Unless a separate act provides otherwise, a written contract or foundation deed is required for establishing a legal person. Legal entities come into being on

35. Decree of the Ministry of Health Care No. 11/1988 Coll.
36. Civil Code §71.

the day when entered in the Commercial Register or in another register as specified by law, unless a separate act has stipulated otherwise.[37]

Legal entities are:

Classification of legal entities in terms of the legal reason for their formation:

- private law legal persons which are established by legal action and are subject to private law regulations
- legal persons governed by public law, which are established by law or administrative decision, are subject to public law regulations, their activities include the direct or indirect exercise of public administration, and the rules of the Civil Code apply to them only if this is compatible with their nature

Classification in terms of substrate:

- a corporation is a community of persons (FO or PO) for the purpose of carrying out a certain common activity, the basis is a personal substrate (members)
- a foundation is an asset set aside for a specific purpose, the basis is a material substrate, there are no members.

Classification in terms of disposal of profits:

- for-profit are those which generate profits mainly for distribution to their members or for their own use, e.g., trading companies
- not-for-profit are those which do not pursue profit-making as their primary purpose and, if they do make a profit, use a substantial part of it for purposes of general benefit.

The classification criteria can be combined:

- private law corporations – association, church, joint stock company, …
- public law corporations – e.g., municipality, region, Czech Bar Association, Palacký University …
- private law foundations – foundation, endowment fund
- public law foundations – State Environmental Fund, State Transport Infrastructure Fund, …

The Civil Code regulates private law corporations (associations), private law foundations (foundations, endowment funds) and institutes (it is classified as a foundation, but it is a hybrid).

---

37. *Ibid.*, §19.

58. An important attribute of legal persons is their name that must be stated upon their establishment. As for protection and good reputation of a legal person's name, this is protected in a manner similar to that pertaining to natural persons.

An inevitable condition of establishing a legal person is also determining its residence.

Legal persons cease to exist, unless specified by a special legislation, by agreement, lapse of time or fulfilling the aim for which they were established. Legal entities filed in the Commercial Register cease to exist as a rule after being struck off from this register.

59. Acts in law of a legal entity are performed in all matters by those authorized to undertake them (management and agents), either on the basis of a foundation agreement, foundation deed or the law. Acts in law can also be performed on behalf of a legal entity by its employees or members if the legal entity's internal regulations so specify or if such employees or members customarily perform these acts. Should such persons exceed their authority, the rights and obligations hereby created will be attributed to the legal entity concerned only if the relevant act in law is related to the objectives of the legal entity's activities and only if the other party could not have been aware of the excess.[38]

§2. Capacity

60. The capacity of an individual to acquire rights and assume obligations through his/her own acts in law (legal capacity) is established when he/she attains majority (i.e., comes of age).

An individual attains majority upon reaching the age of 18. Prior to this time, majority can be acquired by marrying. Majority so acquired will not be lost should the marriage be dissolved or pronounced invalid.[39]

In practice, the majority provision is interpreted in such a manner that a person attains 18 years of age at the beginning (i.e., 0.00 o'clock) of the day which corresponds by number and month to the day when the person was born 18 years ago.

61. Attaining full age by marrying expresses the principle of equality between spouses. However, the legal status of a minor younger than 18 years is rather interesting. To simplify the matter, it can be said that a married spouse is legally capable in matters where the law generally requires full capacity to perform acts in law. Where the law requires expressly the age of 18, he/she may not act independently.

Thus a person of full age below 18 has no right to vote, may not apply for permission to carry on a business, a driving licence, he/she may not be served alcoholic drinks in a pub nor is he/she allowed to see an adult film in a cinema (i.e., as a rule an indecent film). He/she may, as either a buyer or a seller, make a contract of sale involving real estate, make a contract of credit amounting to millions (of course, if finding a bank willing to lend him/her the money), but he/she may not

38. *Ibid.*, §164.
39. *Ibid.*, §30.

make an agreement with his/her employer on a material responsibility in operating a canteen for employees with a monthly turnover of a few thousand crowns as the Labour Law expressly requires the age of 18 for making a material responsibility agreement.

In the case of a court's granting of legal capacity, this is an addition or remission of years (venia aetatis). The law in this matter provides that if a minor who is not fully competent (or his/her legal guardian) proposes that the court grant him/her legal capacity, the court shall grant the proposal if the minor has reached the age of 16, if his/her ability to support himself/herself and to provide for his/her own affairs is proven and if the minor's legal guardian agrees with the proposal (§37 of the Civil Code). In other cases, the court shall grant the application if it is in the minor's best interests for serious reasons. These other cases may be any situation. The only condition to be insisted upon (in relation to the court's proposal) is the minor's ability to support himself or herself and to provide for his or her own affairs on a regular basis. Otherwise, the legislation would be meaningless. The procedure is regulated by the Special Proceedings Act (§466 of the Code of Criminal Procedure).

I. Minors in Czech Law

62. Full legal capacity means that a person is capable of fully acquiring rights for himself or herself by his or her own legal actions and of fully committing himself or herself to obligations (§15(2) of the Civil Code). As a rule of thumb, the law provides that a person becomes fully competent by reaching the age of majority, which is attained by reaching the age of 18 (§30(1) of the Civil Code). Prior to that age, full legal capacity is acquired by conferral of legal capacity (§37 of the Civil Code) or by marriage. Until that time, the person is a minor.

A basis of the legal status of a child derives from constitutional law, as at birth every human being becomes a citizen of a particular state. Recognizing a child to be a citizen (regardless of his/her age) automatically grants him/her entire civil rights enjoyed by any other (i.e., adult) citizen. A child, as a human being and as a citizen of a state, is subject to rights and obligations, and as any other person of full age, he/she may benefit from them or suffer an injury. Entire rights given under the Constitution, as well as in special regulations stipulated by the state for citizens, also concern children and pertain to them.

Regarding the long-term immaturity of a child and its dependence on others (the parents, the society, the state, etc.), in addition to fundamental civil rights, children are also granted special rights under law pertaining to children only and serving to protect them. Thus, children may seem to be granted more rights than people of age. These special rights are mostly of a protective nature; active and positive rights are expressed much less frequently. Besides, civil rights for citizens are intended first of all for adult citizens. A great part of these rights is not available for children in regard to the age at which acquisition of some civil rights is granted (right to work, right to vote and to be elected, etc.).

The fact that a child does not exercise his/her rights by himself/herself makes one presume that a child may be an object of a legal relationship, namely, at the instant when a child is discussed and dealt with by adults. However, dealing 'with' a child is not the same as dealing with an object, and the law, as a rule, provides for special protection of a child employing the institute of custodianship.

63. People of age and state authorities are imposed various special obligations in relation to children which essentially help in carrying out the child's rights, not treating them as an object of rights but as an equal subject. Another problem arises here: in the effort to prevent the child from being an 'object' of their parents or other adults, he/she, as a result, does not become an 'object' of state authorities, namely, courts or state administration authorities responsible for the child's rights protection. The whole matter seems to be very difficult and complex, as a minor child, not enjoying full capacity in acts in law, is always represented by his/her statutory representatives acting in his/her name, or state authorities, acting in the name of the state, respectively.

64. Under the law, a child is generally recognized as enjoying a protective status enabling him/her, with respect to his/her activities and conduct, to escape the consequences normally borne by adults. At the same time, a child is granted certain advantages and is protected from possible irresponsible or inappropriate behaviour and decisions of the adults. This status also has certain disadvantages for the child because some 'advantages' available to adults are not in fact available to children without the consent or action taken by their statutory representatives; a child cannot act independently or make a choice on his/her own. Even though under the law a child is explicitly entitled to address, without the parents being aware, state authorities in order to ask for help. This right is in practice dependent on the child's age and the fact that the child realizes the necessity of intervention or help from state authorities.

65. Various age limits or categories of children in view of their legal status are not recognized under Czech law. If the law uses the term child, it often specifies only a minor child, or this fact may be detected from an order of the relevant provision as stipulated by law, which may raise doubts in some particular cases.

If the law uses only the word child, as a rule, it has in mind the relationship between a parent and a child, regardless of the child's majority.

66. Criminal law distinguishes between minor children up to 15 years and young persons between 15 and 18 years.

The term young person is used in labour law too, denoting a minor employee.

II. Child as an Expression of Relationship

67. The term child is also used in law in relation to predecessors and descendants. In this sense, the question of full age is legally irrelevant. A child born in wedlock, out of wedlock and an adoptive child are all deemed children.

68. For the purpose of the legal rules governing social security, labour law, criminal law, protection of minor children and a number of others, as well as in cases of appointing a guardian or ordering a child to a person's care, a child placed in a natural person's care or foster care is deemed a child.

§3. Absentees

69. A court may appoint a custodian for a person whose whereabouts are unknown if it is necessary for the protection of that person's interest or if public interest so requires. Under the same conditions, the court may also appoint a custodian when it is required for some other serious reason.[40]

Court opinions do not hold a certain person to be of residence unknown in case he/she is merely absent for a certain limited time, even though the address of this person is not exactly known.

Other serious reasons for appointing a custodian may be, for example, mental disorder, but the person involved is not deprived fully or partially of his/her capacity to perform acts in law as a result. Also, a certain serious physical defect can be involved, including insufficient ability to speak clearly to be understood, due to which the person is not capable of performing an act in law by himself/herself, or he/she can do so, but only with immense difficulty and effort (e.g., a condition following a brain stroke).

70. If there is a danger of delay, even the court handling the proceedings may appoint a custodian for a civil lawsuit on behalf of such participant who is unable to act independently. Unless taking other measures, the judge conducting the hearing can appoint a custodian for a participant whose residence is unknown, the serving of a summons to a known address of such party abroad failed, or the participant suffers from a mental disorder or other health condition preventing him/her from participating in the proceedings for a longer time, or is unable to articulate comprehensibly.[41]

71. The court will also proclaim a missing individual dead if it can be assumed, after taking into account all the circumstances of the case, that the person concerned is no longer alive.[42]

The ABGB 1811 stipulated a presumption that a missing person died if seventy years expired from his/her birth and five years had expired since his/her last contact with anyone, or thirty years since he/she was born and ten years since he/she would let anyone know he/she was alive. For war events and shipwrecks, a three-year period for the person missing was stipulated.

The Civil Code 1950 demanded five years for a person missing to be proclaimed dead, or if missing in relation to a very dangerous event, one year only.

Under the current Civil Code, a presumption of death is established in the event that someone can reasonably be presumed to have died (§71(1) of the Civil Code). The court may declare the following to be dead:

---

40. *Ibid.*, §465. The appointment of such persons is subject to §29/3 of the Act of Special Proceedings.
41. Civil Procedure Code §29.
42. Civil Code §71.

- a person who has already been declared missing by a court on the grounds that he has left his home has not reported and is not known to be present, and after the expiry of the statutory time limits (§§66 et seq. in conjunction with §§73 et seq. of the Civil Code);
- one who has become missing by leaving his or her home has not reported and is not known to be present, and after the expiry of the statutory time limits (§§74 and 75 of the Civil Code).

72. The decision must always indicate the date on which the effects of the declaration of disappearance took effect, which is particularly relevant for the application of the first presumption of paternity (§776 of the Civil Code). It is also necessary to specify in the judgment on the declaration of death the date which is deemed to be the date of death or the date on which he did not survive. This is important not only for the application of the first presumption of paternity (§776 of the Civil Code) but especially for the dissolution of a marriage or registered partnership (§71(2) *in fine* of the Civil Code). The law provides that a person who has been declared dead is to be regarded as if he had died (§71(2) of the Civil Code).

73. If a person has been declared dead, this does not exclude proof that he died earlier or later or that he is still alive. If it is established that someone is alive, the declaration of death is not taken into account *ex lege* (however, the decision will be annulled under §64 of the Civil Code); however, the marriage or registered partnership is not revived. A similar procedure is followed if false proof of death has been made (§76 of the Civil Code).

74. Even a death must be registered in the public registers, i.e., in the death register kept by the registry office (§§21 et seq. of the Civil Registry Act).

Chapter 2. Registration of Civil Status

§1. The Registrar

75. Any natural person older than 18 years and an employee of a municipality authorized to keep registers may become a registrar. The law requires that a registrar must not have been convicted and sentenced for an intentional criminal offence.

To be appointed a registrar, the municipality employee must have proved his/her expertise and knowledge of the law related to registries, use of name and surname, citizenship rules and other legal rules related to the activities of a registrar.

Registrars most usually have a secondary school education; typically, they are women.

In regard to the fact that a registrar has access to personal data in registry files and document collections, the law also imposes on registrars a duty of secrecy concerning this data, even after terminating the exercise of this function.[43]

§2. Registry and Certificates

76. Registries belonged to very old population registers originally kept by the Roman Catholic clergy. Their general introduction in Catholic countries was stipulated by the Trident Council 1545–1563, but they were introduced at the same time, or even earlier, by reformed churches too.

Registries in the Czech countries commonly appeared no later than the beginning of the sixteenth and seventeenth centuries. Their original rise probably dates from the twelfth century in relation to the rise of parishes. Altogether, twenty-two registries have been preserved, starting prior to 1563. The oldest registry in our republic is that of Jachymov, which started in 1531. However, care and diligence in keeping registries varied significantly depending on what attention they were paid by the respective priest or authority.

In the years 1627–1781, all registries were operated by the Roman Catholic Church only; from this time, the registries were also kept by protestant clergy. After 1868, civil registries have also been kept in our territory (at first registers of marriage, and after 1870, also birth and death registers).

At the beginning of the rule of the first enlightened monarch, Maria Theresia (1740–1780) on the Austrian throne, the state authorities started to actively interfere in population registries as well as in various lists and registers.

The activities of registries were stipulated for the first time by an Emperor's Patent of Joseph II in 1784 on keeping registries of persons born, married and deceased, by the parish authorities of the Roman Catholic Church.

77. From 1 January 1950, the keeping of registries was entirely passed on to the state. Registries are kept by municipal (local) authorities empowered to do so by law. Not every municipality keeps a registry. A district authority may vest in one of

43. Act No. 301/2000 Coll., Civil Registry Act, §9. Act No. 101/2000 Coll., on Personal Data Protection.

the municipalities the obligation to keep a registry for several municipalities. Several registry districts may exist in large cities.

Registry files upkeep and the respective acts are exercised by the state administration.

Registry extracts on a prescribed form have the nature of a public document.

78. The registry office also issues certificates on legal capacity needed by a Czech citizen to marry abroad.

79. Similar to notaries, the registrars are empowered to authenticate copies as identical with a document as well as authenticate a person's signature.

Chapter 3. Personality Rights

§1. General

80. Under private law, a child may be subject to any legal relationship like any other person. The issue of enforcing the child's rights arising from any particular act in law is, of course, a question of his/her capacity to perform acts in law, that is, rather that of his/her statutory representatives, that is, his/her parents, adoptive parents, a guardian, and to a limited extent that of a foster parent, a person, in whose care the child was placed, or that of a custodian.

81. A minor child, like any other individual, has the right to protection of his/her personality, in particular his/her life and health, civic honour and human dignity, as well as his/her privacy (good) name and expressions of personal nature.[44] The text of the law, demonstrating some examples, also allows the right to personal freedom protection, to free movement and residence to be included on this list.

82. An individual has a particular right to demand that there be no unjustified interference in his/her personal rights, that the consequences of such interference be eliminated and that appropriate satisfaction be rendered.

Should the satisfaction mentioned above prove insufficient, in particular due to the fact that the individual's dignity or reputation in society was diminished to a significant extent, the individual concerned also has the right to monetary compensation of such non-proprietary detriment.

§2. Capacity of Minors to Perform Acts in Law

83. In view of the capacity to perform acts in law, the ABGB 1811 recognized children as being up to 7 years of age, juniors, that is, persons up to 14 and minors, that is, persons who have not yet attained the age of 21.

Also, the Civil Code 1950 resolved the issue of minors' capacity to perform acts in law by stipulating age limits. Children up to 6 years of age were absolutely incapable of performing acts in law; children between 6 and 18 possessed capacity to perform only such acts in law that were exclusively promoting their welfare and to make contracts that were fulfilled immediately and were appropriate to their age.

The Civil Code 1964 did not take over this rule, relying on a very general rule only. Minors possessed the capacity to perform acts in law only if the nature of such acts corresponded to the mental and moral development level of their age.[45] The legal criterion 'if the nature of such acts corresponds to the mental and moral development level of their age' should be understood objectively; that is, each case must be considered not in view of an individual mental maturity (comprising the level of thinking and determining) of a particular minor but consistent with the level of mental development as expected in a minor of a certain age. The nature of an act in law

44. Civil Code §11.
45. *Ibid.*, 1964, §9.

must be considered in this sense as well as the type of item acquired (e.g., a minor has no capacity to buy a live dog in a shop, but he/she can buy a white mouse or aquarium fish), its value, legal consequences of the minor's conduct, etc. Only such an approach enables a balanced view of both the minor's interests and of protecting third persons dealing with a minor in good faith.

84. Today, partial legal capacity is granted to children who are minors and who have not acquired full legal capacity by being granted it (§37 of the Civil Code) or by marriage (§30(2) of the Civil Code in conjunction with §656 of the Civil Code). In this case, it is thus necessary to proceed on the basis of:

- the general positive rule (§31 of the Civil Code);
- the general negative rule (§36 of the Civil Code);
- the provision governing the child's conduct with the consent of the legal representative (§32 of the Civil Code);
- special provisions governing the operation of a commercial establishment (§33 of the Civil Code);
- the provisions laying down the rules on dependent work (§§34 and 35 of the Civil Code); the law provides for the prohibition of dependent work by a minor under the age of 15 or a minor who has not completed compulsory schooling; however, such children are allowed to engage in artistic, cultural, advertising or sporting activities in accordance with a special regulation;
- other special provisions (§95 and 100 of the Civil Code, governing the principles of bodily integrity);
- from special regulations (e.g., §35 of the Health Act) or from international treaties (Article 6 of the Animal Breeding Convention).

85. The acquisition of legal capacity is, by its nature, gradual in relation to intellectual and voluntary maturity. This will be different for newborns, different for children of early school age, and different for secondary school children. However, unlike historical legislation, the law does not set out any age categories for children, e.g., children under 7, 8 to 15, or over 15. The general positive rule is expressed by a rebuttable presumption according to which every minor who has not acquired full legal capacity is presumed to be capable of legal actions of a nature appropriate to the mental and volitional maturity of minors of his or her age (§31 of the Civil Code). This is an objective concept which allows for counter-evidence and thus allows for the specifics of the particular child's intellectual and volitional maturity to be taken into account. The law thus guarantees, on the one hand, certainty and, on the other hand, respects the uniqueness and individuality of each child.

86. If a child has the capacity to perform a legal act, he acts alone, and the legal act is valid if it otherwise complies with the law.

87. However, if the child lacks the capacity to act, a legal representative, i.e., an *ex lege* representative, may act for the child:

a. the child's parent in the exercise of the duties and rights arising from parental responsibility (§892 of the Civil Code; cf. also the rules for resolving possible conflicts, §892 of the Civil Code, and disagreements between parents, §877 of the Civil Code);
b. guardianship (§929 of the Civil Code; cf. also guardianship by court order pursuant to §§934 et seq. of the Civil Code).

88. The general negative rule is that a minor who has not acquired full legal capacity is never, irrespective of the content of the other provisions, capable of acting independently in matters for which his or her legal guardian would also need the court's consent (§36 of the Civil Code). Even if the minor is capable of acting independently, the consequences of a legal act can only be made conditional on the consent of the legal guardian (§36(2) of the Civil Code).

89. The law also regulates the child's actions with the consent of the legal representative (§32 of the Civil Code). It is stipulated that if the legal guardian has given consent to a minor who has not acquired full legal capacity, in accordance with the customs of private life, to a certain legal act or to achieve a certain purpose (expressly or by implication, informally, in advance or after the fact – ratihabice), the minor is able to act legally on his or her own within the limits of the consent, unless this is specifically prohibited by law; the consent may subsequently be limited or withdrawn (with ex nunc effects). If there are several legal representatives, it is sufficient if at least one of them expresses his/her will in relation to the third party. If, however, several representatives act jointly towards another person and contradict each other, the expression of any of them is not taken into account (e.g., §877 of the Civil Code).

90. If there is an excess, i.e., a situation in which a person who is incapable of legal capacity or is not properly represented has acted, the act is absolutely void because it is contrary to law and public policy (§581 of the Civil Code).

In spite of the above, the Civil Law contains a more precise stipulation in defining a minor's capacity in relation to succession law. Minors, who have reached the age of 15, may express their last will only in the form of a notarial record.[46] Minors younger than 15 cannot express their last will at all.

91. The question of the religious upbringing of a child has been stipulated in a specific way. By the time the children have attained the age of 15, this question is decided by their parents.[47] A child over 15 has the right to decide this question by himself/herself.

---

46. *Ibid.*, §1526, *see* below Part IV, Ch. 2, §1.
47. Act No. 3/2002 Coll., on Religious Freedom and Status of Churches and Religious Denominations, §3.

92. Certain variances from general provisions concerning the capacity of a minor in performing acts in law are also contained in the Civil Code, which explicitly allows a minor to perform some acts in law; for example, an express consent must be granted for the adoption of a child by a minor parent older than 16 years. A minor person has the capacity to paternity affirmation too. This affirmation must be made before court (§779(2) of the Civil Code).

93. Capacity in acts concerning civil proceedings is generally connected to attaining the majority. The Act on Special Court Proceedings allows one exception to this rule in case of petitioning the court to grant approval to marry. This petition is brought about by a minor over 16 years of age, by himself/herself, and in the proceedings, he/she is not represented by his/her parents, his/her statutory representatives, or his/her custodian.

94. As regards health interventions, the child's participation rights in general and the child's special rights (§100 of the Civil Code) must be respected in principle. It is stipulated that if the integrity of a minor who has reached the age of 14, has not acquired full legal capacity and seriously opposes the procedure is to be interfered with, even if the legal representative consents to the procedure, the procedure may not be carried out without the consent of the court; if the legal representative does not consent to the interference with the child's integrity, even though the person concerned wishes it, the procedure may be carried out at the request of the child or a person close to the child only with the consent of the court.

95. In the field of healthcare, this also concerns the issue of hospitalization of a child without the consent of the child's parent or the provision of urgent or acute care to a child in the case of treatment for a serious mental disorder and when the health services are necessary to save life or prevent serious damage to health (§38(4) of the Health Services Act). A separate provision regulates the situation in which urgent care may be provided to a minor patient without the consent of his/her legal guardian if abuse or neglect is suspected (§38(5) of the Health Services Act).

96. The question of a minor's consent is stipulated very specifically in connection with abortion.[48]

97. Our law has stipulated, as in some other countries, a limit of 16 years to allow a girl to decide freely on an abortion. In other words, a minor girl over 16 is capable of applying for an abortion without the consent of her statutory representatives.

98. The discrepancy between secrecy requirement towards the parents of a girl over 16 and the parents' obligation to care for their child's health, her physical, mental, emotional and intellectual development and to supervise the minor corresponding to her level of development (and thus their need to be informed) is provided by law in such a way that the medical institute is imposed a duty to notify the statutory

48. Act No. 66/1986 Coll., on Abortions.

representative on the abortion carried out subsequently. It is surprising that this duty exists only in case of abortions applied for, while in cases of serious health condition circumstances indicating the abortion as vital, it may be even more desirable for the parents to be informed.

99. Under the law, in the case of a minor girl below 16, the abortion must be applied for by the statutory representative. Therefore, the consent of statutory representatives will not be required by law in case of abortion in order to protect the minor's health. In a way, this is a violation of the principle that either a minor acts by herself or her statutory representatives act on her behalf. With regard to the regulations by which the Abortion Act is to be carried out (a conception below 15 years of age is always an abortion indication in order to protect the girl's health), the practice has come to the conclusion that for children below 16, the medical facility is not bound by a denial of a statutory representative to grant consent to the abortion, and thus the abortion may be carried out with the girl's consent even without her parents' consent.[49]

100. Dependent work by minors under the age of 15 or minors who have not completed compulsory schooling is prohibited (§34 of the Civil Code). These minors may only engage in artistic, cultural, sporting and advertising activities if such activities are appropriate to their age, are not dangerous to them, do not hinder their education or attendance at school or participation in educational programmes, and do not harm their health, physical, mental, moral or social development (§121 et seq. of the Employment Act). Permission is granted by the labour offices.

101. The employment eligibility of children over 15 years of age is regulated by a special law, which also establishes various restrictions for minors, e.g., with regard to overtime and night work (§243 et seq. of the Labour Code), but especially with regard to the protection of the safety and health of such employees (§§246 and 247 of the Labour Code). A minor under the age of 16 is also protected by the Civil Code, as amended by Act No. 460/2016 Coll., according to which a minor who has reached the age of 15 may undertake to perform dependent work. The date of commencement of work may not be the day preceding the day on which the minor completes compulsory schooling (§35 of the Civil Code).

102. A minor child may also run a business or other activity or engage in self-employment, but only with the consent of the parents and the approval of the court (§33 of the Civil Code).

103. If in the sphere of private law, issues of a minor's capacity to behave consistent with law and to acquire rights and obligations based on his/her own will are typical, in public law, it is typical to allow certain behaviour of a child by stating certain age limits. The age limits differ in nature:

49. Stepan, J., *Pravo a moderni medicina (Law and a Modern Medicine)*, Prague 1989, p. 134. A criticism of this attitude may also be found in: Drgonec, J., *A New Abortion Act*, Pravny obzor 1987, No. 1.

a. on attaining a certain age, the child acquires rights not possessed before, after proving to be capable of certain behaviour (e.g., obtaining a driving licence for a small motorbike at the age of 15; from 1 January 2024, a 17-year-old minor can obtain a driving licence for cars, but until the age of 18 must drive under the supervision of a 'mentor');
b. certain options for the child's behaviour are free from any other limitations (attending film performances, etc.);
c. up to a certain age, children are prohibited from behaving in a certain way that might be dangerous (for their health, life, upbringing – for example, without being accompanied by an older person, a child below 10 years of age may not ride a bike in a public street).

Therefore, in some cases, it is sufficient to attain a certain age; in others, the child is entitled to act in a certain way only on attaining the age, plus a decision of an administrative authority that has inspected the child's capacity for certain behaviour (e.g., obtaining a driving licence) is required.

In a number of cases, observing such bans and restrictions imposed on minors is checked by state authorities in a variety of ways, often only by way of noticing (e.g., the child's right to man a lift without an adult person's supervision).

It should be stated that there exists no complete list of such orders, bans and restrictions in administrative law. At present, when administrative law is subject to numerous substantial changes, indeed, it is not possible for administrative law experts to obtain such a list. However, this question will be acute in the future as it will enable experts to fully review the legal status of children in our system of law.

§3. Liability of Minors for Damages

104. Related to the above concepts are the tort capacity and the partial tort capacity of a minor child who lacks full legal capacity. It is established that every person is responsible for his or her actions if he or she is capable of judging and controlling them (§24 of the Civil Code). A minor who has not acquired full legal capacity is liable to compensate for the damage caused if he or she was capable of controlling his or her actions and assessing their consequences; the injured party is also entitled to compensation if he or she did not resist the wrongdoer out of consideration for him or her. Even if the tort capacity of the minor is not established, the injured party is entitled to compensation for damages if it is fair, taking into account the financial circumstances of the child and the injured party (§2920 of the Civil Code). The party who neglected to supervise the injured party properly shall also be jointly and severally liable for damages with the injured party. If the pest is not obliged to compensate, the injured party shall be compensated by the person who neglected to supervise the pest (§2921 of the Civil Code).

§4. Criminal Liability of Minors

105. The Czech Criminal Code[50] links the start of criminal liability to the age of 15. Thus, the Czech Republic has been placed among the states with a rather high age limit for beginning criminal liability.

106. Prior to World War II, Czechoslovakia had, at that time, a rather modern criminal law concerning juvenile delinquency.[51] This act of law was completely revoked, not to be replaced by another, upon the adoption of the Criminal Act 1950. The Criminal Act[52] of 1961 contained special provisions concerning punishment of minor offenders. Since 1 January 2004, there has been a separate and comprehensive law involving this sphere.[53]

107. On attaining this age limit, however, full criminal liability does not arise, equal to cases of adult criminal offenders. The purpose of punishment involving an offender aged 15–18 is predominantly the minor's upbringing to make him/her a proper citizen in regard to his/her personal properties, character, family upbringing and background. Possible remedial measures can be educational measures, protective measures or punitive measures. By no means may a minor be imposed property forfeiture or an extraordinary punishment (i.e., imprisonment sentence between fifteen and twenty-five years or a life sentence). The imprisonment sentence must be served by a minor offender separated from adult offenders in either special imprisonment facilities or departments.

A minor is punished less severely than an adult offender. The punishment terms for minors are reduced to half of those imposed on adult offenders, and the upper limit of the imprisonment term may not exceed five years. In extraordinary cases, the court may impose a term of five to ten years if it holds that a less severe sentence would not be sufficient to attain the purpose of the punishment.

108. The fact that a criminal offence was committed by a minor offender is also reflected in the procedure, for example, by an obligatory defence, with a representative of the legal and social protection authority present, etc.[54]

109. If a person, having attained the age of 12 and is younger than 15, has committed an act, which would otherwise be deemed a criminal offence, and for which the Criminal Code allows imposing extraordinary punishment (e.g., murder), the

50. Act No. 40/2009 Coll., Criminal Code as subsequently amended.
51. Act No. 48/1931 Coll., on Criminal Jurisdiction over Minors.
52. Act No. 140/1961 Coll., Criminal Act.
53. Act No. 218/2003 Coll., on Responsibility of Juveniles for Crimes and on Jurisdiction in these Cases.
54. Act No. 141/1961 Coll., Criminal Procedure Code.

special juvenile court in civil proceedings is bound to impose a protective care order involving the child.[55]

Protective care is exercised in special facilities.

55. Act No. 218/2003 Coll., on Responsibility of Juveniles for Crimes and on Jurisdiction in these Cases, §93(2).

Chapter 4. Names

§1. Names

110. The name and surname of a natural person are his/her essential identification denotation. The right of a child to have a name denoted is, in addition to others, also embedded in Article 7 of the UN Convention on the Rights of the Child.

Denoting the name and, in some cases, also a surname of a child, comes within parental rights, constituting the substance of the legal relationship between parents and children.

A natural person is entitled and bound to employ the name (or names) and surname stated in his/her certificate of birth, issued by the registry office, before public authorities.[56]

§2. Forename

111. Parents are bound to agree on the child's name (names).

If a child is born to an unmarried woman and if within one month the paternity is not established based on an affirmation of both parents, then the mother's declaration on the child's name will be sufficient. The registry office is bound to notify the court if the parents do not agree on the child's name, or will not denote the child's name at all, or they denote a name that cannot be entered in the birth register, or if the child's parents are not known, within one month.[57]

Such cases, when the parents (typically when only the child's mother is known) do not denote the child's name at all, occur, for example, when the child immediately following the delivery is placed in a baby care institute and the mother agrees with adoption, regardless of the future adopters.

112. The parents may not select any name whatsoever for their child; their selection is restricted by law.

Operative on 1 July 2001, a maximum of two names of a child, that may not be the same, can be entered in the register; a child whose parents are not Czech Republic citizens may have more than two names entered.

Special provisions of the Civil Registry Act enable entry of a second name for a natural person; as in 1950–2001, this option did not exist, and a person could have only one name. In case of a child over 15, his/her express consent is required for entering his/her second name in the register. The parents may not enter a second name in the register without this consent.[58]

It is not possible to enter as a name an expression denoting days or things. Male natural persons may not have a female name entered, and vice versa. The registry office will not enter the name if it is aware that this name is used by a living sibling

56. Act No. 301/2000 Coll., Civil Registry Act, §§61, 68.
57. *Ibid.*, §18(4).
58. *Ibid.*, §62(3).

or if the siblings have a parent in common. For example, a man, married for the third time, may have a son of the same name from each marriage.

In case of doubts concerning the correct form and spelling of the name, the applicant is bound to submit a relevant expert's opinion.[59]

The parents' education and the related professions are reflected in selecting names in the Czech Republic. As shown in a recent survey, parents with primary education prefer both the names traditionally considered to be 'Czech', that is, the names of Slavonic origin, and Czech versions of non-Slavonic names long occurring in our territory. However, these parents rather often select names that are striking, foreign or newly introduced from abroad, namely, based on popular foreign soap operas and films (Esmeralda, etc.).

Parents with secondary and university education prefer names used here earlier and today revived, having a certain tradition in the Czech language in the past. These parents select striking or foreign names less frequently.

In comparison to others, for parents engaged in agriculture, they frequently select names commonly found in the countryside of the early twentieth century.

§3. Surname

113. A surname of a child is usually decided prior to his/her birth. The following rules apply in denoting a child's surname.

114. In particular, the law stipulates that the child has the surname determined at the time of the marriage of his/her parents for the joint children of the spouses (§860 of the Civil Code).

115. If the child was not born into the marriage, or if the fiancés did not agree on the surname of their joint children at the time of the marriage, the parents choose the surname of one of them for the child (§862 of the Civil Code); the child may thus have both the mother's surname and the father's surname, but not a double surname, as is customary in some foreign jurisdictions or as is possible in the case of adoption (§835 of the Civil Code). An exception is the situation where the mother or the father of the child has a double surname. When registering the birth of a child, at the request of the parents, the surname of the female child may be given in the male form (§69(3) of the Civil Registry Act).

116. If the child has only a mother, or if only one parent is known, the child has his/her surname (§861 of the Civil Code). In the case of a child whose mother has requested that her identity be kept secret in connection with the birth, the child bears her surname.

117. If no parent of the child is known, e.g., in the case of a baby in a baby box, the surname is determined by the court. A similar procedure is followed if the parents of the child do not agree on the child's surname (§860 of the Civil Code).

---

59. *Ibid.*, §§62, 63.

§4. Change of Name and Surname

I. Changing a Minor's Name or Surname under the Family Code

118. The change of a child's surname under the Civil Code occurs as follows:

a. if the mother of a minor child whose father is unknown marries, the child's mother and her husband may declare unanimously before the registry office that the surname intended for their other children will also be given to that child (§862(2) of the Civil Code);
b. as a result of adoption or annulment of adoption, *ex lege* (§§835, 842 of the Civil Code);
c. by the nature of the case if:
   - the mother marries the father of the child;
   - the paternity is established by a decision by consent of the parents or by a court decision, and the parents determine by agreement a surname different from the surname the child has hitherto borne;
   - there is a denial of paternity, and the mother has a surname different from the former 'legal' father of the child.

119. If the child was adopted, then the court ruling also comprises a statement that the child will bear the surname of his/her adopters. A common adoptive child of a married couple will have the surname denoted for their other children. This also applies in the case when the adopter is the adoptive child's parent's married spouse.[60] If the adoptive child has reached the age of 12 years, the adoptive parent may, with the consent of the adoptive child, declare that the adoptive child shall add the adoptive parent's surname to his or her own surname. If the adoptee has an appended surname, the adopter's surname may be appended only to the adoptee's first surname; if the adopter has an appended surname, only the adopter's first surname may be appended to the adoptee's surname. If adoption were revoked, the change of the adoptive child's surname to his/her previous one, which he/she bore at the time the court was deliberating on the adoption, would be a resulting legal consequence too.

II. Changing the Name or Surname under the Civil Registry Act

120. In order to change a minor child's name or surname, both parents' consent is necessary. If the child is over 12, his/her consent is always needed for his/her name or surname to be changed.

In case of name or surname changing in cases other than those so far mentioned, this change would be decided upon by the registry office in an administrative proceeding, after receipt of payment of the appropriate administrative charge.

60. Civil Code §835.

121. In deciding by the registry office on changing the name or surname based on an application of a natural person, the point of registry is, namely, cases of shameful or ridiculous surnames or if there is a serious reason for the surname to be changed. The reason must be proved by the applicants to the registry office, and the registry office will consider whether the reason is indeed so serious as to justify the surname change.

The change of name or surname of a minor child will not be permitted by the registry office if the change were contrary to the child's needs and interests.[61] In order to judge whether the name or surname change is consistent with the needs and interests of the minor, the registry office may demand an opinion of a relevant authority of social and legal protection of children, an expert report of a paedopsychologist, etc.

122. To change a child's name or surname, both parents' agreement is necessary. Most often, there is an effort to change the child's surname in a situation when the child's mother remarries and changes her surname to that of her husband. This change of the mother's surname has had no influence on the child's surname. In a new family, a new child was born, bearing, of course, a surname different from that of his/her half-sibling. In order to change the name of the first marriage child, the mother needs the consent of her former husband, that is, the child's father. If the child's father disagrees with the child's surname being changed, there is no other choice than to address the court with a petition to substitute the father's consent in the application for changing the surname in a registry office.[62]

The court should substitute the other parent's consent in the application for changing a minor's surname only if there are serious reasons to do so. This will be, for example, if a parent who disagrees with the child's surname being changed does not meet his/her obligations towards the child, shows no genuine interest in the child, has evidently lost any emotional bonds with the child or if for any other serious reason strengthening the child's feeling of appurtenance to this parent, does not promote the child's welfare.[63]

It should be noted that the registry office is not bound by the court decision, as the court did not rule on the surname changing of the child, but merely that the application for a surname change could be made even without the other parent's consent. In practice, the registry office will allow this change as the question of whether the surname change promotes the child's welfare and interests has already been deliberated by the court.

The other parent's consent to change the minor child's name is not required when:

a. the other parent has died; in that case, the application shall be accompanied by his or her death certificate; or
b. if the other parent has been deprived of the right to determine the name or names and surname of the child, in which case the application shall be accompanied by a final judgment; or

61. Act No. 301/2000 Coll., Civil Registry Act, §72(4).
62. *Ibid.*, §76(2).
63. Supreme Court Decision No. 11/1973.

c. the place of residence of the other parent is unknown.

123. In case of adoption, the possibility of changing the child's name is stipulated separately. As already stated, the surname is changed upon the court's decision on adoption. The change of name has not yet been stipulated, although adopters often are interested in the adoptive child's name changing. This was decided by the registry office based on general provisions on name changing; that is, the adopters were not entitled under the law to have the child's name changed. Operative on 1 July 2001, the Civil Registry Act now expressly entitles the adopters to select another name or names for the adoptive child by an affirmation before a registry office within six months from the court ruling on adoption becoming effective, but no later than when the child comes of age. If an adoptive child has only one name entered in the register of births, his/her adopters may select a second name for him/her. Also in this case, this name change or entering a second name is subject to the minor's express consent.[64]

The registry office in this case does not allow the name changing; it will only examine whether the name selected (names) is capable of being entered in the registry, and if so, the office is bound to do so. Adopters are relieved from paying administrative charges for name changing.

If an adoption were revoked, unlike the surname, the name of the adoptive child will not change.[65]

124. Under the rules of Czech grammar, in the majority of cases, it is quite unambiguous whether the name and surname pertain to a male or to a female. Therefore, a natural person, undergoing a change of sex, will be allowed by the registry office to use a neutral name or surname,[66] based on his/her application. The certification of a medical facility, that is, that it has been licensed to carry out the respective treatment in order to change the person's sex, must be attached to the application. There are a few names that may be used for both males and females, namely, those of foreign origin, for example, Rene. For surnames, such will be used, not requiring the feminine ending -ova.

125. A natural person, who is not a Czech Republic citizen, may be allowed to have a surname changed only if this person has been granted permission to reside permanently or in the long term in the territory of the Czech Republic.

64. Act No. 301/2000 Coll., Civil Registry Act, §64.
65. *Ibid.*, §65.
66. *Ibid.*, §72a.

Chapter 5. Nationality

126. Determining a child's nationality (citizenship) is a question of public law.[67] A child's nationality is attached to the existence of a legal relation in a family.

127. A child acquires Czech nationality by birth, providing that at least one of the parents is a Czech Republic national. To acquire Czech nationality, it is not decisive whether the child was born in or out of the territory of the Czech Republic. If the parents are lacking any citizenship and at least one of them permanently resides in the territory of the Czech Republic, the child acquires Czech citizenship, if born in the territory of the Czech Republic.

If at least one of the adopters is a Czech Republic citizen, the child acquires Czech citizenship upon the court ruling on adoption becoming effective.

If the mother is an alien or is lacking any citizenship and the father is a Czech citizen, the child acquires Czech citizenship upon establishing paternity either by the parents' affirmation or by an affiliation proceeding.

The child acquires citizenship also by being found in the territory of the Czech Republic if the child is below 3, unless proved that the child had acquired citizenship of another state by birth. This means that the children found, after the search for their parents failed, acquire Czech citizenship.

67. Act No. 186/2013 Coll., on State Citizenship as later amended.

Chapter 6. Domicile and Residence

128. The express definition of domicile is contained in the provisions of §80 of the Civil Code: 'a person is domiciled in the place where he resides with the intention of living there permanently, subject to a change of circumstances; such intention may arise from his declaration or from the circumstances of the case'. The concept of habitual residence should be used as a threshold determinant for the international jurisdiction of the courts in relation to the exercise of parental responsibility. This is a factual concept which has no legal definition, and its interpretation therefore depends primarily on the case law of the Court of Justice of the EU (CJEU) and national courts, in our case primarily the Supreme Court of the Czech Republic. In its decision,[68] the CJEU stated that when assessing the habitual residence of a child, it is necessary to take into account the integration of the child within the social and family environment and set out the aspects according to which this integration must be assessed – the duration, regularity, conditions and reasons for residence in the territory of the Member State and the family's move to that State, the nationality of the child, the place and conditions of schooling, the language skills and the family and social ties of the child in that State. It also stated that the place of habitual residence must always be assessed in the light of the specific facts of the case.

129. Local jurisdiction of the court deciding on the child is related to the child's domicile. Pursuant to §467(1) of the Act on Special Court Proceedings, the general court of the minor child is competent for the proceedings. The general court of the minor party is, in accordance with §4(2) of the Act on Special Court Proceedings, the court in whose district the minor resides on the basis of the parents' agreement or a court decision or other decisive facts. Only such a court is locally competent to decide on matters concerning the custody of minors.

130. Stipulation of so-called permanent residence is a matter of public law. Public law regulations and those concerning social security are based on the fact that a minor child has, as a rule, the same residence as his/her parents if they live together; otherwise, the child's residence rather automatically evolves from the residence of the parent in whose custody the child was placed.

131. Minor children receive an identity card after attaining 15 years of age, with their permanent residence entered. Until that time, there is no written document confirming the child's place of residence.

68. Judgment of the CJEU of 2 Apr. 2009 in Case C-523/07 ('A').

Chapter 7. Mentally Handicapped Persons

132. The person whose legal capacity has been restricted by the court has limited legal capacity (§§55 et seq. of the Civil Code). The basic premise is that any decision must be made in the interests of the person concerned after having seen him or her and with full recognition of his or her rights and personal je-dynamics; in doing so, the extent and degree of the person's incapacity to take care of his or her own affairs must be thoroughly taken into account. Furthermore, the law provides that a person's legal capacity may be restricted only if he would otherwise be at risk of serious harm and if less restrictive measures would not suffice in view of his interests. Thus, the principle of proportionality must be applied in any decision (*see also* IV.ÚS 412/04, II.ÚS 934/16 and IV.ÚS 1580/16). The new law therefore provides for a whole catalogue of support measures, e.g., preliminary declarations, assistance in decision-making, representation by a household member. If someone has been limited in his or her legal capacity, a court-appointed guardian acts on his or her behalf. The procedural regulation is the Act on Special Court Proceedings (§§31 et seq. of the Code of Civil Procedure).

133. The Act lays down further rules, in particular, that the aim of the restriction of legal capacity is the person's interests. The grounds for the restriction are a mental disorder that is not merely transitory and the extent to which the person is unable to act legally because of the mental disorder, which is not merely transitory. In the last order, however, it is possible for a maximum of three years. If it is clear that the person's condition will not improve within that time, the court may limit the person's capacity for a longer period, but not longer than five years.

134. The second part of the Civil Code contains special provisions relating to persons who have been deprived of their legal capacity. These include, in particular, the capacity to marry (§673 of the Civil Code), the right to consent to adoption (§812 of the Civil Code) and the rules on the exercise of parental responsibility (§868(2) of the Civil Code).

Part II. Family Law

Chapter 1. Marriage

§1. The Nature of Marriage

135. Traditionally, the law stipulates that marriage may only be entered into between a man and a woman (§655 of the Civil Code). The legislation is mandatory because it is a status relationship (§1(2) of the Civil Code). Since 1 January 2025, there has been one change in Czech family law that fundamentally changes the status of same-sex unions. Same-sex unions entered into after 1 January 2025, i.e., partnerships under the Civil Code, continue to be treated in the same way as marriage and the obligations and rights of the spouses.

136. Prerequisites and requirements for marriage may be defined as follows:

a. personal assumptions, e.g., the absence of obstacles on the part of the fiancées;
b. the essential elements of a marriage declaration of will, e.g., the non-existence of free and complete consent expression of will;
c. the essential elements of the procedure, i.e., the formal requirements.

137. The basic principles on which the legal regulation of marriage is based include voluntariness, monogamy, permanence, equality (parity), autonomy of the will, solidarity, protection of the weaker party and dissolubility.

138. When it comes to the purpose of marriage, the law stipulates that setting up a family, proper upbringing of children and mutual support and help are the main purposes (§655 of the Civil Code).

§2. The Capacity to Marry

I. Betrothal

139. Betrothal (*sponsalia pro futuro*) is an ancient legal institution, which in our country was quite thoroughly regulated by historical legislation (in particular, §45 ABGB, i.e., the then Civil Code of Austria). It was a matter of great social importance that had a number of consequences, e.g., a prenuptial agreement could be concluded, and a dowry stipulated within it.

140. There is no doubt that even today, betrothal may still be understood as an institution based on trust and having a moral obligation or as a certain stabilizer of expectations.

141. Betrothal is not enshrined in the current legislation, although the law uses the term betrothal in many cases, however only as a legislative abbreviation (e.g., §659 of the Civil Code). In fact, betrothal more or less takes place, even if it does not have a ceremonial form.

142. Betrothal may be understood as an expression of the consent of a man and a woman to enter into a marriage at a time that is either precisely determined or appropriate according to circumstances, customs, etc. The betrothed shall agree that they will enter into marriage in the future, they shall announce this to each other, respectively be aware of another's notice.

143. Since the current legislation does not explicitly regulate betrothal, the consequences of breaking the promise to marry are not enshrined either. If there was an agreement to conclude a marriage and then there was a withdrawal from that agreement, certain negative legal consequences may be taken into consideration, especially in the property sphere. It is, for example, possible to demand the return of the engagement ring (if the recipient harms the donor and clearly violates good morals, etc., in accordance with §2072 of the Civil Code).

144. Damages may also be requested if they arise in causal connection with intentional conduct against good morals (§2(3) and §2909 of the Civil Code). It may be an act that is not illegal, but which harms the interests of the other spouse and causes harm to them. Their personal sphere may also be affected.

II. Different Sex

145. Marriage may be, as arises from its nature, made by a man and a woman only. Marriage between two persons of identical sex cannot come into being at all (*non matrimonium, matrimonium putativum*).[69] On 1 January 2025, Act No. 123/2024 Coll. came into force, which fundamentally changes the Civil Code with regard to unions of same-sex couples; as of 1 January 2025, it is no longer possible to enter into a registered partnership in the Czech Republic. Same-sex couples can enter into a civil partnership under the Civil Code. This union has similar obligations and rights as marriage, but is not called marriage.

146. However, the problem of transsexuals is addressed by law only in terms of how to change sex.[70] For the contracting of a marriage, the sex that is stated on the register of birth is decisive. If, after marrying, one of the partners demands sex-conversion surgery, the marriage must first be dissolved. If this does not happen, the

69. *See* Family Code, §15a and §3.
70. Act on Specific Health Services No. 373/2011.

marriage is dissolved by a change of sex.[71] As soon as hormonal treatment has begun in the course of changing gender, the registry office will allow such person to change his/her name and surname into such name and surname from which it does not show in the Czech language whether the person is male or female. After carrying out the surgery, the registry office will again allow the change of name and surname into the opposite gender, adjust the data in the register of birth and issue a new birth certificate with the sex changed.

Under Czech law, the person, after having officially changed his/her sex, may contract a valid marriage with a person having, in his/her birth certificate, the opposite sex.

III. Prior Marriage

147. Marriage may not be contracted by a person who has been married before if this marriage legally exists (is valid). Such marriage is declared void by the court ex officio.[72] The same barrier applies to registered partnerships.

For this reason, the Civil Code stipulates expressly that a person wishing to contract a new marriage is bound to show that his/her previous marriage has ceased to exist or has been declared void.[73] In case of a new marriage, the person has to submit either a certificate of death of the former husband or wife or a legitimate court ruling on divorce (divorce certificate) or a legitimate court ruling declaring the previous marriage void.[74]

148. The monogamy principle is also protected under criminal law. The person who contracts a marriage while his/her former marriage still exists shall be punished by imprisonment for up to two years. The person who contracts a marriage with a person already married shall be equally punished.[75]

Under both the Criminal Code and the Civil Code, bigamy occurs in case the person involved in fact becomes a husband or a wife of two different persons. It is a criminal offence, regardless of the fact that the previous marriage is also void, for example, due to the fact that it was contracted by a minor without court consent. In the view of criminal liability, it is not substantial that the second, a bigamous marriage, is void due to some other impediment, for example, a mental disorder.

The crime of bigamy is an intentional crime, which means that the offender must be aware of the fact that his/her previous marriage still exists, as well as of the consequences arising from contracting a new marriage while the previous one still exists ('hopefully nobody will find out'). The same concerns the other spouse contracting marriage with the bigamist, although he/she is aware of the fact that the previous marriage has not legally ceased to exist.

71. Civil Code §29.
72. Family Code §11(1).
73. *Ibid.*, §6(2).
74. Act No. 301/2000 Coll., Civil Registry Act.
75. Criminal Code §194.

IV. Consanguinity

149. The parties must not be related within prohibited degrees. Marriages of parties within prohibited degrees of relationship are:

a. marriage between a person and an ancestor or a descendant of the person;
b. marriage between a brother and a sister (whether of whole blood or half-blood).

The persons having obtained the above-stated relationship through adoption may not marry, supposing the adoption legally exists, even though their biological origins are quite different.[76]

However, consanguinity may not be revoked by a legal rule. Even though this is not expressly stipulated under the Family Code, a brother and a sister who have been irrevocably adopted by different families may get married. Regarding the Czech provisions of irrevocable adoption aiming at maintaining anonymous adoptions, this fact may be found out after the marriage has been contracted. Such marriage shall be declared void ex officio.

V. Marriageable Age

150. A person over 18 years of age (age of majority) may marry. Minor persons between 16 and 18 may petition the court for permission to marry. The court grants its consent to the marriage if there is a substantial reason in favour. It has been held that this phrase means more than the mere fact that the girl is pregnant. The Family Code considers the possibility of granting consent to marry to a minor as an exception if it is consistent with the purpose of marriage.[77]

It is not provided by law that the other party to be married must be an adult. Judicial decisions admit granting consent to marry to two minor persons over 16.

151. The court hearing is attended by the minor's parents, and the other person to be married must also be questioned. Parental consent to the marriage is not required; however, the court always considers carefully whether to permit the marriage or not, providing the minor's parents present serious dissenting reasons. The court ruling must contain precisely the name of the person to be married.[78]

The marriage would be void if contracted with a person different from the one named by the court in its permission. Such marriage shall be declared void by the court ex officio.

In the instant of contracting marriage, the minor becomes an adult. He/she would become an adult even in case the marriage was contracted without court permission. Majority so acquired is not lost should the marriage be dissolved or pronounced void.[79]

76. Civil Code §675.
77. *Ibid.*, §672.
78. Civil Procedure Code §194.
79. *Ibid.*, §8(2).

Recently, the number of marriages of minors has decreased significantly. While in 1993, the court granted permission to marry 264 16-year-old brides and 1,202 17-year-old brides, in 1999, there were only 29 16-year-old brides and 99 17-year-old brides.

VI. Mental Disorder

152. The legislation stipulates that marriage shall not be concluded by a person whose legal capacity in this area, i.e., in the marital sphere, has been limited by the court (§673 of the Civil Code). If, in a specific case, the judgment does not contain restrictions on a certain person's capacity to marry, they will be able to marry without further ado, i.e., without having to go through the procedure of permission to marry, as it was under the previous regulation. After all, even the procedural regulation regulates this procedure only for minors who have not acquired legal rights and have reached the age of 16 (§367 Special Proceedings Act).

153. However, if a person whose legal capacity is limited in terms of their capacity to marry enters into a marriage, such a marriage will be concluded. The court could not declare this marriage invalid upon the motion of anyone who has a legal interest in it (in particular, §680 *in fine* of the Civil Code), neither ex officio (§685 of the Civil Code, which defines the range of cases in which a court declares a marriage null and void even without an application). However, the court may declare such a marriage invalid upon the suggestion of the second spouse, e.g., when the spouse is subject to fraud (§684 of the Civil Code).

154. Law *expressis verbis* establishes the grounds for validation, namely the dissolution of a marriage, e.g., by death, or the correction of this deficiency (§682 of the Civil Code) or the conception and birth of a living child (§683 of the Civil Code).

155. In the case of persons who, according to the previous regulation, have been deprived of their capacity to perform legal acts, it shall be stated in accordance with the transitional provisions that they are considered to be persons limited in their capacity according to the Civil Code (§3032(1) of the Civil Code). As it regards persons limited in their capacity to perform legal acts (§10(2) of the Civil Code 1964), it will depend on the extent of the limitation or the area in which they were limited to perform legal acts – it will be important whether it is a property sphere or personal items or status (§3032(2) of the Civil Code). A person's freedom to marry as a basic rule shall be derived from the value base of the Civil Code, the Charter and human rights conventions in general (§2(1)) of the Civil Code in connection, in particular, with Article 12 of the European Convention on Human Rights (ECHR). In the case of doubts about whether a marriage was concluded or not, or in the matter of a null and void marriage, only the court may decide, in accordance with the law, in relation to the specifics of the case or following the specific extent of the limitation of a person in their legal capacity.

156. Under the conditions stipulated by law, the marriage of a certain person could also be fraudulent (§677 of the Civil Code). This could be a situation where the fiancé's will is completely absent or when the fiancé is unable to express their will.

VII. Duration of Guardianship, Custodianship and Fosterage

157. The existence of guardianship (§928 of the Civil Code), custodianship (§953 of the Civil Code) and fosterage (§958 of the Civil Code) is a completely new legal obstacle to marriage, which takes into account the state of dependence. A marriage concluded in violation of the prohibition of marriage between a person in care and a person providing care (§676 of the Civil Code) may be declared invalid upon the proposal of anyone who has a legal interest in it (§680 of the Civil Code).

158. However, the law stipulates that if rectification occurs, the marriage may not be declared invalid (§682 of the Civil Code). In the considered cases, convalidation always occurs, as these obstacles disappear due to the nature of the matter when the child entrusted to guardianship, custodianship and fosterage acquires legal capacity, in this case, precisely by concluding a marriage (§30(2) of the Civil Code, *see* explicitly §970 and §935(1) of the Civil Code).

VIII. Failure to Consent

A. *Lack of Free Will*

159. The marriage does not arise if the man or the woman has been forced to marry under physical duress (*vis absoluta*). With the regard that marriage is contracted with two witnesses and a priest present, or in civil marriage with a municipality mayor and the registrar present, this possibility is highly improbable, perhaps only in case one of the affianced would have been served a drug and he/she would not be aware of his/her acts.

160. The marriage is void if the marriage declaration has been made under wrongful threat (under duress, *vis compulsiva*).[80] Wrongful threat results in manifesting the will on the part of the agent; however, his/her will is modified by the will of another person, for example, the other party or a third person who may be in no legal relationship to either or both persons to be married.

Wrongfulness of the threat may arise from not only the essence of the threat (reporting criminal offence which was not even committed) but also threatening to do something the person threatening is entitled to do (e.g., a right of a creditor to sue his/her debtor) if the threat is to influence the other fiancé/fiancée (may he/she be so-called at all?) to marry.

80. Civil Code §684.

It is not inevitable that the harm as threatened must occur directly to the person threatened; it may concern another close person, for example, a threat to kidnap a child.

In theory, it is not a wrongful threat if a person to be married acts under the influence arising from natural respect (e.g., a very well-brought-up young lady) and also in case of threatening by minute harm or such harm that cannot arouse reasonable fear.

B. Error

161. An error may concern:

a. an identity of either of the parties to be married;
b. legality of the matrimonial ceremony.

Both possible errors are provided for under Czech law only since the family law reform in 1998.

162. An error in identity of either of the parties to be married means that the marriage is contracted with a different person than intended. Predominantly, these are cases when a person submits another person's or forged identity documents. This fact has been growing in significance in the past ten years, namely, in relation to marriages with foreigners or with refugees, who have no identity documents.

However, the identity error may not concern situations with the erroneous gender of the other party, in which case the marriage has not arisen at all.

Nevertheless, an error concerning the expected character of the other party has no effect.

163. An error in the nature of ceremony can involve predominantly the church wedding. Certainly, a person to be married who is not a member of a particular church or congregation might hold a particular ceremony to be another church act, not a marriage contracting (e.g., engagement).

In civil marriages with regard to the presence of the registrar, possibly also an interpreter (for foreigners), neither of the spouses can be excused from his/her non-considerate acting by alleging he/she had no idea he/she was getting married. A possibility of claiming the right to have the marriage declared void might arise only in case it were contracted without an interpreter present, although an interpreter is expressly prescribed by law for such cases.

C. Others

164. Czech law does not in any respect sanction marriages contracted with the purpose of circumvention of the law (*in fraudem legis*). These are mainly marriages with foreigners with the aim of obtaining a residence permit in the territory of the Czech Republic, etc.

Even though the intentions of the man and wife are not to cohabit but merely to obtain certain advantages arising from marriage, the Czech law holds such marriages valid. However, this act may constitute the offence of aiding and abetting an unauthorized stay in the Czech Republic.[81]

§3. Formalities of Marriage

I. Declarations

165. Marriage is created by the fiancés making their free, identical expressions of will to each other in front of a competent marriage celebrant.

166. The legislation builds on and clarifies the previous legislation in relation to Article (1) of the New York Convention,[82] which provides that 'no marriage shall be legally contracted without the full and free consent of both parties, expressed in person after due publicity in the presence of the authority competent to perform the marriage ceremony and of the witnesses prescribed by law'.

167. The law lays down the rule that the marriage celebrant (§658 of the Civil Code) asks the betrothed whether they wish to enter into marriage together. The order is not specified. The affirmative answer of both, namely the word 'yes', or the hearing of the nuptial expression of will, will create the marriage. Subsequent acts, e.g., the mutual exchange of rings, have no legal effect.

168. A new feature is that marriage is no longer created merely by the declaration of marriage but by the free and full consent of the betrothed to enter into marriage together (§656 of the Civil Code). The new legislation is thus more general and liberal. Marriage can also be established in other ways if it is clear that the spouses have made their marriage intention (§659 *in fine* of the Civil Code). The will must always exist, be real and genuine, serious and free from mistake (Pl. ÚS 16/15).

169. Marriage is established when the spouses express their will to enter into marriage in other than words. In particular, it may be some ritual that is typical of a particular legitimate church. It may also be a vow or various promises made by the betrothed to each other or to the one who is marrying.

170. Without a conjugal expression of will, the marriage does not come into existence (§677 of the Civil Code; *see* IV.2.2).

171. If the freedom of will is violated, e.g., by coercion consisting in the use of violence or the threat of violence, or if the marital expression of will is made in error

81. Act No. 40/2009 Coll., Criminal Code, §341.
82. Convention on Consent to Marriage, Minimum Age for Marriage and Registration of Marriages, New York 7.11.1962.

as to the identity of the betrothed or as to the nature of the marital act, the court could declare the marriage null and void (§684 of the Civil Code, which is *lex specialis* to §587 of the Civil Code; *see* IV.3.2.6).

172. It is necessary to distinguish between the formation of the marriage and its registration, i.e., the registration of the marriage in the civil registry (§11 of the Civil Registry Act).

173. Before marrying, the persons to be married are bound to make several other declarations contained in the questionnaire to be filled out by them prior to marriage. All these declarations are read out by the registrar in the course of a civil marriage.

The persons to be married are bound to declare that they are not aware of any circumstances barring their intended marriage. This declaration substitutes the traditional public announcement of two persons intending to marry (bans).

174. The Civil Code imposes the duty on persons to be married to know in advance each other's character and health condition so they can create a marriage which will fulfil its aims.[83] In the course of the marriage ceremony, the parties only declare that they know each other's health conditions. This declaration, however, has no legal consequences as Czech law does not require obligatory medical checks prior to marriage. The fact that the persons to be married did not know each other's health conditions, that, for example, one of them concealed a serious disease or disorder, has no effect on the validity of the marriage.

The persons to be married are also bound to declare that they have considered the future arrangement of their property relations, dwelling and providing for the family after marrying. This declaration has no legal effects, either. The affianced are not bound to enter into any contract concerning matrimonial property or a contract concerning matrimonial cohabitation.[84] The declarations, as mentioned, are rather an attempt to prevent non-considerate marriages.

The persons to be married are also bound to declare how they have agreed to use their surnames after marrying.[85]

II. Types of Marriage Solemnization

175. The ABGB 1811 originally provided for church weddings only. In 1868, the so-called exigency civil wedding was stipulated for cases when a priest of the church recognized by the state refused to administer the marriage for reasons not recognized by the Civil Code. In 1870, an obligatory civil wedding was established for persons who were not members of any of the churches recognized by the state and for non-believers.

83. Civil Code §665.
84. *See* below Part III, Ch. 3.
85. *See* below Part II, Ch. 2, §3.

After the rise of the Czechoslovak Republic in 1918, marriage and divorce were provided under the law in a new way, enabling both civil and church weddings to take place with equal legal consequences.[86]

176. Since January 1950, only the civil wedding has been stipulated by law.[87] The couple to be married could go through a 'religious wedding ceremony' only after having been married by a civil wedding. The Criminal Code stipulated sanctions for priests who would administer a religious wedding ceremony prior to the civil wedding. This provision was taken over by the Family Code of 1963.

177. An obligatory civil wedding also applies to Czechoslovak citizens in case of marrying abroad. Should a Czechoslovak citizen marry abroad by a church wedding only, such marriage would be considered in the territory of the former Czechoslovakia as non-existent (*non matrimonium, matrimonium putativum*).[88]

178. After the 'Velvet Revolution' in 1989, an effort in society was made to provide for a church wedding to be equal to a civil wedding. The Family Code Amendment, operative on 1 July 1992. stipulated both marriage solemnizations by a civil ceremony and a religious ceremony.

The Family Code Amendment[89] was adopted by the Federal Assembly after being proposed by the deputies, and thus it did not pass through the usual commenting procedure of the relevant governmental departments and an expert committee. The Amendment suffered from a number of drawbacks that could be settled only within the family law reform in 1998:

> At present a man and a woman intending to marry have the option to choose either a civil or church solemnization of marriage. Both forms are equal. The law stipulates expressly that if a marriage was contracted as a civil one, a religious wedding ceremony may follow, although with no legal consequences. If a marriage was contracted through a church solemnization, no civil wedding may follow.[90]

III. Civil Wedding

A. Marriage Solemnization Before a Local Authority

179. Marriage is administered by an appropriate local authority, keeping the register in any place within the Czech Republic.

The persons to be married may also administer the marriage in front of an authority, which does not keep the register.

---

86. Act No. 320/1919 Coll.
87. Act No. 365/1949 Coll., Family Law Act.
88. Act No. 97/1963 Coll., Private International Law and the Related Procedural Law Act, §20(2).
89. Act No. 234/1992 Coll.
90. Civil Code §670.

The solemnization of marriage must be carried out by the persons to be married before the mayor, his/her deputy or an authorized member of the local council, with the registrar present. As of 1 January 2024, a declaration of entry into marriage may also be accepted by a Member of Parliament or a Senator, who must declare in writing in advance that he or she will accept the declaration of entry into marriage (§11a(2) of the Civil Registry Act).

B. Consular Wedding

180. A citizen of the Czech Republic may also solemnize the marriage abroad before a diplomatic official of the Czech Republic.[91]

If the life of a person wishing to solemnize a marriage is under an immediate threat, he/she may solemnize the marriage abroad also before a captain of a ship sailing under the flag of the Czech Republic, a captain of an aeroplane registered in the Czech Republic or a commander of a military unit of the Czech Republic abroad. In the third case mentioned above, at least one of the parties must, however, be a citizen of the Czech Republic.[92]

IV. Church Wedding

181. A church wedding may be solemnized only before a church or religious congregation recognized by the state. At present, altogether twenty-one churches and religious associations are registered by the Ministry of Culture, the appropriate authority in the Czech Republic.[93]

182. To solemnize a marriage by a church wedding, equal terms given by law apply as in civil weddings. Matrimony law of a particular church, for example, the Roman Catholic Church stipulating certain terms to marriage in a way different from that of the law (e.g., age), is decisive only whether the church or religious association will enable the parties to solemnize their marriage. If the parties did not comply with the requirements of the particular church even though complying with the terms given by law, they would have no other choice but to solemnize the civil marriage.

The affianced are bound to submit to the person administering (the priest) a certificate showing they have complied with all requirements for marriage as stipulated by law. The certificate is issued by the register office in the district in which one of the parties resides. The certificate may not be older than six months.[94]

---

91. *Ibid.*, §668.
92. The option to marry before the persons as stated was stipulated only within family law reform in 1998. *See* Civil Code §667.
93. Act No. 3/2002 Coll., on Religious Freedom and the Status of Churches and Religious Denominations.
94. Civil Code §677(2).

If a priest solemnized the wedding without such certificate, the marriage will not come into being.[95]

A new feature since 2012 is that a marriage can also be celebrated as a church wedding if one or both of the spouses are in immediate danger of death.[96]

Within three working days, the priest is bound to deliver the record of marriage solemnization to the register office in the district in which the marriage was contracted. The register office will file the marriage contract in the marriage register and issue a certificate of marriage to the married couple.

However, no sanctions are stipulated for not carrying out this duty.

V. Power of Attorney

183. For important reasons, a local authority may permit an attorney to declare the marriage on behalf of one of the parties. A party's attorney may only be a fully legally capable natural person of the same gender as the party represented.

An important reason may be, for example, a long-term absence of a party in his/her residence and an urgent need to marry at the same time; for example, the other party is seriously ill, pregnant, etc.

184. Power of attorney must be given in writing with the signature attested by a notary. The other party to be married must be expressly and precisely named in it. Power of attorney must also contain all declarations made by the persons to be married in the course of marriage solemnization.

The power of attorney cancellation is effective only if the other party is informed about it prior to his/her declaration that he/she is marrying.

Failure to meet any of the terms as stipulated by law, including the failure to obtain permission from the local authority, has the effect that the marriage will not come into being at all.

This way of marriage solemnization is very rare.

VI. Other Formalities

185. The Civil Code requires the declaration of marriage to be carried out in public and solemnly.[97] 'The public' is deemed as the opposite of so-called clandestine marriages (*matrimonium clandestinum*), provided for by canon law. As the persons to be married may choose any place for the ceremony, the 'publicity' is seen in participating of the administering person, the registrar and the witnesses in the ceremony. Church weddings are public in the sense that they are solemnized in places used for religious ceremonies.[98]

---

95. *Ibid.*, §17a(3).
96. *Ibid.*, §667.
97. *Ibid.*, §656(2).
98. *Ibid.*, §663(2).

186. The Civil Code also requires the marriage to be solemnized with two witnesses present. In an exceptional case when witnesses will not take part in the ceremony, this has no effect on the validity or existence of marriage.

The presence of witnesses at the ceremony has a long history. However, Czech law today does not specify any details concerning the witnesses. Witnesses are generally expected to be adults. Their possible family relationship to the affianced is not decisive. Names of witnesses are written in the record of marriage and in the register of marriage, but not in the certificate of marriage.

187. Under Czech law, there is no statutory term prescribed for persons to be married, between deciding to marry and the wedding following. No waiting period must lapse between filling out the questionnaire that, since 1 July 2001, replaced the previous application to solemnize marriage, submitting the prescribed documents and the ceremony. Thus, Czech law does not prevent in any way non-considerate marriages from arising.

§4. Effects of Marriage

I. Name

188. On marriage solemnization, the parties are bound to declare how they agreed on the surnames to be used after marriage. They have three options under Czech law:

1. common surname for both of them;
2. both husband and wife will retain his/her original surname;
3. the parties may announce that one of them will use the common surname of the two with his/her original surname as a second one.

189. Under the constitutional principle of equality of men and women, a married couple may select as a common surname the surname of either the man or that of the woman. The parties may not choose another surname, for example, the maiden name of one of their mothers.

Traditionally, the woman adopts her husband's surname. A couple usually selects the woman's surname as a common surname if the husband's surname is ridiculous or pejorative.

190. If the parties decide to retain his/her original surnames respectively, they must also declare which of these surnames will be that of their common children. They cannot agree that if a girl is born within wedlock, she will take her mother's name and a boy, his father's name, respectively. The same surname must, as a rule, be borne by all common children of the married couple.

191. Since the family law reform in 1998, either spouse may have a double surname. If his/her previous surname consisted of two surnames, only one of them may be used as a second surname.

The double surname option is not very frequent. It is usually used by women well known in the public, unless they retain their present surname upon marrying. *Example*: Mr Adam Jagr marries Miss Eva Navratilova. The surnames of the couple after marrying may be as follows:

a. Adam Jagr and Eva Jagrova.
b. Adam Navratil and Eva Navratilova.
c. Adam Jagr and Eva Navratilova. Their children will bear either the surname Jagr(ova) or Navratil(ova).
d. Adam Jagr and Eva Jagrova Navratilova.
e. Adam Navratil Jagr and Eva Navratilova (this option will not be too frequent, but it is not excluded by law).

Mrs Eva Jagrova Navratilova has been divorced and is contracting a new marriage with Mr Alan Jones. As the wedding is solemnized in the territory of the Czech Republic, her name after marriage may be:

a. Eva Jonesova.
b. Eva Jagrova Navratilova.
c. Eva Jonesova Jagrova.

192. The woman's surname has, under the contemporary standard of Czech grammar,[99] the ending -ova, resp. -a, sometimes omitting the previous vowel. Therefore, the wife of Mr Havel is not Havelova, but Havlova. Sometimes, the previous records in the register prevail, and the wife's surname is formed following the tradition within a particular family. Thus, Mr Karel's wife may be either Mrs Karlova or Mrs Karelova.

The ending -ova may not as a rule be used for surnames with vowel endings other than -a, for example, Wallo, Schlee, Janku, etc.

If the spouses agree on a common surname of that of the woman, the feminine ending -ova is, of course, omitted in the man's surname. However, it is very hard to explain this principle in English- and German-speaking countries. Supposing I would like to marry Mr Schmied in Germany and we would agree that our common surname will be my surname, the German registrar will not write my husband's surname Hrusak as would be commonly done by a Czech registrar, but he will use its feminine form Hrusakova. In the territory of the Czech Republic, my husband will then be subject to ridicule, and the Czech registrar recording the name in a special register will automatically correct the surname into the grammatically proper form. Of course, it is not certain whether my husband would be able to have such surname corrected in his foreign passport as well.

On the marriage of a Czech female citizen to a foreigner, the registrar will record that the spouses have decided to use a common surname Müller – Müllerova, noting that the form Müllerova is a female form of the name Müller.

99. Act No. 301/2000 Coll., Civil Registry Act, §69.

As of 1 January 2022, there is no condition for the right of registration in the form without -ova. Simply request registration without any justification.

II. Personal Rights and Duties of the Spouses

193. The ABGB[100] imposes upon spouses the duty to cohabit, that of sexual intercourse, the duty to be faithful to each other, and the duty to treat each other decently. Nevertheless, the man is considered the principal in the family. The husband is bound, besides others, to maintain his wife appropriately consistent with his property situation and authorizes him to act on her behalf in all cases.

194. Since 1 January 1950, both spouses have equal rights and duties. Their equality arises from the constitutional principle of equality of men and women.[101] Even with the adoption of the new Civil Code in 2012, the obligations and rights of the spouses remained defined (§687).

195. Mutual legal obligations and corresponding rights are of great importance both for the spouses themselves and for their children and other family members.

196. The law is primarily based on the constitutional equality of men and women (especially Article 1 of the Charter of Human Rights), which is developed through the diction claiming that *'Spouses have equal duties and equal rights'* (§687(1) of the Civil Code). Other provisions also build on this principle. However, in many places, due to the principle of solidarity and the protection of the weaker party, the law balances the actual inequality in order to achieve a fair balance, especially in the property sphere. Some other duties and rights of spouses are also elaborations of other key principles of family law and private law in general. They capture the very essence of marriage. In their interpretation and application, the purpose of marriage shall always be followed, which is primarily the establishment of a family, the proper upbringing of children, and above all, mutual support and assistance (§655 of the Civil Code).

197. The personal rights and obligations of spouses are traditionally defined. The law follows from the equality of men and women in marriage, family and society in general. Spouses are obliged to respect each other, live together, be faithful to each other, respect each other's dignity, support each other, maintain the family community, create a healthy family environment and take care of children together (§687 of the Civil Code), represent each other (§696 of the Civil Code) and take care of family matters together (§693 of the Civil Code and §694 of the Civil Code).

198. However, in the property sphere, many innovations against the previous adjustment are anchored. In particular, the law stipulates that each of the spouses

100. ABGB §§90, 91.
101. Charter of Fundamental Rights and Freedoms, Art. 3.

has the legal right to have the other spouse provide them with information regarding their income and the condition of their assets, as well as their current and contemplated work, studies and similar activities (§688 of the Civil Code). This corresponds to a legal obligation of the other spouse, enforceable, for example, upon fines imposed by the court in the context of proceedings on the spousal duty to support and maintain. This is further related to the provision according to which when choosing their work, study and similar activities, each of the spouses is obliged to take into account the interests of the family, the other spouse and a minor child who has not acquired full legal capacity and who lives together with the spouse in the family household, or other family members (§688 and §689 of the Civil Code). Regarding other property aspects of marriage, the new Act stipulates that each of the spouses contributes to the needs of family life and the needs of the family household according to their personal and property circumstances, abilities and possibilities, so that the standard of living of all family members is fundamentally comparable. The provision of monetary performance has the same meaning as personal care for the family and its members (§690 of the Civil Code). In addition to the obligation to contribute to the needs of the family, the law also regulates the mutual obligation of support and maintenance between spouses within the scope of the right to the same standard of living (§697 of the Civil Code). The community property of spouses as a statutory property regime, which may be contractually excluded or modified both before and during the marriage (§§708 et seq. of the Civil Code), remains the core concept of matrimonial property law. The autonomy of the spouses will be widely respected here. Limits protect the spouses themselves, as well as third parties (e.g., §718(3), §732, §738 of the Civil Code).

199. The provisions governing the family business (§700 of the Civil Code) are another innovation.

The Nature of the Spouses' Mutual Obligations and Rights

200. Each subjective obligation corresponds to a right, which is endowed with a claim and enjoys judicial protection.

201. As regards the classification of obligations and rights:

a. Many obligations and rights corresponding to them derive as natural rights from human dignity and the right to family life, which is linked to the recognition of the free human will to live a family life according to one's own preference; these include in particular the duty to respect, the duty to respect each other's dignity (§687(2) of the Civil Code).
b. Property ones, e.g., arising from the community property (§§708 et seq. of the Civil Code), the common family business (§§700 et seq. of the Civil Code) or the customary furnishings of the family home (§§698 et seq. of the Civil Code) or the aforementioned mutual obligations of support and maintenance between the spouses (§§697 et seq. of the Civil Code).

On the Enforceability of Rights and Penalties for Breach of Obligations

202. Rights arising from the law are vested; i.e., they are judicially enforceable. In practice, however, all the circumstances of each case shall be taken into account. The duty of mutual fidelity, the failure to comply with which may cause a qualified breakdown between the spouses and lead to the dissolution of the marriage, is a special case. In this case, there is a conflict between different values protected by law.

203. If there occurs a breach of other legal obligations, e.g., the obligation to disclose information about one's income and the condition of one's assets (§688 of the Civil Code), the right to this information may be claimed before the court and enforcement of the decision may be sought, e.g., by imposing fines. This may be particularly relevant in connection with the enforcement of the right to an equal standard of living in the context of mutual obligations of support and maintenance between spouses before the court (§§697 et seq. of the Civil Code).

204. Other breaches of statutory obligations may result in the application of relative voidability by the spouse who has been omitted from the decision-making process or even has to face bullying or other contemptible conduct on the part of the other spouse, e.g., in the case of the sale of certain items constituting the usual equipment of the family household (§698(3) of the Civil Code) or in the case of such a burden on the house in which the household of the spouses is located as to be incompatible with the spouses' housing (§747(2) of the Civil Code).

205. It should be mentioned here that the limitation period between spouses does not start or run while the marriage lasts (§646 of the Civil Code). If the protection of rights is to be decided by a court, the Civil Procedure Code will be the procedural norm; in the case of domestic violence, it would be the Special Court Proceedings Act.

Basic Rights and Obligations of Spouses

206. Above all, it is established that spouses are obliged to respect each other, live together (to cohabit), be faithful to each other, respect each other's dignity, support each other, maintain the family community, create a healthy family environment and take care of children together (§687(2) of the Civil Code). An obligation of one always corresponds to a right of the other.

A. To Cohabit

207. Marriage is a lifetime union. Therefore, legal rules, namely, those concerning social care, commonly presume that the spouses cohabit in a common home. However, the wife is no longer bound to follow her husband as had been imposed by the ABGB.

The Family Law Act 1949, as well as the Family Code 1963 in the wording effective until 1998, stipulated expressly that a spouse does not need the consent of the other spouse to exercise his/her profession and career. Within the family law reform, this provision was revoked as redundant.

Cohabitation is deemed a personal and property union; that is, the spouses share their worries and pleasures, practise sexual intercourse, cover jointly all common expenses, etc. Thus, spouses may live in a common home without cohabiting, or they may live separately but cohabit.

208. The spouses are not legally bound to practise sexual intercourse. Therefore, a husband may be prosecuted for raping his wife.

B. Duty to Be Faithful

209. Duty of faithfulness arises from the nature of matrimony as a cohabitation of one man and one woman. It has, however, only a moral aspect. Violation of the duty to be faithful is not sanctioned, nor is it a ground for divorce by itself. It may, however, cause a breakdown of the marriage.

C. Duty to Respect One Another's Dignity

210. This duty was expressly stipulated by law only within the family law reform in 1998. It emphasizes equal status of both spouses, regardless of whether one of them 'only' looks after the home, household and children, and the other earns money.

D. Duty to Help One Another

211. This duty also arises from the nature of matrimony as a lifetime union. The duty to help one another in the sphere of property is expressed by mutual duty to maintain that which involves the spouses and possibly also divorced spouses, as well as by stipulations concerning further property relations between the spouses.

E. Duty to Jointly Care for the Children

212. There is no distinction under law whether this involves common children of the spouses or a child/children of only one of them. A step-parent living in a common home with a child in fact supports him/her as his/her child and has a right to share the living standard of his/her parents, and his/her real parent has the right to share the same living standard with his/her spouse.

In case of divorce in such marriage, any legal relationship between the child and his/her step-parent ceases to exist.

F. Duty to Create a Sound Living Environment and Background

213. Creating a sound living environment is a prerequisite not only for harmonious cohabitation of a man and a woman but also for bringing up their minor children.

G. Obligation to Inform

214. It is enshrined that a spouse has the right to have the other spouse provide them with information on their income and the condition of their assets, as well as on their current and contemplated work, study and similar activities (§688 of the Civil Code).

215. A spouse's right to be informed corresponds to the other spouse's legal obligation to disclose that information. As mentioned above, it is legally enforceable.

H. Duty of Consideration

216. This legal obligation is an elaboration of the aforementioned obligation of mutual respect and support, maintaining the family community and creating a healthy family environment (§687 of the Civil Code). The law stipulates that when choosing their work, study and similar activities, a spouse is obliged to take into account the interests of the family, the other spouse and a minor child who has not acquired full capacity and who lives together with the parents in the family household, or other family members (§689 of the Civil Code).

I. Legal Representation

217. The rule is that a spouse has the right to represent their spouse in ordinary affairs (§696(1) of the Civil Code). This corresponds to the other's right to representation. There is no need for a power of attorney because such representation is created *ex lege.*

218. Exceptions to the rule are provided by Act Three (§696(2) and (3) of the Civil Code). The right to legal representation does not arise or expire:

a. if the spouse who is to be represented informs in advance the person with whom their spouse is supposed to act legally or intends to act legally that they do not agree with the representation;
b. if the court cancels the right to legal representation of the spouse upon the proposal of the other spouse;
c. if the spouses do not live together (for the situations listed in §691(2) of the Civil Code).

219. If the spouse is to be represented in a matter which is not ordinary, it will be necessary to conclude a contract of representation and draw up a power of attorney (§§436 et seq. of the Civil Code).

J. Right and Obligation to Co-decide Family Matters

220. The law places emphasis on the agreement of the spouses in family matters, including the choice of the location of the family household or the household of one of the spouses and other family members, especially children who have not acquired full legal capacity and on the way of life of the family (§692(1) of the Civil Code). This is an expression of the equality of the spouses in marriage (§687(1) of the Civil Code) and the principle of autonomy of the will. If there is an agreement between the spouses, the spouses' agreement shall be respected in the spirit of the saying *'family life is to be fortified'*.

221. In the case of absence of an agreement on an essential family matter, the law lays down a rule (§692(2) of the Civil Code) according to which the court may, upon the application of one of the spouses, substitute its decision for the agreement in the two following cases:

1. if they refuse to give their consent in such a matter of family life without serious reason and contrary to the interests of the family;
2. if they are unable to manifest their will.

K. Duty to Attend to the Family Matters

222. First of all, it is stipulated that family matters are to be taken care of by the spouses jointly or by one of them (§693 of the Civil Code). This is again an expression of the equality of man and woman in the family (§687 of the Civil Code), while the law presupposes an agreement. It lays down clear rules in the event of a disagreement or conflict.

223. The law further divides matters into:

a. ordinary family matters (§694(1) of the Civil Code), where the legal act of one spouse binds and entitles both spouses jointly and severally (i.e., with regard to solidarity); however, this does not apply:
   - if the spouse who has not acted legally communicates in advance to a third party that they did not agree with the legal action;
   - the court may, upon the application of a spouse, exclude the consequences of future legal acts of the other spouse vis-à-vis third parties; such measures do not apply to legal acts by which the spouse provides for the normal necessities of life of the family and its members, in particular, children who have not acquired full legal capacity.

b. other than ordinary family matters, i.e., other family matters where the legal act of one spouse binds and authorizes both spouses jointly and severally (i.e., with regard to solidarity), however, only in a situation where the other spouse gives their consent to the legal act of the other spouse; the law further provides for an analogy in this matter (i.e., similar application of §692(2) of the Civil Code), whereby, in the absence of an agreement on an essential family matter, the court may substitute its decision for the consent of the other spouse on the application of one of the spouses:
   - if they refuse their consent in such a matter of family life without good cause and contrary to the interests of the family;
   - if they are unable to manifest their will.

224. If, however, the spouse who does not consent to the legal act of the other spouse does not obtain the assistance of the court beforehand, they may invoke the voidability of the legal act (i.e., relative voidability).

225. However, if the spouses do not live together (in the situation referred to in §691(2) of the Civil Code), a legal act of one spouse in family matters (both ordinary and other) does not bind or entitle the other spouse without their consent (§694(3) of the Civil Code).

III. Meeting the Needs of the Family

226. Each spouse is obliged to contribute to the needs of family life and the needs of the family household according to their personal and financial circumstances, abilities and possibilities so that the standard of living of all family members is essentially comparable.

227. Even personal care for the family and its members (§690 of the Civil Code) is of a property nature, which may be either a pecuniary or non-pecuniary one (cf. evaluability or substitutability in the form of social services). This obligation corresponds to the right of the other spouse to performance which may be enforced before the court.

228. If the spouses live together in the same dwelling and maintain a family household (regardless of whether they live together; §758 of the Civil Code regulating separation), they are obliged, in accordance with the principle of solidarity, to share the essentially same standard of living with each other and with the members of their family, while family means anyone (children in common or in custody, their parents, etc.).

229. However, if the spouses do not live together, i.e., if they are permanently separated and do not have a family household, the principle applies that each of them bears the costs of their own household. The law provides that they are still obliged to help and support each other (§691(1) of the Civil Code). Other provisions regulate the mutual maintenance obligation between spouses (§697 of the

Civil Code), which should be aimed at meeting all the reasonable needs of either spouse so that they share the same standard of living as the person liable for support and maintenance, and not at meeting the needs of other persons, in particular children, who have independent rights vis-à-vis their parents regulated by law (§910 of the Civil Code). Nevertheless, it is with regard to the children (hereinafter specified more closely) that a different provision is made in relation to the unilateral abandonment of the family household (§691(2) of the Civil Code). If no agreement is possible, the abandoned spouse may request the court to order the other spouse, who left the family household without any special reason and refuses to return, to contribute to the costs of the former common family household. The condition is that the children continue to live in the household with the abandoned spouse. These shall be joint dependent children towards whom the spouses have the obligation of support and maintenance (regardless of age) or minor children without legal capacity entrusted to the care of one or both spouses. The court shall assess the matter in the light of good morals and the principle of decency.

IV. Usual Family Household Furnishings

230. This is a new term in matrimonial property law. Its purpose is to ensure the good functioning of the family, the family household and family life in general. The new regulation of the usual furnishings of family household protects the family as a whole (and also the economically weaker one) and follows the general principles expressing family solidarity, even though it may appear to restrict the exclusive right of ownership. However, this limitation of the right to property is fully justified in value terms. Cf. also the new provisions restricting, for example, the (co-)owner of a house or flat from exercising their right of disposition (§747 of the Civil Code) or directly in connection with domestic violence (§§751 et seq. of the Civil Code).

231. The usual furnishings of a family household consist of a set of movable items that serve the normal necessities of life of the family and its members. It should be emphasized here that ownership or joint ownership (whether or not in shares, cf. §1115 of the Civil Code, cf. also §1236 of the Civil Code governing community of property). The purpose (§698(1) of the Civil Code) and the special regime are relevant as well. The legislation is cogent. The protection under the legislation under review ceases with the dissolution of the marriage.

232. The scope of the usual family household furnishings regulated under matrimonial property law in Part Two of the Civil Code is broader than the right of the surviving spouse to acquire only the basic family household furnishings, even if they are not an heir (§1667 of the Civil Code), although the law uses the diction *'necessities of life'* in the first case. Both statutory terms reflect an objectifying aspect which, in principle, expresses average conditions at the time and place (cf., e.g., the term fair market value). In the case of evidence, indicative reference may be made to data from the National Statistical Service or other similar data or to expert judgment, particularly in the case of borderline conditions, or evidence may be based on general experience.

233. The law stipulates that irrespective of the ownership of goods which serve the normal necessities of life of the family and its members, one spouse needs the consent of the other spouse to dispose of them; this does not apply if the goods are of negligible value (§698(2) of the Civil Code). A spouse may invoke the voidability of a legal act upon which the other spouse disposed of an item which forms part of the normal furnishings of the family household without their consent (§698(3) of the Civil Code). This is called relative voidability (§586 of the Civil Code). If the right to assert the invalidity of the act is time-barred, the time limit does not start to run during the marriage (§646 of the Civil Code).

234. The provisions governing the regime of the usual furnishings of the family household may not be contractually modified or excluded, either before or during the marriage; an exception is provided for permanent abandonment of the household with the intention not to return (§718(3) of the Civil Code). If this occurs and no contract is concluded, the one who has left the household and who is also the sole owner of the furnishings constituting the usual household furnishings may demand that the other spouse hand them over to them (§699(1), the first sentence, the Civil Code). If these items are jointly owned, they shall be divided equally, if possible, or the joint ownership of them shall be dissolved and settled (§699(1), the second sentence of the Civil Code). However, the above rules do not apply if the abandoned spouse needs the property, in particular, also for the joint minor child of the spouses who is not fully capable of exercising their legal capacity (§699(2) of the Civil Code).

V. Duty to Maintain

235. In a harmonious marriage, however, the spouses not only voluntarily provide for the needs of the family and children to the best of their abilities and capacities but also provide for their own needs, in particular within the framework of the community of property (§§708 et seq. of the Civil Code). The mutual support and maintenance obligation between the spouses supplements these property rights (§697 of the Civil Code). The aim and purpose of the reciprocal support and maintenance obligation between spouses is to ensure a fundamentally equal standard of living for both spouses and not for other persons. Several basic principles influence the legal regime of the support and maintenance obligation between spouses. The voluntary nature of performance based on the general principle of family law is one of them, i.e., solidarity, or the principle of mutual help and protection of the weaker party. However, if one of the spouses does not voluntarily fulfil their obligation of support and maintenance, it is determined by the court on the basis of an action brought by the other spouse. The principle of reciprocity is another principle. This means that the law scrupulously respects the constitutional equality of men and women. It establishes that spouses have the mutual obligation of support and maintenance. In practice, however, it is mostly wives who assert the right to maintenance against their husbands. This is a consequence of women's generally lower incomes, part-time work, maternity and parental leave, however, not of the inequality established by the law. The equal standard of living between spouses is the final principle.

236. The principle of mutuality and the equal standard of living of both spouses distinguishes the support and maintenance obligation between spouses from other types of support and maintenance obligation, which are always based on a certain degree of dependence on the support and maintenance of the person entitled to it (§911 of the Civil Code). The mutual obligation of support and maintenance between spouses precedes the obligation of support and maintenance of children with respect to their parents (§697(1) *in fine* of the Civil Code). This means that if someone is married, they are primarily entitled to support and maintenance from their spouse. However, if the spouse is unable to fulfil their obligation of support and maintenance, the children's obligation of support and maintenance with respect to the parents may be invoked to the extent of decent support and maintenance (§915(2) of the Civil Code).

237. Similarly, if a child gets married and is unable to support themself, the spouse is primarily responsible for the child's maintenance. Only if the spouse is unable to fulfil this obligation of support and maintenance at all or only to a limited extent, the parents' obligation of support and maintenance continues in the alternative. This may be particularly in the case of student marriages.

Creation of the Obligation of Support and Maintenance Between Spouses

238. The following prerequisites for the creation of a mutual obligation of support and maintenance between spouses may be deduced from the law under the following conditions:

a. the existence of a marriage;
b. an unequal standard of living of the spouses;
c. conformity with good morals or not obvious abuse of the law.

239. A. The obligation of support and maintenance between the spouses arises from the conclusion of the marriage and lasts, in principle, for the duration of the marriage. The mutual obligation of support and maintenance arises even in a marriage which was concluded despite the existence of one of the obstacles to marriage, even in a marriage which be declared void. The obligation of support and maintenance does not apply in a putative marriage since such a state of affairs does not produce any legal consequences at all. Nor may a legal obligation of support and maintenance arise between cohabitants. The obligation of support and maintenance between registered partners is governed by a special law (§10 RP).

240. B. In the case of obligation of support and maintenance between spouses, dependence on support and maintenance is not required, although it may not be excluded (cf. the general §911 of the Civil Code). The purpose of the legal regulation of obligation of support and maintenance between spouses is to ensure a fundamentally equal standard of living for both spouses. The prerequisites for the application of a mutual obligation of support and maintenance also exist if both spouses are in principle, able to meet their material and cultural needs themselves, however, to a different extent.

241. C. Obvious abuse of rights does not enjoy legal protection (§8 of the Civil Code); therefore, the court may not award support and maintenance. The same applies in the case of a breach of good morals (§2(3) of the Civil Code).

Scope of the Obligation of Support and Maintenance Between Spouses

242. The extent of the obligation of support and maintenance is based on general criteria, i.e., the capacities, possibilities and financial circumstances of the obligor and the justified needs of the beneficiary (§697(2) in conjunction with §913 of the Civil Code). These general criteria apply to all types of obligations of support and maintenance provided for by law.

243. However, in determining the maintenance obligation between spouses, an account shall also be taken of the care of the family household (§690 of the Civil Code). The court should base itself not only on the actual but also on the potential possibilities and abilities of the obligor. The specific extent of the obligation of support and maintenance between the spouses should be determined, taking into account the above, so that the material and cultural level of both spouses is essentially the same. The determination of the obligation of support and maintenance between the spouses is a matter not only of ensuring the support and maintenance of the beneficiary but also of providing the means to meet all other personal, cultural, recreational needs, etc. The support and maintenance does not have to be of a consumptive nature; i.e., it may also be stipulated in such a way as to enable the beneficiary to build up savings, make investments, etc.

Termination of the Obligation of Support and Maintenance Between Spouses

244. The obligation of support and maintenance between spouses lasts essentially for the entire duration of the marriage. The termination of the obligation of support and maintenance is, in principle, linked to the dissolution of the marriage, i.e., death of one of the spouses, the declaration of death of one of the spouses, divorce, change of gender or declaring the marriage null and void. The obligation of support and maintenance between spouses may also be terminated by the court, in particular, if the prerequisites and grounds for its provision no longer exist. If the marriage is dissolved by divorce, a new obligation of support and maintenance, namely support and maintenance between the divorced spouses, may, however, be imposed if the conditions stipulated by law are met (§760 of the Civil Code).

VI. Domestic Violence

245. For a long time, there was no special legal regulation in the Czech Republic concerning the unwelcome social phenomenon of domestic violence. The first legislative step was to introduce a law that, since 6 January 2004, has been regulating new crime in the Criminal Code, the maltreatment of a person living in the common home.[102] The next step was the change of the police directives,[103] which allow police to act very quickly. Private law provisions (since 2014) against domestic violence provide for protection of spouses living in the family household together, whatever the reason. The law provides that if the continued cohabitation of the spouses in the house or flat in which the matrimonial household is located becomes intolerable for one of them because of physical or mental violence against the spouse or another living in the family household, the court may, upon the application of the spouse concerned, restrict or, if necessary, exclude for a specified period the right of the other spouse to reside in the house or flat (§751(1) of the Civil Code). The same may be applied in the case of divorced spouses, as well as in the case of spouses or divorced spouses living together elsewhere than in the family household (§751(2) of the Civil Code) and in the case of persons other than spouses (§3021 of the Civil Code).

246. The limitation or exclusion of the spouse's right to reside in the house or flat shall be determined by the court for a maximum period of six months. The court shall decide again on application if there are particularly compelling reasons for doing so (§752 of the Civil Code). However, this is not a deprivation of the right of ownership or divided co-ownership but a restriction on its use (*us utendi*). Property interests shall often be set aside in favour of the protection of life and health on the basis of the proportionality test.

247. The Special Court Proceedings Act regulates preliminary proceedings for protection against domestic violence and, within its framework, interim measures (§§400 et seq. of the Special Court Proceedings Act) and the extension of interim measures (§§410 et seq. of the Special Court Proceedings Act). There is no regulation of proceedings on the merits (the procedural reflection of §§751 et seq. of the Civil Code is only §§400 et seq. of the Special Court Proceedings Act). However, procedural protection is broader than protection of substantive rights since the obligations listed under sub-paragraphs c) and d) below are obligations which relate to the protection of personality.

248. These are application proceedings, while the Act specifies what the application shall contain. The Act also contains a provision requiring the court to make appropriate requests to supplement the application (§402(2) of the Special Court Proceedings Act). Where evidence is involved, the investigative principle applies.

249. In particular, the court may order (§405 of the Special Court Proceedings Act) that the violent person:

a. leave the common dwelling and its immediate vicinity, not to stay in the common dwelling or not to enter it;
b. not enter or stay in the immediate vicinity of the common dwelling or the applicant;

102. Act No. 40/2009 Coll., Criminal Code, §199.
103. Act No. 237/2008 Coll., Police Code, §§44–47.

c. be refrained from meeting the applicant;
d. refrain from unwanted surveillance and harassment of the applicant in any way (prohibition of stalking).

250. The court shall rule on the application within forty-eight hours without a hearing. The interim measure lasts for one month from its enforceability, i.e., from the date of issue.

251. If the decision on the application for an interim measure is preceded by a restraining order (§§44 et seq. of the Police of the Czech Republic) and if the statutory period of ten days does not expire before the interim measure becomes enforceable, the duration of the interim measure shall be extended by the period which has not expired before the interim measure becomes enforceable (§408(2) of the Special Court Proceedings Act).

252. Before the lapse of the one-month period, the applicant may file an application to extend the duration of the interim measure. The filing of the application extends the duration of the interim measure until the court decides on the application for extension.

253. The court may extend the duration of the interim measure only for as long as strictly necessary, up to a maximum of six months after the interim measure has become enforceable. It is not necessary to file any application on merits, e.g., for the dissolution and settlement of the joint ownership of the house or flat, to obtain an extension. However, the court shall take into account whether the applicant has made any other submissions on merits in addition to the application for the extension of the interim measure.

254. An application for an interim measure (not for its extension) may be filed again.

255. In the case of a child at risk of domestic violence, the law regulates the specifics of the case, in particular the possibility for a legal representative, a child welfare authority or a lawyer to file a petition on behalf of the child, as well as the procedural capacity of a child over 16 years of age (§403(2) of the Special Court Proceedings Act) and the appointment of a guardian ad litem (§406 of the Special Court Proceedings Act).

Public Law Protection: Excursus

256. First of all, the authority of the police to expel a person from a shared residence for the necessary period is enshrined if, according to the established facts, especially with regard to previous battering, it may be reasonably assumed that the person will commit a dangerous personal crime against life, health and/or freedom or a particularly serious attack against human dignity (§44(1), the Police of the Czech Republic). The expulsion period is a maximum of ten days. A violent person may be expelled ex officio even in their absence.

257. In this context, the Criminal Code regulates a whole range of crimes, e.g., battering of a person living in a common dwelling (§199 of the Criminal Code) or battering of a person entrusted to one's care or custody (§198 of the Criminal Code), restriction of personal freedom (§171 of the Criminal Code) or the crime of stalking (§354 of the Criminal Code), further, e.g., the crime of bodily harm (§146 of the Criminal Code) or the criminal offence of serious bodily harm (§145 of the Criminal Code).

258. According to the Criminal Order, a person accused of a crime may be prohibited from having contact with the victim, persons close to them or other persons, especially witnesses, or even a prohibition from entering a common dwelling inhabited with the victim and its immediate vicinity and staying in such a dwelling, etc. (§88c of the Criminal Code).

259. If domestic violence does not reach such an intensity that it may be qualified as a crime, it may be assessed as an offence against cohabitation (§49 of the Offense Act).

260. The Crime Victims Act was adopted in relation to EU regulation, in particular Directive 2012/29/EU of the European Parliament and of the Council of 25 October 2012 establishing minimum standards on the rights, support and protection of victims of crime, and replacing Council Framework Decision 2001/220/JHA. It regulates, among other things, the provision of financial assistance to victims of crimes by the state (§§23 et seq. of the Crime Victims Act).

VII. Family Business

261. This is not a new type of business, but a special case of a business plant, a collective matter (§501 of the Civil Code). Its purpose is economic, or often even the subsistence protection of family members permanently working for the family and the family business. Since an employment relationship may not be established between the spouses, the family business may ensure protection for the spouses in the property sphere (cf. also §730 regulating the distribution of income in the case of business under the regime of separate assets of spouses).

262. According to the law, a family business is considered to be a business in which spouses or at least one of the spouses work together with their relatives up to the third degree or persons with spouses who are of affinity to the second degree and which is owned by one of these persons. A family business is not owned by the family. Those of them who work permanently for the family or for the family business (without a partnership or employment or similar contract) are regarded as family members participating in the operation of the family business. As a consequence, these persons participate in the profit from it and in the assets acquired from this profit, as well as in the growth of the family business to the extent corresponding to the amount and type of their work. This right may only be waived upon a person with full mental capacity by means of a personal statement (§701 of the Civil Code).

263. If the family business is to be divided during the division of the estate by the court, the family member involved in its operation has a priority right to it (§704(1) of the Civil Code).

§5. Void and Voidable Marriages

I. Void Marriage

264. In the Czech Republic, a marriage is either valid or void (*matrimonium nullum*) or not existing (*non matrimonium, matrimonium putativum*). The grounds for a void marriage are as follows:

a. Prior marriage (bigamy) or registered partnership.
b. Consanguinity.
c. Non-age (minor).
d. Limited legal capacity with express interference with conjugal capacity.
e. Relationship of dependence.
f. Wrongful threat and error.

265. A marriage contracted in spite of one of the circumstances as stated is void. It is considered valid until the court holds this marriage null and void in its ruling.

266. Declaring a marriage null and void is ruled by the court ex officio for the grounds of prior marriage and consanguinity.[104]

267. If a marriage was contracted with a married man or a married woman or man or woman in registered partnership, or between ancestors and descendants, or between siblings, the court may declare the marriage null and void also when it already ceased to exist. In other cases of void marriages, the court may not declare such marriages null and void after they ceased to exist.

268. Void marriages may become valid if the original impediments causing the marriage to be void will cease to exist by the time the court has held the marriage void.

The marriage void due to bigamy becomes valid at the instant the previous marriage or registered partnership ceases to exist.[105] However, criminal liability for bigamy is not affected.[106]

Marriages void due to non-age or limited legal capacity with express interference with conjugal capacity become valid when the spouse who was under 18 years of age turns 18 years old or the wife becomes pregnant and the child is born alive.[107]

104. Civil Code §685.
105. *Ibid.*, §682.
106. Act No. 40/2009 Coll., Criminal Code §194.
107. Civil Code §683.

A spouse may claim to declare his/her marriage null and void on the grounds of being contracted upon a wrongful threat only within one year from the time he/she has learnt about this fact.[108] After the lapse of this period, the marriage is deemed valid.

II. Effects of Declaring Marriage Null and Void

269. As soon as the ruling declaring a marriage null and void is effective, this marriage is deemed to have never come into being.[109] If this were a first marriage, the personal status of the former spouse would be 'single' again.

The spouse who changed his/her surname upon marriage is bound to use his/her former surname as soon as the court ruling declaring the marriage null and void is effective.

The rights and duties of spouses to their common child and their property relations are provided in the same way as in the case of divorce.[110]

III. Non-existing Marriage

270. The Civil Code provides that the marriage will not come into existence unless such requisites have been fulfilled as are to be insisted upon unreservedly.[111]

271. The following list of such situations that can lead to the non-existence of marriage has been created by legal science.[112]

272. A marriage has not come into being if:

a. it was contracted between individuals of the same sex;
b. man and woman were forced to marry under physical duress (*vis absoluta*);
c. it is contracted by a person younger than 16;
d. the certificate required for a church wedding was not issued or was older than six months;
e. the wedding was solemnized before a church or religious denomination not registered by the state;
f. in case of marriage by proxy, no permission of the local authority was issued or the power of attorney was inchoate.

---

108. *Ibid.*, §684.
109. *Ibid.*, §681.
110. *Ibid.*, §686.
111. *Ibid.*, §677.
112. Hrušáková, M., Králíčková, Z. & Westphalová, L. *a kolektiv. Rodinné právo. 2. vydání.* Praha: C. H. Beck, 2017, pp. 44–48.

273. Courts rule in cases of doubt whether a marriage has come into being or not based on petitioning the court to determine personal status. The court can determine that there is no marriage, even without a petition.[113]

113. Civil Code §678, Act on Special Court Proceedings, §371.

Chapter 2. Divorce

§1. Grounds

I. Protection of Minor Children

274. Minor children cannot be protected from their parents' divorce – divorce of parents of minors would then have to be directly banned. Legal rules must necessarily protect the child's interests effectively in relation to its parents' divorce.

The basic idea of the legislation is to avoid long-term 'fights' over children after the divorce. Therefore, the court cannot grant a divorce before the judgment of the juvenile court on the regulation of the relations to the minor children for the period after the divorce or the judgment by which the court approved the parents' agreement on the regulation of the relations has become final.[114] Deciding on the exercise of parental responsibility for the period after the divorce, on the parents' maintenance obligation towards the children[115] and, where applicable, on the parents' personal contact with the children[116] places significantly higher demands on the custody judge. It is, however, in the interests of the minor child, whose circumstances are already finally settled at the time of the dissolution of his parents' marriage.

Contemporary law relies on the fact that if a married couple wants a divorce, they are forced to agree on the child's custody or at least to accept the relevant court ruling and not to prolong the custody proceedings forever.

Court hearings concerning children separate from divorce hearings on the one hand prolonged the total time of hearings; on the other, it brought about better decision-making on the child's custody. The divorce proceeding by itself has thus been significantly simplified and made more formal.

A significant role in protecting the rights of the child in divorce proceedings is the hardness clause in favour of the child. Special grounds for which the dissolution of the marriage is contrary to the interests of the child may be, in particular, the child's disability, physical or mental handicap.[117] In some cases, the decisive facts may already be apparent from the grounds of the decision of the juvenile court on the post-divorce arrangement of the child or from the objection of the spouse who opposes the divorce, irrespective of whether the child has been granted custody for the post-divorce period. Where one of the spouses opposes the divorce on the grounds of conflict with the best interests of the child on special grounds, the court may ask the guardian appointed for the child in the post-divorce proceedings for an additional report on the current family situation. There may have been some changes, without those changes constituting such a substantial change in circumstances as to require a new decision of the court on the adjustment of the minor child's relations.

---

114. *Ibid.*, §755/3, §906.
115. *Ibid.*, §910.
116. *Ibid.*, §887.
117. *Ibid.*, §755/2a).

II. The Breakdown of Marriage

275. The law stipulating divorce arises from an objective principle of the breakdown of a marriage. Under Czech law, the court cannot investigate who is at fault in the breakdown of the marriage; neither is it possible to obtain a divorce on the basis of mutual agreement of the spouses.

276. The court may divorce a married couple on petitioning filed by either of the spouses if the marriage has broken down so deeply and permanently that no recovery of matrimonial cohabitation can be expected.[118]

Finding the grounds of the breakdown may prove practical in regard to further deciding on maintaining one of the spouses divorced.[119] However, statistically, the most frequent cause of the breakdown has been for decades a 'discord of interests and characters' which is very general and formal.

The law does not require separation of spouses for a specified period as proof of breakdown.

In divorce proceedings, the court may not concurrently decide on possible family assets settlement, dwelling or duty to maintain the divorced spouse.

277. Married couples may be divorced even if one of the spouses disagrees because it is sufficient to satisfy the court by submitting proof of an existing breakdown of the marriage. However, since 1998, the family law contains a hardening clause (*Härtelklauzul*). Even though breakdown of the marriage has been objectively shown, the court will not grant divorce if one of the spouses opposes (disagrees with the divorce). Nevertheless, it must be the spouse who has not contributed predominantly to the breakdown of the marriage. This should not mean that the other spouse is responsible for the breakdown, and it need not be shown to what extent this spouse has contributed, violating matrimonial duties, to the breakdown of the marriage. In theory, breakdown of the marriage might arise due to objective causes, for example, sterility of one of the spouses. The spouse opposing divorce must also show that he/she would suffer a very serious loss as a result of divorce. This loss shall not only be of a financial nature but a personal loss in the first place. Extraordinary circumstances must exist in favour of preserving the marriage.[120]

If the married couple has not lived together for longer than three years, the court will grant a divorce in spite of the other spouse still refusing the divorce.

278. However, present law allows a married couple, without searching for the causes of breakdown of the marriage, to obtain a divorce very decently, including an overall resolution of all legal effects following the divorce.

---

118. *Ibid.*, §755/1.
119. *See* below Part II, Ch. 2, §3, Civil Code §762.
120. Civil Code §755/2a). This provision is an evident effort to protect an old and deserted wife who would be in a difficult social situation after divorce. This way of divorcing has been practised very rarely so far.

In courts, this type of divorce is called 'uncontested or agreed divorce'.[121] It is not, however, the type of divorce based on the principle of mutual agreement of spouses known in a number of Western countries. Based on certain facts, the law only allows to create an irrefutable presumption of breakdown of the marriage, which in return will not have to be proved before the court. The court does not investigate the breakdown causes either.

To grant an agreed divorce, it is presumed that:

a. the marriage lasted at least one year;
b. the couple has not been cohabiting for more than six months;
c. the other spouse will come to line with the divorce petition.

While meeting the presumptions as stated, the court holds that there has been a breakdown between the spouses and will grant a divorce if the spouses submit:

a. an effective decision by which the court has approved the agreement of the parents concerning the custody of a child and the maintenance of a child; and
b. an agreement concerning the family assets settlement and a settlement of their rights and duties concerning their common dwelling (matrimonial home) and possibly an agreement on maintaining the divorced spouse.

Signatures of spouses must be officially verified. The agreements may be made in the form of a public notary record. The agreements include a suspensive condition; that is, they are effective only on the day of the divorce coming into effect. The court does not approve of these agreements; it only takes them into account and of course must deal with their validity.

The agreement on family assets settlement and the agreement on settlement of rights and duties concerning the common dwelling must always be submitted. In a number of instances under Czech law, one spouse is protected from being moved out from the common flat providing for his/her right to obtain a substitute flat.[122]

In this type of divorce, the court hearing is very short and formal. However, the court shall hold a hearing at which it shall hear the parties. The hearing of the parties may be dispensed with if it would involve great difficulty. At the hearing, the court shall guide the spouses in eliminating the causes of the breakdown and seek to reconcile them.[123]

As the particular divorce types differ from one another only by the presence or absence of the necessity to prove qualified breakdown of the marriage before the court, it is possible, and it occurs rather often, that a divorce petition is filed with the inclusion of decisive facts displaying the breakdown. Before the court orders a hearing to be commenced, the couple agrees on future family assets settlement. In this situation, proving the existence of breakdown and its causes will not be necessary. However, it may happen that even though the spouses have made all necessary agreements, the court handling custody disputes will not approve of their

121. Civil Code §757.
122. *See* below Part III, Ch. 2, §4.
123. Act on Special Court Proceedings, §389.

agreement concerning custody and maintenance, and they will have no other choice but to prove the breaking down of the marriage before the court. The opinion prevails that the agreements made may not come into force, and after the divorce is granted and effective, the family assets settlement must be agreed again.[124]

§2. PROCEDURE

279. The Act on Special Court Proceedings regulates the proceedings for divorce.[125] If divorce has long been understood as a legitimate solution to the crisis between the spouses, the legal rules contained in both substantive and procedural law should correspond to this concept. It is generally acknowledged that the course of divorce proceedings in many cases has a direct bearing on other post-divorce relations between the former spouses, including their legal solutions. That is also why the former designation of the divorcing spouses as 'plaintiff and defendant' has been replaced by the word 'spouses'. Divorce proceedings may be initiated not only on the application of one of the spouses but also by a joint application.[126] Divorce proceedings have also been made somewhat more rigorous, as a mandatory hearing in the presence of both divorcing spouses has been established. The examination of the parties, which is usually the most important evidence of the existence of a breakdown of the marriage, may be dispensed with only if its conduct would involve great difficulty. However, divorce proceedings remain adversarial.

280. The court of the district in which the married couple has resided together in the Czech Republic is appropriate to handle the divorce if at least one of the spouses has resided within the court district; if there is no such court, the appropriate court is the general court of the respondent and if there is no such court, then it is the general court of the petitioner.[127]

The marriage is dissolved on the day the divorce granted has come into effect. As the court decision involves personal statuses and contracting new marriages may be in question, no extraordinary judicial remedies like re-appeal or re-opening the case are available.[128]

§3. EFFECTS

I. Surname

281. The spouse who took the surname of the other spouse on the marriage may, within six months after the divorce granted comes into effect, announce at the

124. Civil Code §757/1c).
125. Act on Special Court Proceedings, §383 to §398.
126. *Ibid.*, §384(1).
127. *Ibid.*, §383.
128. *Ibid.*, §398.

register office that he/she takes his/her former surname or that he/she gives up using the common surname beside the former surname.[129]

Change of surname of a divorced spouse is his/her personal right; the other spouse may not force him/her to change it or to keep it. Of course, change of surname has no effect on the surnames of children coming from the marriage. The change is carried out by mere announcement; the register office does not consider or approve of it.[130] It only issues a certificate that the announcement on taking the former surname has been taken into account and recorded in the marriage registry.

II. Property Relations

282. On divorce, the joint property of the spouses ceases to exist and must be settled. In some specific kinds of tenant relations involving the use of a flat, joint tenancy of the flat also ceases to exist upon divorce.[131]

III. Duty to Maintain the Divorced Spouse

283. The maintenance obligation towards a divorced spouse is a traditional concept of family law. Its aim and purpose is to compensate, at least in part, for the unequal economic opportunities and the different standard of living in the period after the divorce. The law emphasizes the voluntary nature of the relationship, which is based on the general principle of solidarity or the principle of mutual assistance and protection of the weaker party. At the same time, it expressly contains certain limits, thereby emphasizing the exceptional nature of the statutory maintenance obligation between divorced spouses. Indeed, the property aspects of divorce may already be regulated in a prenuptial, marriage or pre-divorce agreement.

284. The basic prerequisite is, as a general rule, a state of dependence on maintenance originating in or in connection with the marriage[132] with reference to the general provisions on maintenance.[133] However, the Act also contains other prerequisites, taking into account the passage of time and other subjective and objective considerations. Some of the innovations, such as the explicit recognition of the origin of the inability to support oneself during or in connection with the marriage or domestic violence are a direct response to the case law in this matter. The new legislation also includes penal maintenance.[134]

285. In order for a maintenance obligation to arise for the period after the divorce, the following basic conditions must be met:[135]

129. Civil Code §769.
130. Supreme Court Decision No. 11/1951.
131. *See* below Part III.
132. Civil Code §760(1) and the diction 'if he is … unable to support himself'.
133. §911 of the Civil Code provides similarly.
134. Civil Code §762.
135. *Ibid.*, §760/1.

a. the divorced spouse entitled to maintenance is unable to support himself or herself;
b. his or her inability to support him or herself has its origins in the marriage or arose in connection with it;
c. fairness of the claim or conformity with good morals or not manifest abuse of rights.

286. The state of dependence on maintenance, or the inability to support oneself, is a key prerequisite for the application of maintenance obligations between divorced spouses. The legislation reasonably imposes this requirement in order to ensure that no one is dependent on another.

287. Circumstances originating in or relating to the marriage are another necessary prerequisite. The wording of the law is intended to prevent the right to maintenance from being exercised for a very long period of time without direct connection to the marriage or the period preceding it in the form of unmarried cohabitation.

288. On the part of the obligor spouse, the condition of whether maintenance can be fairly claimed from him, in particular having regard to his age or state of health at the time of the divorce, is expressly emphasized. That condition is also linked to the obligation to exercise the right in accordance with good morals or not to manifestly abuse the right.

289. The law also explicitly states other prerequisites or specific criteria for the establishment and determination of the divorced spouse's maintenance.[136] This is more or less based on established practice and takes into account European standards. The court must thus take into account in particular:

a. the duration of the marriage and the time interval since the divorce;
b. whether the divorced spouse has (not) secured adequate employment;
c. whether the divorced spouse was able to provide for his or her own maintenance by managing his or her own property properly;
d. whether the divorced spouse contributed to the maintenance of the family household during the marriage;
e. whether the divorced spouse has not committed an offence of a criminal nature against the other spouse or a person close to the other spouse;
f. whether there is any other compelling reason.

By divorce, joint property (family assets) of the spouses ceases to exist. This was supposed to be settled, namely, by a pre-divorce agreement of the spouses. Even though a divorced spouse, who is otherwise unable to support himself/herself, had obtained a larger financial amount through property settlement, under judicature rules of cases decided he/she might claim maintenance from his/her former spouse

136. *Ibid.*, §760/2.

supposing the other spouse would be capable of providing him/her with the maintenance allowance. Thus, the dependent divorced spouse should not be bound to sell a family house he/she lives in, or furniture and other equipment he/she uses as well as the items that contribute to his/her reasonable living standard in order to support himself/herself in case the other spouse, the person liable, is capable of providing him/her with a maintenance allowance. This may not, however, apply to the property that would exceed beyond this framework of reasonability.

290. A divorced spouse may not be granted maintenance if this were contrary to morality (*contra bonos mores*). Therefore, along with determining maintenance, the court will also have to deal with the grounds that led to the breakdown of the marriage. Court practices hold that it would be inconsistent with the principles of social morality if the spouse who had significantly contributed to the breakdown of the marriage were entitled to be maintained by the spouse who did not cause the breakdown. In considering whether maintenance providing is consistent with morality, it should be decisive as to not only how the breakdown of the marriage occurred but also the spouse's conduct after divorce.

291. Claims for maintenance after divorce are stipulated by law as so-called reasonable maintenance.[137] Court practices hold 'reasonableness' as considered in relation to the abilities and situation of the person liable, that is, his/her living standard, health condition, age, etc.[138]

292. The divorced spouse who did not share predominantly in the breakdown of the marriage by violating matrimonial duties and who suffered a serious loss by the divorce may claim maintenance from the former spouse in such an amount that the material and cultural living standard of both spouses would be principally the same, that is, as though no divorce occurred. Maintenance so extended may be granted for no more than three years following the separate living. In determining the extent of maintenance, the court does not investigate whether the divorced spouse is able to support himself/herself. Therefore this type of maintenance is called (not very precisely) a 'sanctioning maintenance' in court practice.[139]

293. The right of the divorced spouse to be maintained may cease to exist also by receiving a lump sum of money based on a written agreement.[140] This agreement is most frequently made, along with other necessary agreements, in an agreed divorce. In this way, it is possible to 'buy' the divorce.

137. *Ibid.*, §761.
138. Supreme Court Decision No. 45/1985.
139. Civil Code §762.
140. *Ibid.*, §921, §761/1.

IV. Housing after Divorce

294. The law provides protection to the spouse after divorce in relation to housing. This may be a premarital agreement (§718(2) of the Civil Code), a pre-divorce agreement (§757 of the Civil Code) or an agreement concluded after the dissolution of the marriage. The issue of housing can be settled comprehensively in connection with the settlement of the matrimonial property (§736 of the Civil Code) and the determination of maintenance obligations between the divorced spouses (§§760 et seq. of the Civil Code).

295. If no agreement is reached, the matter shall be decided by the court in an adversarial proceeding under the Civil Procedure Code. The legal basis for the spouses' cohabitation must always be assessed.

296. This may include:

a. joint ownership within the community of property (§§708 et seq. of the Civil Code);
b. joint ownership of the family home, e.g., acquired before the marriage (§§1115 et seq. of the Civil Code);
c. a derivative legal right of residence from one's spouse, i.e., the spouse's right of residence (§§744 and 767 of the Civil Code);
d. the right of joint commitment (§745 of the Civil Code);
e. another right of residence, e.g., derived from a third party (parents of one of the spouses, etc., §770 of the Civil Code); a sublease (§2274 of the Civil Code); an easement (§§1257 et seq. of the Civil Code); a maintenance contract (§2701 of the Civil Code).

297. The law provides that if the marriage was dissolved by divorce and the spouses had equal rights (e.g., joint ownership) or joint rights (e.g., joint tenancy) and if they do not agree on who will continue to live in the house or apartment, the court shall, on the application of one of them, according to the circumstances of the case, cancel the existing right of the divorced spouse who can be fairly required to leave the house or apartment, or, if necessary, at the same time decide on the method of compensation for the loss of the right. In doing so, it shall take into account, in particular, which of the divorced spouses has been entrusted with the care of a minor child who has not acquired full legal capacity and for whom the spouses have been caring, as well as the landlord's opinion (§768(1) of the Civil Code). In the case of a divorced spouse who has to leave the house or apartment, he or she has an *ex lege* right to live there until the other spouse provides him or her with alternative accommodation. If he has not been granted compensation by the court, he has the right to live in the house or apartment for a maximum of one year (§768(2), first sentence of the Civil Code).

298. If, however, he has been entrusted with the care of a minor child who has not acquired full legal capacity and who was cared for by the spouses during the marriage, or a dependent child who lives with him, the court may, on the application of the spouse, establish a right corresponding to an easement in his favour (§768(2), second sentence, with reference to §767(2) of the Civil Code).

V. Exercising Parental Responsibilities

299. Divorce has no effect on parental responsibilities; only carrying out the particular rights and duties involved is changed.

As stated, prior to divorce, custody and maintenance of the common minor children must be ruled on. Custody and maintenance may be ruled on based on the court authority, or the parents' agreement is approved by the court if this agreement is consistent with the child's interests. The following three options are available:

1. The court shall decide or approve the parents' agreement on granting custody of the child to one of the parents. In essence, it is only a question of executing childcare in person as deciding substantial matters concerning the child is preserved for both parents.
2. The court may approve the parents' agreement on joint custody. In this case, the parents must have agreed on maintenance as well. The court cannot specify its amount. Joint custody in the view of the Civil Code means nothing else than that the child's terms are not settled for the time following the divorce, that is, as though the parents were not divorced.
3. The court may also approve of the parents' agreement or decide on alternating custody.

Joint custody and alternating custody are a result of the family law reform of 1998. Joint custody may not be ruled by the court against the will of one of the parents; the court may only approve of their agreement as a ruling irrespective of whether the attitude of one of the parents would be contrary to the child's interests.[141]

300. The rules and criteria for entrusting a child to personal custody are laid down by law in very general terms.[142] First of all, the court is to decide in such a way that the decision is in the best interests of the child and takes into account:

- the personality of the child, in particular his or her abilities and aptitudes in relation to the developmental possibilities and living conditions of the parents;
- the child's emotional orientation and background;
- the educational abilities of each parent;
- the current and expected stability of the child's future educational environment;
- the child's emotional attachment to his or her siblings, grandparents and, where appropriate, other relatives and non-relatives;

141. *Ibid.*, §907/1.
142. *Ibid.*, §907/2.

- the fact that which parent has hitherto properly cared for the child and properly provided for his or her emotional, intellectual and moral upbringing;
- which parent has the better prospects for the child's healthy and successful development;
- the right of the child to the care of both parents and to maintain regular personal contact with them;
- the right of the other parent to whom the child will not be entrusted to receive regular information about the child;
- the ability of the parent to agree on the upbringing of the child with the other parent; good communication between the parents is crucial for the child.

301. It follows from the nature of the case and the case law of the Constitutional Court that there are no family life models.[143] The court must therefore take into account the above-mentioned statutory rules, the opinion and wishes of both parents and, in particular, the opinion and wishes of the child in each particular case and assess everything in such a way that the post-divorce arrangement is in the best interests of the child. If the views of the child's parents are irreconcilable, the State must not resign from its positive duty to protect the minor child. It must, *inter alia*, make efforts to improve the relationship between the child's parents and address the reasons for their negative attitudes.[144] A whole range of means are available for this purpose, e.g., family mediation, family therapy, meetings between the parents and the child with an expert in the field of paedopsychology.

302. Every child is different, and this must be taken into account above all, as well as the child's right to the care of both parents, or to regular personal contact with them, to security, background and the prospect of successful development and family life in general. This is primarily about preserving family ties and minimizing interference with them, as well as a whole range of other aspects.[145] However, it must always be borne in mind that the child is not the subject of the agreement or court decision. The child must be an active subject with all the rights of a party to the proceedings and must be represented by a conflict guardian.[146] His opinion and wishes must be taken into account.

303. In the case of alternating personal care, both the mother and the father care for the child at intervals that may or may not be of equal length (e.g., a week or a month; for young children, e.g., two to three days). Alternating care may then be close in nature to individual care with very extensive contact with the non-individual parent. Alternate care can take many forms. No provision of the law prevents the child from remaining in the family home and the parents from coming to the former common home or taking turns in the personal care of the child. If the parents agree on this form of care, they should also agree on the fulfilment of the

143. Constitutional Court decision, No. II ÚS 363/03; I ÚS 420/05.
144. *Ibid.*, No. III ÚS 1206/09; I ÚS 2482/13.
145. *Ibid.*, No. I. ÚS 2482/13.
146. *Ibid.*, No. I. ÚS 3304/13.

maintenance obligation. The agreement may also include an arrangement for the child to have contact with the other parent during the period of custody of the first parent.

304. This form is not suitable for every child. It is not and cannot be considered a one-size-fits-all arrangement, as every child is different, has different needs and wants, etc. After all, there are no set models for family life either. Particularly for young children or children with various health problems, experts prefer the stability of a nest, the primary carer. However, if alternating care actually works in a particular family before the court's decision, there is usually no reason not to approve the parents' agreement on alternating care.

305. In practice, it is often discussed whether the court can decide on alternate custody authoritatively, against the will of one or both parents. The law does not explicitly require parental consent in the case of alternate custody. However, it is always necessary to base oneself on the above-mentioned criteria and, above all, to take into account the best interests of the child and his or her welfare, the factual (in)functioning of this form, etc., as well as the ability of the parents to reach an agreement, to prioritize a compromise over their personal interests, new partners, etc. One can agree with the opinion that 'alternating care is not always in the best interests of the child'.[147]

306. If one parent does not agree to alternate care, the reasons for his or her refusal must be addressed.[148] They may be different. The decision must be up-to-date on the date of the decision, but it must also take into account a longer-term perspective, the prospect of care, etc.

307. If there is a substantial change in circumstances, e.g., the child starts primary school or studies at secondary school, there is no bar to res judicata, and it is possible to change both the parents' agreement and the court decision.

308. As for the option to visit the child placed in the custody of one of the parents, the law prefers agreement of the parents which need not be approved by the court. The contact of a parent with a child is ruled on by the court only when the parents are unable to arrive at an agreement. Repeatedly and unfoundedly obstructing the other parent to contact the child may be deemed such a substantial change of terms that might allow a change in the original ruling charging the child into the custody of one of the parents.[149]

The court may restrict or ban the other parent to contact the child if such a decision is in the child's interests. These are the cases when either no personal relations exist between the parent and the child or the parent's influences upon the child's upbringing prove harmful, etc.

---

147. *Ibid.*, No. II. ÚS 169/16.
148. *Ibid.*, No. III. ÚS 1206/09.
149. Civil Code §889.

309. The court may also adjust the contact of the child with his/her grandparents or siblings if such adjustment would be in the child's interests.

Chapter 3. Cohabitation Without Marriage

§1. Definition

310. Although marriage is highly valued in our environment, the number of persons living as unmarried couples has been growing. The pool results show that more and more people wish to live with his/her partner without marriage in so-called factual cohabitation, or independently without a partner. To a great extent, it is a reaction to a previous closed society where family life based on marriage considerably prevailed as a way of life.

A number of legal rules use the term unmarried spouses; that is, factual cohabitation of two persons without marriage is taken into account to a certain extent. If so, factual cohabitation is equalled to marriage as legislation as a rule uses the term 'married or unmarried spouse'.

311. There is, however, no unified law in regard to the duration of the cohabitation to make this relationship legally relevant. Either the necessary period of cohabitation is not directly stated or the question of whether there is a factual cohabitation or not is left to the interpretation of an appropriate authority (e.g., criminal law) or is stipulated to three months (state social allowances) or one year (Civil Code in relation to inheritance).

Unless expressly specified, the prevailing period of cohabitation arises from the minimal period of cohabitation as stipulated within social security provisions; that is, a man and a woman living together can be deemed a factual cohabitation if they have lived together in a common home for longer than three months.

312. In some instances, it will be significant for the relationship of unmarried spouses that the provision of the Civil Code defining so-called close persons will be taken into consideration. A close person is a relative in the direct line of descent, a sibling or a spouse; other persons within a family or similar relationship shall be considered as close persons if a detriment suffered by one of them may be justly felt by the other person as his/her own detriment.[150] Where the law does not mention expressly unmarried spouses but mentions close persons, the relationship between the unmarried spouses must be taken into consideration because in the light of the definition stated unmarried spouses are no doubt close persons.

313. Factual cohabitation of a man and a woman is not recorded anywhere. As a rule, a declaration of the man and woman towards the relevant authority that they have been living in a common household, or perhaps an affidavit, is sufficient.

150. *Ibid.*, §22.

§2. Duty to Maintain

314. There is no legal right between unmarried spouses to be provided maintenance. If the spouses manage their finances together, their personal needs are factually satisfied within this framework too. After the extinction of such a relationship, they have no legal claims to one another, not even in a situation where they have had a common child. The Family Code provides for the claims of an unmarried mother towards her child's father only to a very limited extent. The duty to maintain the mother is limited to a period of two years.[151]

315. Factual voluntary maintenance although not provided for in the Civil Code may, however, be of significance in regard to recovery of damages. If a physical injury resulted in death, the defendant is bound to refund, by monetary allowances, maintenance costs of the survivors whose maintenance was factually provided or was owed under law by the deceased person.[152]

Voluntary maintenance is taken into account also by social security regulations in determining the specific amount of the social allowance provided.[153]

§3. Property Relations

316. No property relations similar to joint property of married spouses may arise between unmarried spouses based on law or on contract. With regard to the explicit provision of the Civil Code under which joint property may arise only between married couples,[154] an *analogue legis* cannot be applied.

Even though unmarried spouses have lived together in a factual long-term union, each of them acquires property into his/her own individual ownership and may dispose of this property without the consent of the other spouse.

Of course, co-ownership may arise between the two of them in a way similar to that between other persons. If not stipulated by law or otherwise agreed upon by the parties, the portions of the property owned are equal.[155] The difference between co-ownership and joint property of spouses arises in the instant of its settlement.[156]

§4. Common Dwelling

317. Unmarried people can live together on several legal grounds, mainly arising from a contract. These include joint tenancy of a flat (§2270 of the Civil Code), subletting of a flat or a part thereof (§§2274 et seq. of the Civil Code), or joint ownership of a flat or a property used for living purposes (§§1115 et seq. of the Civil

---

151. *See* below Part II, Ch. 4.
152. Civil Code §2966.
153. Act No. 117/1995 Coll., on State Social Benefits, §7.
154. Civil Code §708.
155. *Ibid.*, §1122(3).
156. *See* below Part III.

Code). The spouse and the partner may also live together on the basis of a right corresponding to an easement or an easement (§§1257 et seq. of the Civil Code) or on the basis of an unnamed contract. Another possibility of living together is related to the derivative legal grounds of living together by virtue of close persons (§22 of the Civil Code).

318. Special provisions regulate the issue of the transfer of tenancy (§§2279 et seq. of the Civil Code) and the right to free provision for three weeks after the death of the deceased in his/her home (§1669 of the Civil Code).

Protection against domestic violence may be invoked by anyone, including a spouse (§3021 of the Civil Code, with reference to §§751 to 753 of the Civil Code).

§5. Right to Inherit

319. In view of the succession law, the surviving unmarried spouse is not favoured in any way as compared to other heirs. Having a status of so-called co-living person, he/she may be a co-heir in the second group of succession or a universal heir in the third group.[157]

Here, it is necessary to note that if a child was born during cohabitation of an unmarried couple, on the death of one of the partners, the surviving spouse is completely excluded as heir.

§6. Social Allowances

320. Regarding social allowances to families with a poor economic background, unmarried spouses are deemed to be so-called jointly considered persons if they live together permanently and jointly cover expenses for their needs, and only in case they have been living together for a period longer than three months.[158]

321. An unmarried spouse may not claim any allowances arising from the deceased spouse's pension insurance, regardless of the length of their cohabitation. This can be claimed by a widow or a widower only supposing the marriage was legally effective on the death of the other spouse.[159]

322. Here, a so-called pension contract as provided for in the Civil Code (§2701 of the Civil Code) should be mentioned. A written contract grants the right to pay certain allowances to a person for life or for a period of uncertain duration stated otherwise.

157. *See* below Part IV, Ch. 1, §3.
158. Act No. 117/1995 Coll., on State Social Benefits, §7, Act No. 110/2006 Coll., on Subsistence Level.
159. Act No. 155/1995 Coll., on Pension Insurance.

Unmarried spouses might accordingly conclude a written contract granting the right to pay certain allowances for life or for a period stated otherwise of an uncertain duration (e.g., for the time they will be 'together'). Allowance in this respect is any repeated payment (annuity), the amount of which or at least the way of its calculation should be explicitly mentioned in the contract. The reason need not be specified in the contract. Paying such allowance need not be related to any consideration.

§7. Criminal Law

323. Under criminal law, the rights of the accused to a defence are secured, besides others, also by stipulating the rights of the persons of separate defence rights among whom unmarried spouses are explicitly mentioned under criminal law.[160] Such persons may appeal in favour of the accused, not, however, to his/her detriment. Under court practices, they may not appeal against the will of the accused.

An unmarried spouse is explicitly granted the right to refuse to testify in court.[161]

324. Criminal prosecution for rape should be mentioned here as well. Under criminal law, a criminal prosecution of the perpetrator – a husband or an unmarried male spouse – may start or proceed in a pending criminal prosecution only with the consent of the female victim.

160. Act No. 141/1961 Coll., on Criminal Court Proceedings, §247(2).
161. *Ibid.*, §100.

Chapter 4. Partnership

325. On 1 January 2025, Act No. 123/2024 Coll. came into force, which fundamentally changes the Civil Code with regard to unions of same-sex couples; as of 1 January 2025, it is no longer possible to enter into a registered partnership in the Czech Republic. Same-sex couples can enter into a civil partnership under the Civil Code. This union has similar obligations and rights as marriage, but is not called marriage.

§655 of the Civil Code is added of section (2) to read:

> (2) A partnership is a permanent union of two people of the same sex which is entered into in the same way as marriage. Unless otherwise provided by law or other legislation, the provisions on marriage, rights and obligations of spouses, widows and widowers shall apply mutatis mutandis to a partnership and the rights and obligations of partners.

This is the new legislation, which is very sketchy and raises more questions than answers. We will try to outline some of them, as the situation, for example, regarding the formation of a partnership, is not as simple as it may seem at first sight. In particular, the question of the marriageable age. A person under the age of 18 could not enter into a registered partnership. A minor under the age of 16 can enter into a valid marriage with the permission of the court. Can the court rule on the permission of a 16–18 year old to enter into a civil partnership? Logically, such a procedure cannot be ruled out.

326. Another problematic aspect may be the conclusion of a partnership between two foreigners under Czech law. Taking into account the different approach of national regulations, the Czech legislator has stipulated in the provisions of Article 4(2) of the RegP that at least one person entering into a registered partnership must be a citizen of the Czech Republic. Can two foreigners enter into a partnership in the Czech Republic? It can be stated that under the same conditions as for spouses, yes.

Furthermore, the legislation does not clearly reflect the issue of church marriage. It is a well-known fact that some churches do not allow same-sex unions. However, the proposed legislation defines that the partnership is to be entered into in the same way as marriage. This includes the form of a church marriage.

Another change is the addition of §778 of the Civil Code, which reads as follows: 'If a child conceived by artificial insemination is born to an unmarried woman or a woman in a civil partnership, the man who gave consent to the artificial insemination shall be deemed to be the father of the child.' We understand this provision to mean that a woman in a civil partnership is regarded as unmarried, so the first presumption does not apply. The partnered mother will still have to come forward with a man who consents to artificial insemination and will subsequently be registered as the father of the child on the basis of that consent, regardless of whether his sperm was actually used. The mother's partner will then be able to be registered on the basis of the father's consent to the adoption. Another possible scenario is that, after the birth, the mother of the child in the civil partnership will not indicate that the artificial insemination has taken place, no father will be entered in the register, and the mother's partner will then be able to adopt the child with the mother's consent.

The new §800 of the Civil Code also poses major problems. Its new wording reads: 'Spouses or one spouse may become adoptive parents, or a partner may also become an adoptive parent if the other partner is the child's parent. Exceptionally, another person may also adopt; in this case, the court will also decide that the registration of the other parent is deleted from the register.'

What did the legislator want to express by the term 'if the other partner is the parent'? There can be great debates on the topic of parenthood. What is certain, however, is that, in legal terms, it is not only the biological parent who is the parent. It is worth recalling the provisions of §771 of the Civil Code, according to which: 'Parenting is a relationship based on blood ties or created by adoption.' Therefore, we stress that the adoptive parent also becomes the minor child's parent with all obligations and rights upon the legal force of the adoption judgment. Thus, the interpretation of this provision must be that if one of the partners is registered as the parent of the child , his or her partner will be able to 'adopt' the child.

It should be summarized that if the partners are aware of the legislation, then one of them will 'adopt' the child, by whatever means, including adoption prior to entering into partnership, and then his or her partner will adopt the child. This will burden the courts with double adoption proceedings which will in effect be the same as if they had adopted together.

As far as joint foster care is concerned, here we consider that the obligations and rights of the spouses apply to the partners and the law does not explicitly state anything regarding joint foster care. We believe that if in the provisions of §964 of the Civil Code the law allows for joint foster care to be entrusted to spouses, this must be understood to include partners.

As regards the rest of the obligations and rights, it can be generally summarised that the partners have the same obligations and rights as spouses, i.e., they are entitled to joint property, a widow's pension, etc.

Chapter 5. Registered Partnership

327. As of 1 January 2025, the situation with registered partnerships in the Czech Republic is as follows. It is no longer possible to enter into it, but registered partnerships already concluded continue and have legal consequences. Dissolution can occur when registered partners enter into a partnership under the Civil Code or when a registered partnership is dissolved by a court.

With regard to the historical development of same-sex unions, it should be pointed out that the adoption of the Registered Partnership Act in 2006 was a milestone which conferred certain obligations and rights on such persons. Although the original intent of the 2024 amendment was to create marriage for all, some compromise, as described in the previous chapter, was eventually pushed through. On the obligations and rights of registered partners, see the following text.

§1. Rights and Duties of the Partners

328. The Czech lawmaker followed the example of Germany by enumerating the rights and duties of the partners. However, I am afraid that these rights and duties exist up to a strict limit. The partners have the same rights and duties. Concerning matters related to mutual decision-making, they should agree, and if not, the court can decide.[162]

One of the partners is entitled to represent the other partner in his/her trivial matters unless stated otherwise by a special regulation.[163] These may be, for example, the acts related to common management of assets (partners can have assets only in divided co-ownership), receiving common payments of the other partner. However, they cannot file a suit on behalf of the other one without power of attorney.

Acts of one of the partners in managing common family matters hold both partners liable jointly and severally. A partner can expressively exclude the other partner's title to act on his/her behalf. This exclusion is effective only if a third party is aware of it.

Partners are principally entitled to an equal living standard. If one of the partners does not pay his/her contributions, the court can decide about his/her support with an eye on the situation within the common household. If one of the partners has a child, then the support between partners has priority over the support of the child. Only if the partner is unable to pay, the children are then obliged to pay the support for their parents.

Common property does not play the same role as in marriage.

162. §8(2) RP.
163. §9(1) RP. Special regulation is, e.g., Labour Code No. 262/2006 Coll., §142(5). A partner can receive the others partner's salary only upon a written power of attorney.

§2. Rights in Relationship to Minor Children

329. The existence of the partnership has no effect on parental responsibilities and is also no handicap in the case of decisions in which custody of the parents the child should be.[164] The partner that is a parent has the same rights and duties to the child as the other parent.

In case that one partner has a child in his/her custody, the other partner (step-parent) participates in the child's upbringing.

The original regulation stipulating that 'an ongoing partnership prevents one of the partners from becoming the adoptive parent of a child' has been abolished (Constitutional Court Decision Pl. ÚS 7/15, abolishing §13(2) of the RegP, since 22 July 2016). What remains is the prohibition of joint adoption, whether of another's child or of a partner's child – *step-parent adoption* (only spouses can do this; §800 of the Civil Code).

However, at present (2023), the Czech Republic is discussing the possibility of registering same-sex parents in the Czech civil registry if the parentage was established abroad, either through recognition of parenthood or adoption. As there are great differences in these possibilities and some are registered and some are not, there is a great interest in changing the legislation so that the interests of the child are protected regardless of the gender or status of the parents.

§3. The End of the Registered Partnership

330. Registered partnership has the same reasons for extermination as in the case of marriage. It terminates with the death of one of the partners, with one of the partners declaring the death and with the court's decision to terminate the partnership.

The court decides that the partnership is terminated if one of them files a suit and brings evidence that the partnership relationship does not exist anymore.[165] This definition results from the fact that the partners do not have the same duties as spouses yet implies the duty to cohabit and to be faithful. However, the evidence of a non-existing relationship mostly refers to the evidence that they do not cohabit anymore in accordance with the Family Law Code. It means they do not have to live together in a common home, yet they have to have a personal union, maybe a plan to live together later if it is not now possible, to call one another and so on. If one of them does not want to live in this way, then the court has to end the partnership.

We can also find parallels with agreed divorce in the registered partnership code.[166] If the other partner comes to agreement with the suit to end the partnership, the court will not investigate if the partnership relationship exists or not.[167] The court will end the registered partnership. With the other partner's consent, there is

164. §13(1) RP.
165. §16 RP.
166. Civil Code §757.
167. §17 RP.

a legal title for ending the partnership. There is no need to put forward agreements of the settlements of common assets and common dwellings as joint property and joint tenancy of property do not play a relevant role such as between spouses.

After the ending of the partnership, there may be a legal claim by one of the partners for support if he/she is not able to support himself/herself after the end of the registered partnership. The law as so-called reasonable support in this case stipulates claim for support.[168] Reasonable refers to the needs and the situation of the person entitled to certain things, that is, his/her living standard, health condition, age, etc., also to the abilities, situation and property of the person liable. The court has to prove that the person liable did not refuse any profit or a more lucrative job or if he/she is not undergoing the property risks.

The ex-partner who did not contribute towards the breakdown of the relationship and who suffered a serious loss by ending the partnership may claim support from the ex-partner to such an amount, which relates to the material and living standard of both partners would be principally entitled to the same (as in existing partnership). Support so extended may be granted for no more than three years following the end of the partnership.[169]

The right of the ex-partner to be financially supported (both types of support) may cease to exist through receipt of a lump amount of money based on a written agreement.[170] It also ceases if the liable ex-partner has died or the entitled ex-partner closes a new registered partnership or marriage.

An ex-partner may not be granted support if this were contrary to morality (*contra bonos mores*). In this case, the court must investigate why the partnership has broken down.

Support payments are set on a monthly basis from the first day of the initiation of the procedure.

I. Registration of the Partnership

331. The local authority, which is certified to look after the register, registers the partnership. They have special books for registered partnerships. They are similar to those for marriages, births and deaths.

168. §11(1) RP.
169. §11(2) RP.
170. §11(5) RP.

Chapter 6. Filiation

332. Czech law does not distinguish between the legal status of children born in wedlock or out of wedlock. Shortly after World War II, the unequal status of illegitimate children regarding the execution of parental rights and obligations, duty to maintain or right to succession was removed.[171]

The contemporary Civil Code stipulates parents' rights and obligations towards children, regardless of whether the parents are married or not.

333. Filiation, with regard to a child, is generally established on the basis of three basic legal presumptions (*pater est quem nuptiae demonstrant*), which are refutable. But it is necessary to explain that this system of presumptions is internally articulated. The two basic presumptions are directly the legal fact by which paternity is determined. The third presumption is relevant for the evidence in the proceedings for the establishment of paternity; the legal fact that establishes the status relationship of paternity is the court decision. The system is supplemented by a presumption that the father of a child born to an unwed mother from artificial insemination is the consenting father.

334. A child is, as a rule, entitled to affiliation. It has, however, no right to deny paternity. This right is granted to his/her legal parents only.

335. Since the family law reform in 1998, the legal regulation also stipulates the determination of motherhood. The law has reacted to growing options of so-called assisted reproduction (*artificial fertilization, fertilization in vitro*). The woman who delivers a child through childbirth is always considered a mother.[172] Thus, Czech law has completely excluded any possibility of surrogate motherhood a legal option for direct determination of motherhood. In case of surrogate motherhood, adoption has to be applied. Surrogacy is not regulated as an institution, but in practice it is generally not excluded. The law mentions it only in the provision of §804 of the Civil Code, which allows adoption between relatives in the case of surrogacy.

The law does not explicitly provide other instances of objectionable motherhood. If, however, a newborn baby is mistakenly identified or misplaced in the hospital, the respective motherhood could be ruled on by the court in proceedings on determination or denial of parenthood.[173]

In the Czech Republic, some hospitals have so-called baby boxes. These do not have any legal regulation, and if the mother puts a baby into this box, the baby becomes a foundling. It means the court decides upon his/her name and surname and the child becomes a Czech citizen. If a woman files a suit for her motherhood, she should bring evidence that she has given birth to the foundling child.

171. Constitution of 9 May 1948, Act No. 265/1949 Coll., on Family Law.
172. Civil Code §775.
173. §417 Act on Special Judicial Proceedings.

Since 2004, the so-called child's delivery with the identity of the mother being held confidential has been established.[174] It is necessary to say that the private statutory law was changed through a public act without thinking about the far-reaching consequences. Only an unmarried mother may request this confidential child delivery. She can come to the hospital and request to give birth to a child with her identity being held confidential. Her name and surname are dealt with separately from the child's documentation. The identity of the mother can be first known only after a court decision. The problem of this regulation is that this woman is, in Czech legal system, still a mother of the child because she gave birth to him/her. So, the child has a mother, but she is confidential. The child should also have a surname of the mother.[175] She is a legal representative of the child, but she cannot act for the child and that is why the court should appoint a custodian to the child. The court cannot appoint the guardian because the child has a representative. The lawmaker wanted that these children be quickly adopted. However, the court has to wait for two months if the mother does not demonstrate any interest in the child. If she does not, the court may decide that the child can be adopted without her consent. In the opposite case, when she gives birth to the child and she is written down as a mother of the child, but she wants the child to be adopted, she can give consent to adoption with no relation to prospective adopters after six weeks after the child's delivery. This means that the child can be adopted quicker than in the case of confidential birth. This new regulation does not respect the rights of the father of the child.

§1. Children Born in Wedlock

I. Filiation

336. If a child was born within the time of contracting the marriage and the 300th day following its termination, the mother's husband is deemed the father. The same applies if a child was born during a void marriage or no later than 300 days following the marriage being declared void.[176]

If a child is born to a woman married again, the latest husband is deemed to be the father even though the child was born before the lapse of the 300th day after the previous marriage terminated or was declared void.[177] If the later husband successfully denied his paternity, the presumption of the former husband shall apply automatically.[178]

337. The mother's husband's paternity is recorded in the register of births automatically, regardless of possible allegations of the mother or her husband that the father is another man. The fact that the marriage legally existed at the moment of the child's birth is decisive.

174. Act No. 372/2011 on health services.
175. §14 Act No. 301/2000 Coll., Civil Registry Act .
176. Civil Code §776.
177. *Ibid.*, §776.
178. *Ibid.*, §788.

II. Paternity Denial by the Mother's Husband

338. The denial of paternity of the mother's husband is limited by a time limit. If the husband denies paternity, he may do so within a subjective period of six months, which begins from the moment he becomes aware of the circumstances giving rise to doubt. However, the latest the father may file the petition is 6 years of age of the child.

339. The mother may file a petition to deny paternity within six months of the birth.

340. The specific regulation of the denial of paternity of the mother's husband is contained in the provisions of §777 of the Civil Code, according to which, if the child is born after the commencement of the divorce proceedings, the mother, the former husband and the putative father may, after the divorce, declare before the court or the registry office that the husband is not the father, but it is the putative father who acknowledges paternity.

341. After the expiry of the period of denial, a claim for denial of paternity is not completely excluded but can only be successful if the court excuses the missed period of denial. A waiver is only possible if the best interests of the child and public policy so require.

342. Although the procedural rules do not lay down any binding rules in terms of possible evidence in proceedings for the denial of paternity, the biological link between the father and the child is actually proved by an expert opinion in the field of genetics. As the proceedings are newly uncontested, the parties do not bear the subjective burden of proof.

§2. Children Born Out of Wedlock

343. The number of children born out of wedlock has been constantly growing. No legal rule uses the term 'illegitimate child'. Only the expression 'child whose parents are not married' is used, which may denote not only a child born out of wedlock but also a child whose parents are not married anymore because they are divorced.

I. Affiliation by the Parents' Affirmation

344. If a child is born to an unmarried woman, or more than 300 days after termination of the previous marriage or after this marriage was declared void or the mother's husband denied successfully his paternity, the man whose paternity was established by the parents' common affirmation is deemed the child's father.[179]

Affirmation must be taken in person before a court or registry office. A written statement about paternity is not sufficient, and such an affirmation may not be made on behalf of either party through a power of attorney. The parents are not, however, bound to appear together in order to affirm, even though it is mostly done in this way.

However, a consensual declaration of paternity cannot be made before the registry office if paternity proceedings are pending.

If one of the parents were a minor, his/her paternity affirmation may be made before a court only.[180] The attitude or possible consent of his/her parents to the affirmation is not substantial.

The mother is not bound to name her child's father, and paternity may not be established by affirmation against her will.

If the mother is unable, because of mental disorder, to assess the meaning of her declaration or if the measure of her declaration involves an obstacle which is difficult to overcome, it is not possible to establish paternity by a declaration of consent.[181] The law states that if the father does not have the capacity to act, the court shall according to §780 of the Civil Code assess whether the father who lacks full capacity is able to act on his or her own or whether his or her guardian will act for him or her. However, the doctrine has held that it is not appropriate for a guardian to make a declaration on behalf of the putative father. Therefore, if the father is unable to make a declaration, proceedings to establish paternity must also be brought.

345. A situation may occur when paternity is established by common affirmation of the parents before the child is born (*nasciturus*), but the mother contracts marriage with another man before the child is born. Thus, the paternity presumption suits both men, for one based on the common affirmation, for the other based on marriage.

In practice, it is the mother's husband who tends to be named as the child's father in the birth register. If the mother's husband succeeded in paternity denial, the paternity of the father established by common affirmation would probably apply.

346. Another question is to what extent the authorized body taking the parents' affirmation is entitled or bound to investigate whether this legal paternity is consistent with natural paternity.

The authority keeping the registry or court probably should not accept paternity affirmation in case it was made by the man whose paternity was already excluded by, for example, a legitimate court ruling, for example, the mother's husband who successfully denied his paternity in a suit, a man whose paternity suit has been lawfully dismissed, a man whose paternity, was excluded in a pending paternity suit based on an expert report, etc. However, such allegations do not rely on a legal rule

179. *Ibid.*, §779.
180. *Ibid.*, §779.
181. *Ibid.*, §781.

as the law presumes only that the man who affirms, together with the mother, to be the child's father will be named as the father in the birth register. Investigating further facts, namely, if in the time decisive for conceiving the child sexual intercourse occurred, is not in our view up to the registry office or the court.

Although the Civil Code, in an attempt to improve the situation, introduced a regulation according to which a declaration of consent is to be treated as a legal act and may be void, the legal regulation created more ambiguity.[182] It is not clear which grounds of invalidity are applicable and in which proceedings. However, the Supreme Court has ruled that the invalidity of a declaration is to be invoked only in proceedings for the denial of paternity.

II. Paternity Denial

347. The man whose paternity was established based on common affirmation of the parents may deny his paternity in court, but only if it is excluded that he might be the child's father.[183] This right is of course granted to the mother as well.

The statutory limit for paternity denial is also six months running:

a. six months after establishing paternity by common affirmation;
b. if paternity of a not yet born child (*nasciturus*) was established in such a way, the statutory time limit would not expire sooner than six months after the child's birth.

Even in the case of paternity established by a declaration of consent, it is possible to file a petition for denial after the expiry of the period of denial with a request for waiver of its delay. The conditions are the same as for the denial of the paternity of the mother's husband, i.e., compliance with public policy and the best interests of the child.

III. Paternity Denial by Court Without a Petition

348. If paternity has been established by a consent declaration, proceedings for the denial of paternity may be initiated by the court even without a petition if the interests of the child and the protection of human rights so require. At present, this provision is the only chance for the so-called putative fathers, as they do not have the right of denial.[184]

182. *Ibid.*, §782.
183. *Ibid.*, §790.
184. *Ibid.*, §793.

IV. Affiliation by Court Ruling

349. Whereby paternity is not established by marriage or by the common affirmation of the parents, the father may be established on the basis of court proceedings.

350. The law states that the man who had intercourse with the mother in the time between no more than 300 days and no less than 180 days prior to the child's birth is deemed the father unless his paternity is eliminated by serious circumstances.[185]

351. In fact, however, the procedure is already underway to verify the child's origins by means of an expert opinion in the field of DNA profiling.

352. The father, the mother and the child can file a petition to initiate proceedings. The proceedings are uncontested, and the child is represented by a conflict guardian, who is usually a child welfare authority.

353. The court decides the case by judgment. The proceedings are also linked to the child custody and maintenance proceedings. Logically, however, if the parents agree on this, there is no need for proceedings.

V. Name and Surname

354. The parents are bound to agree on the child's name and surname. If no agreement has been arrived at, the name or surname shall be determined by the court.

VI. Inheritance

355. In regard to succession law, it is not decisive whether the child was born in or out of wedlock. All testators' children inherit equally.[186]

VII. The Rights of an Unmarried Mother Toward Her Child's Father

356. The child's father whom the mother is not married to is bound to contribute appropriately to cover the costs for her maintenance during the period of two years and to cover the costs related to pregnancy and child delivery.[187]

The costs related to pregnancy and child delivery are the costs of the mother to purchase clothing and shoes for the period of pregnancy, medical care costs that are,

185. *Ibid.*, §783.
186. *See* below Part IV, Ch. 1, §3.
187. Civil Code §920.

for any reason, not covered by her health insurance, etc. However, the cost incurring from purchasing the necessary items for the child, such as a baby pram, baby cot, diapers, and baby clothing, do not belong here, making the cost covered within the maintenance owed by the child's father.

The mother may claim the cost as stated if and only after the child has been delivered and paternity established either by common affirmation of the parents or by a court ruling. The mother may claim these rights also against her divorced husband, supposing the child was born within three hundred days following the divorce.

The right to claim such costs will expire three years after the child's delivery.

357. As the prospective mother may find herself in a difficult social situation and she may need to buy the items necessary for the expected child, the law allows a pregnant woman to claim the costs for her maintenance and the costs related to pregnancy and child delivery also against the man whose paternity is probable. At the same time, the costs for the child's maintenance shall be reimbursed for the time of thirty-seven weeks (predominantly the costs concerning the baby's outfit).[188]

The claims as stated must be asserted in court prior to the child's delivery. The relevant amount is as a rule decided by the court only after the child has been born. The court may rule that the probable father will be obliged to reimburse these costs as a lump sum and in advance.

358. If it is later proved that the probable father who had covered the expenses for the mother's maintenance, her costs related to pregnancy and child delivery as well as the child's maintenance costs is not the child's natural father, this man may sue the person who was obliged to cover the costs as stated, that is, the real father as established to recover all his costs incurred. If paternity were not established at all, in theory, he might claim the costs paid by him from the child's mother.

VIII. Situation of Putative Fathers

359. As it follows from the above, the right of denial belongs only to the legal parents. One who feels himself to be the biological father of the child cannot deny the paternity of another man. He has only the possibility to ask the court to deny paternity without a petition if it has been established by a consent declaration. It is not possible to deny the paternity of the husband in this way. That is why Czech practice has created an action for the establishment of consanguinity by which only the blood relationship is declared. The putative father may also be granted access to the child under §927 of the Civil Code.

188. *Ibid.*, §920.

Chapter 7. Adoption and Foster Parent Care

§1. Introduction

360. If a child may not permanently grow up in his/her natural family, the state, keeping in mind the child's welfare, must intervene in the relations between the child and his/her parents. These are, namely, the cases when natural parents are unable for objective or subjective reasons to bring up the child, are not willing to live with him/her or are unable to create a favourable family environment and background. The utmost solution of the critical relation between the parents and the child is to remove the child from his/her family by court order and to place him/her in another substitute place, in a family, if possible.

Czech law provides for an overall system of substitute care of the child out of his/her original family. Depending on the particular social situation of the child, this system enables the selection of the most suitable form of substitute care for the child.

For very young children of relatively good health who will never be able to grow up in their original families (social orphans), adoption is most suitable.

For older children, groups of siblings and children impaired physically or mentally who will never be able to grow up in their original families, the most suitable is a form of state-subsidized foster parent care.

If the parents are not statutory representatives of the child, a guardian is appointed who personally looks after the child. This care is also state-subsidized.

If the parents themselves are not able to look after the child but other relatives (most often the grandparents) are, the court may place the child into their care and specify in its ruling the extent of their rights and obligations towards the child.

361. If a child cannot be placed in a substitute (surrogate) family or by the time a suitable family for him/her has been found, he/she shall be placed in an institutional care facility.

Local authorities search for persons interested in taking the child into substitute care, investigate their abilities and motivation to take a strange child into their own care, and they also search for children in need of being placed in a substitute family. Earlier, the substitute care was mediated by the Ministry of Labour and Social Affairs. Since 1 January 2002, these activities have been passed on to regional authorities.[189]

§2. Adoption of the Minor Child

I. General

362. Adoption of a minor child with full legal capacity (also referred to as adoption of a child) is one of the traditional institutions of Czech family law. As in many

189. Details being stipulated in Act No. 359/1999 Coll., on Social and Legal Protection of Children (Children Act).

European legal systems, adoption began to be conceived in this country after World War II as a service, especially to the orphaned child, or the adoption of another's child as one's own. The Civil Code builds on this concept; however, by its systematic classification and explicit diction, it emphasizes the status nature of adoption (§794 of the Civil Code). As a return to tradition, it introduces the adoption of an adult, which was rejected in 1949 as a 'bourgeois survival'. Since 1 January 2014, Czech law has returned to the adoption of an adult.

363. The goal of adoption of a minor child is to establish such a relationship between the adopter and the adopted child equal to one between natural parents and children and thus to create a permanent and harmonious home for the minor child.

Through adoption, such a relationship arises between the adopter and the adoptive child as between parents and children, and a family relationship arises between the adoptive child and the adopter's relatives (*adoptione natura imitatur*). Adopters have parental responsibility.[190] The adoptive child obtains the adopter's surname.[191]

364. Czech law stipulates so-called complete adoption (*adoptio plena*) in the two following manners: as an adoption that may be revoked for very important reasons (so-called simple adoption, first-degree adoption) and the so-called irrevocable adoption, which cannot be revoked. In both types of adoption are the adopters named in the register of births as the child's parents. It means the court decision of the adoption sounds that the child is adopted, the child has a surname of the adopters and the adopters will be written down in the register of birth as parents. Although the original parents' names remain in the register, on the child's birth certificate (abstract of birth), the adoptive parents are named as the child's parents; therefore, no personal document of the child will show that the child was adopted. Only adopters and the adopted child after the age of 12 years, unless the court has ordered the concealment of the blood parent and his or her consent to the adoption; if the court has ordered the concealment of the blood parent and his or her consent to the adoption, the adoptee may consult the record only after he or she has acquired full legal capacity.[192]

II. The Personality of an Adopter

365. Selecting a suitable person for a prospective adoption is decisive for the adoption to successfully meet its goals. Therefore, only such natural persons may become adoptive parents who guarantee by way of his/her lifestyle that adoption will be in favour of both the child and the society. Only a person who has reached the age of majority and is fully competent may become an adoptive parent if his or her personal characteristics and way of life, as well as the reasons and motives which lead him or her to adopt, guarantee that he or she will be a good parent for

190. Civil Code §832/2.
191. *Ibid.*, §835.
192. §8(8), §25(2) Act No. 301/2000 Coll., on Registers, Name and Surname.

the child to be adopted. The state of health of the adopter or of both adopters must not limit the care of the adopted child to a significant degree.[193]

The adopter must guarantee a permanent and harmonious environment and background for the child by his/her character, his/her motivation to adopt a child as well as by his/her dwelling conditions and property situation.

In determining adoption, the court is bound to investigate the health conditions of the adopters, their character, personal properties and motivation to adopt on the basis of medical checks and other necessary examinations and to consider if these are not contrary to adoption.[194] A child may be adopted only if the adoption promotes his/her welfare.[195]

In order to ascertain the personal properties and characters of the prospective adopters, the courts mostly require psychological examinations. These examinations are carried out as a rule in the period when the persons apply to the social and legal care authority to be included in the list of applicants for substitute family care.[196]

366. The adoptive parent must enjoy full legal capacity; that is, be of age (18 years) and may not be restricted for acts in law.[197] Czech law does not stipulate any age limit for adopters; it only requires a 'reasonable age span', normally not less than 16 years of age between the adoptive child and adoptive parent. If the custodian representing the child in the proceedings agrees to the adoption and if the adoption is in the best interests of the child, the age difference between the adopter and the adopted child may exceptionally be less than sixteen years.[198]

367. It is generally held that there must be no relationship between the adopter and the adoptee which would make the adoption unreasonable and superfluous. The adoption of a child by a grandparent would also be prevented by the age difference, which could not normally be regarded as reasonable (§803 of the Civil Code). In such cases, the legal consequences of adoption, i.e., the establishment of a kinship relationship between parents and children, would also lead to a serious distortion of family relations, including practical complications related to inheritance law, for example.

368. The barrier of consanguinity is now expressly expressed in the law (§804 of the Civil Code), but it applies only to persons related to each other in the direct line and to siblings, with the exception of surrogacy. The law does not provide any specifics for the adoption of a child from a surrogacy, e.g., specifics for granting consent or shortening of time limits, etc. It follows from the nature of the case that it will be a direct adoption.

193. Civil Code §799.
194. *Ibid.*, §827.
195. *Ibid.*, §795.
196. Act No. 359/1999 Coll., on Social and Legal Protection of Children, §§20 and the following.
197. Civil Code §799.
198. *Ibid.*, §803.

369. Only married spouses may adopt a child together.[199] Besides individual adoption, the Civil Code also stipulated joint adoption, but by a married couple only, not by, for example, non-marital partners or by persons of the same gender. Married spouses may adopt a child jointly or consecutively; that is, one of the spouses adopts the child first and then is followed by the other spouse. In cases of joint adoption by a married couple, the courts investigates into the length of duration and the course of the marriage, etc.

If only one of the spouses were to adopt the child, he/she will have to do so only upon the approval of the other spouse. The consent of the other spouse is not needed if his/her legal capacity is limited in this right. To grant consent is the other spouse's personal right; the court is not entitled to examine reasons for the other spouse's consent or his/her denial to consent.

370. Czech law also stipulates adoption by a step-parent of the child, that is, by a new mother's husband or by a new father's wife. This type of adoption is called in practice 'an improper adoption'. Through this adoption, the question of substitute family environment and background is not resolved as the child has been living in a complete family created by his/her parent and his/her spouse, but its aim is rather to settle the legal relationship of the child and his/her step-parent. The child's parent's spouse would otherwise be bound only to share the duty of care owed to the child under the Civil Code.

From 1 January 2025 it is possible for a partner to adopt his/her partner's child (§800 of the Civil Code).

III. Adoptive Child

371. Historical provisions in our territory allowed the adoption of adults, even a married woman.[200] The adopter might not have children of his/her own and must have been more than 40 years old. The adopter and adoptive child were viewed as a parent and a legitimate child; the right to inherit in the original family was preserved; however, the adopted child inherited from his/her adopter as well. The adoptive child also retained other rights in his/her original family, for example, the right to be supported and the right to be given a dowry (*dos*). However, the adopter did not acquire any property rights towards his/her adoptive child. As for becoming a member of the adopter's family, no legal relations and no property rights arose towards the members of the adopter's family.

372. Since 1 January 1950 to 1 January 2014, adoption of a minor person exclusively has been possible under Czech law.[201] The purpose of adoption is predominantly for the child to become part of a new adopting family. That is why mainly

199. *Ibid.*, §800.
200. Act No. 56/1928 Coll., on Adoption.
201. Family Code §65(2). The fact that adoption as reserved to minors only does not violate the constitutional principle of equality has been supported by the Opinion of the Constitutional Court of CR No. 295/1996 Coll.

the children of preschool age are most suitable for adoption as it is not a serious problem for them to adapt to the new family. Older children are adopted mainly in relation to their parents' new marriages (so-called improper adoption).

373. Since 1 January 2014, it is possible to adopt an adult. This issue is described below.

374. When it comes to the adoption of a minor and not fully capacitated child, international treaties and the Civil Code imply that the child must be at the centre of the matter. His or her welfare must be paramount. Every child is different, has different needs, comes from a different family background. Adoption can be, and often is, the best solution to his or her plight. However, it must not be seen as the only solution. However, what is in the best interests of the child, or the child's welfare, must be evaluated by the court in a particular situation. The Convention on the Rights of the Child guarantees the right of the child to the care of his or her parents, or to other individual care, so that the child grows up in a family environment, in an atmosphere of happiness, love and understanding, and so that his or her health, physical, emotional, intellectual and moral development is cared for. If the child cannot live with his/her parents or relatives or close persons, the child must be cared for by a person who is not a stranger to the child. Adoption is not always an appropriate solution for the difficult life situation of a minor child. The child's needs may be different.

375. The child's health handicap must not be an obstacle to adoption or any form of foster family care due to inertia of thinking. An applicant for adoption has the right to learn about the child's medical condition, as ignorance could be to the child's disadvantage. However, the good health of the child is relevant in relation to the possibility of the prospective adoptive parents to transfer the child to optional immediate care (§823 of the Civil Code, *see* the dictum 'as soon as the child's health permits … '). The court is obliged to request a report on the child's physical and mental health, including a prognosis, in the adoption proceedings (§827 of the Civil Code).

376. In relation to the participation rights guaranteed by international treaties of the child (especially Article 12 of the CRC), it is necessary to deduce the rule that the consent of the adopted child is required for adoption (§805 of the Civil Code). It must be informed consent (especially §807 of the Civil Code).

377. The law differentiates between children in relation to their age so that if the child:

a. has attained at least 12 years of age, his or her personal consent is always required; before the adopted child expresses his or her consent, the court shall duly instruct him or her on the purpose, content and consequences of the consent to the adoption (§806 of the Civil Code); an exception is made for situations where:

  - it is beyond any doubt that a procedure requiring the personal consent of the adopted child would be fundamentally contrary to the interests of the child (we consider that this must not be a situation where the child is not informed of who his parents are; the law elsewhere provides that the child must be informed of his adoption no later than the start of school; §806 of the Civil Code);
  - the child is unable to assess the consequences of consent (e.g., due to an adverse psychological condition).

b. has not attained the age of at least 12 years, the guardian shall consent to the adoption on his/her behalf, who shall be appointed by the court, as a rule, by the child welfare authority (before giving consent, the guardian shall ascertain all the relevant facts which lead him/her to the conclusion that the adoption will be in accordance with the interests of the child); if possible (unless the child is of a young age), the court shall also hear the adopted child and take his/her comments into account with regard to the child's degree of mental development.

378. This arrangement more or less takes into account the child's right to a fair trial or his or her rights of participation in general (Article 12 of the CRC, Article 3 of the European Convention on the Exercise of the Rights of the Child). The child is a party to the proceedings and, in view of the procedural standard, must be given a place in the proceedings.

379. The adopted child may withdraw his/her consent to the adoption until the adoption decision is made (§808 of the Civil Code).

IV. Parental Consent for Adoption

380. Parents are both obliged and entitled to keep their children with them, to bring them up, to exercise their parenthood through parental responsibility, etc. (§858 of the Civil Code in conjunction with §§865 et seq. of the Civil Code). However, they also have the right to consent to the adoption of their child (§809 of the Civil Code). In the case of adoption, the consent of the child's parent is the rule. This right to consent to the adoption is not part of parental responsibility (*see* the list in §858 of the Civil Code) but arises from the natural rights of the parent or parenthood in general (cf. §856 of the Civil Code). It belongs to the parent who is legally determined (maternity on the basis of birth pursuant to §775 of the Civil Code and paternity on the basis of one of the three legal presumptions of paternity pursuant to §§776 et seq. of the Civil Code). It is irrelevant whether the minor child is in the direct custody of his parent or not, whether his parents were married or not, whether paternity was established against the will of the father or mother, etc. If the child has both parents, consent is required from both of them.

In principle, the right to consent to adoption is vested in a parent who is fully competent, i.e., who has attained the age of 18, married after the age of 16 or has been granted legal capacity by a court (§30, §37 of the Civil Code). The law also grants the right to consent to adoption to a minor parent who is not fully autonomous in connection with the general regulation of partial autonomy (§31 of the Civil

Code). However, a parent under 16 years of age may not give consent at all (§811(1) of the Civil Code). It follows that the court may not accept consent from such a parent. Such consent would be null and void (§581 of the Civil Code). Representation by a guardian is excluded by law (§811(2) of the Civil Code). Representation by a parent or guardian of a minor parent is excluded by the nature of the case since consent to adoption is a personal act.

A parent with limited legal capacity may act only to the extent of his or her judicial limitation (§812 of the Civil Code). Therefore, if a parent of a minor child has been restricted in his or her capacity to adopt by a court ruling, including the granting of consent to the adoption of his or her child, this ruling must be relied upon without further reference. If a parent has not been deprived by the court of the right to act legally in matters of adoption of his or her child, including the granting of consent to adoption, it must be assumed that such parent is entitled to grant consent or to take a negative position in the matter. This must be respected both in the course of any adoption mediation and in the course of the court proceedings. The legislation also takes into account the reality of the adverse health condition of the child's parent. It stipulates that the consent of the child's parent is not required if he or she is factually incapable of expressing his or her will, of recognizing the consequences of his or her actions or of controlling them (§818(1)(b) of the Civil Code). The factual condition of the parent in this exceptional situation is assessed by the court.

The legislation contains an express provision according to which the court may, if it relieves a parent of parental responsibility, also decide to deprive the parent of the right to consent to the adoption (§873 of the Civil Code, cf. also §818(1)(a) of the Civil Code). These are sanctions that often complement criminal sanctions.

The law also regulates the rules for the content and form of consent to adoption, certain time limits, location, the possibility of withdrawing consent, etc. First of all, a parent gives consent to the adoption of his/her child by a personal declaration (§810(1) of the Civil Code). It can be deduced from the wording of the law that the consent must be expressed only by the child's parent (representation by the other parent or a third party is excluded by the nature of the case), orally (not in writing), and must meet the general requirements of a legal act (in particular, certainty, clarity), be unconditional and unlimited in time (it may not be subject to the fulfilment of any condition or be limited in time under the sanction of an apparent act, §554 of the Civil Code) The consent must be instructed, i.e., before the declaration, the court must duly instruct the parents on the nature and consequences of the declaration of consent and on the nature of the adoption (§810(2) of the Civil Code).

As regards the content of the declaration of consent to adoption, it must be clear who makes the declaration, which child is involved and whether consent is given to adopt the child:

- by a specific person, e.g., the mother's sister; practice speaks of consent for direct adoption;
- without a specific person – in practice, the term blanket consent is used.

This division is important in relation to the possibility of its revocation, withdrawal or rejection, or its expiry (§§815, 816, 817 of the Civil Code). This classification is also important for the purposes of mediating adoption. If the consent to adoption is given in connection with a particular person, mediation of the adoption is excluded by the nature of the case. Practice speaks of direct adoption.

Only the court is competent to accept consent to adoption.

With regard to the passage of time, the law provides that the mother of the child may consent to the adoption no earlier than six weeks after the birth of the child (§813(1), sentence 1 of the Civil Code). If she had given her consent earlier, before or shortly after the birth, such an act would not be taken into account (cf. §813(2) of the Civil Code) because it would be contrary to the law and would be an apparent act without any effect (cf. §554 of the Civil Code). The father of the child, who is legally appointed, may give his consent at any time after the birth of the child (§813(1), second sentence). If he had given consent before the birth of the child, this would have been an apparent act (§554 Civil Code).

Although the law speaks of the necessity of informed consent to adoption so as to avoid any haphazard and ill-considered actions on the part of the parents of the minor child, it provides for the possibility of revoking the consent. The rule is that consent to adoption may be revoked for a period of three months from the date on which it was granted (§817(1) of the Civil Code). It is irrelevant whether it was a blanket consent or a consent to adoption by a specific person, e.g., the mother's sister. As an exception to the rule, the law provides that consent to adoption may be revoked at a later date, after the expiry of three months from the date on which it was given, namely:

- if the child to be adopted has not yet been placed in the care of the adoptive parent prior to the adoption;
- if the adopted child is to be handed over by the person to whom it has been entrusted with custody pursuant to a court decision issued on the parents' petition because it is in the child's best interests to be with his or her parents (cf. §817(2) of the Civil Code).

The law further provides that the provisions on how, against whom and with what effects consent to adoption is given apply *mutatis mutandis* to the revocation of consent (cf. §817(3) of the Civil Code).

Another provision regulates the expiry of the adoption consent. If the consent to adoption was given with the designation of a certain person as the adoptive parent in the case of a direct adoption and if the adoption proposal is withdrawn by the prospective adoptive parent or rejected by the court (e.g., due to the child's disagreement), the consent will cease to be effective (§815 of the Civil Code). If the consent to adoption for a particular person is withdrawn by the parent, the child may not be adopted either by that person or by anyone else (§816 of the Civil Code).

If someone else gives consent to the adoption on behalf of the parents, i.e., a guardian, e.g., if the child's parents have died or have been deprived of parental responsibility, or a guardian (§818(2), §821 of the Civil Code) or a competent public authority in the case of adoption from or to a foreign country (§796(1) of the Civil Code), the adoption can only be decided if all the persons referred to in the law have consented to the adoption.

381. The law provides for exceptions to the rule of consent of the child's parent to the adoption. Parental consent is not required if:

a. the parent has been deprived of parental responsibility and also of the right to consent to the adoption (§818(1)(a) of the Civil Code);
b. the parent is factually incapable of expressing his or her will, recognizing the consequences of his or her actions or controlling them (§818(1)(b) of the Civil Code);
c. the parent is restricted in this right by a court decision on the issue of his or her legal capacity (§812 of the Civil Code);
d. the parent is in an unknown place (§818(1)(c) of the Civil Code);
e. the parent manifestly and consistently fails to take an interest in the child and thereby in fact persistently and culpably violates his or her parental duties (§819 of the Civil Code in relation to the duties laid down in particular in the context of parental responsibility, i.e., the duty of personal care for the child, personal contact with the child, ensuring the child's upbringing and education, etc.). We are talking about gross or manifest lack of interest, where no remedy is possible, which the explanatory memorandum describes as 'no interest at all …, even to the extent of endangering the child's physical or psychological or moral health'; as regards its duration, the law provides for a rebuttable presumption of manifestness, according to which a parent's lack of interest in the child is deemed to be manifest if it lasts for at least three months from the last manifestation of genuine interest;
f. obvious, persistent, gross and irremediable neglect is distinguished from remediable (removable) neglect by means of active social work; if the parent's behaviour cannot be regarded as a gross violation of his or her obligations, he or she must be instructed by the child welfare authority on the consequences of his or her behaviour, provided with counselling and assistance and at least three months must have elapsed since such instruction (§820(1) second sentence of the Civil Code); the duration of the lack of interest may vary depending on the time elapsed before the instruction.

382. Parental notification is not required if:

- the parent's behaviour can be seen as a gross violation of his or her obligations (§820(1) of the Civil Code);
- the parent has left the place where he or she used to reside without having communicated his or her whereabouts, and it has not been possible to locate the parent's whereabouts even after three months (§820(2) of the Civil Code). This is, for example, the case of flight from the maternity hospital soon after giving birth on someone else's identity document.

383. It follows from the nature of the case that the consent of the parent is not required even if the birth was an anonymous birth and the child was placed, for example, in a baby box, or the child has the status of a foundling for another reason. If the child does not have parents because of their death, the situation is similar.

384. There are further consequences associated with the above. If the child does not have a legal parent as a result of being found, being placed in a baby box or the death of the parents, if the parent has been deprived of parental responsibility by the court and also of the right to consent to the adoption (§818(1)(a) of the Civil Code), the child may be included in the list of children suitable for adoption for the purpose of adoption mediation without further consideration in other court proceedings and the adoption may be decided positively by the court in relation to other prerequisites and conditions, in particular the consent of the guardian. If a parent's right to consent to the adoption of a child is limited by a court decision on the issue of his or her legal capacity (§812 of the Civil Code), the guardian of the child shall consent to the adoption on his or her behalf;

385. If the birth was a clandestine birth, if the parent is factually incapable of expressing his or her will, of recognizing the consequences of his or her actions or of controlling them (§818(1) lit. b) of the Civil Code), if he or she is staying in an unknown place or if he or she does not show any interest in the child, whether gross (§819 of the Civil Code) or remediable (§820 of the Civil Code), the court must decide on the matter in a special procedure, in practice called an injunction procedure (§821 of the Civil Code). It is irrelevant whether or not the parent is fully competent.

V. Disinterest of the Extended Family in Caring for the Child

386. In relation to international treaties, it is stipulated that if the child's parents are unable or unwilling to provide all-round care for the child, the state must try to ensure that the child is cared for by a substitute family, preferably within the extended family. In particular, if the consent of the parents to the adoption is not required, all the facts concerning the child and his or her family must be ascertained, especially whether the child has close relatives and whether they are interested in caring for the child; the person with whom the child is staying shall be heard (§818(2) of the Civil Code).

387. If a close relative of the child is willing and able to care for the child personally and expresses a proposal to that effect to the court, he or she must be given preference over a person interested in adoption who is a stranger to the child, if this is in accordance with the interests of the child and if it is clear that this person is able to care for the child (§822 of the Civil Code). Thus, it may not only be adoption by a relative, which is excluded by law in the case of close relatives (§804 of the Civil Code), but also trusteeship (§953 of the Civil Code) or foster care (§958 of the Civil Code), or guardianship with personal care (§928 of the Civil Code).

388. Only if it is not possible to arrange care for the child by a close relative, or a relative who is a relative of the child or a person close to the child (§954(2), §962(2), §931(1) of the Civil Code), mediation of the adoption of the child by a completely foreign person may be initiated.

VI. Principle of Adoption Mediation Except for Direct Adoption

389. Intermediation of adoption by a state authority is a legal prerequisite for the legality of adoption. Intermediation consists in finding children suitable for adoption and suitable and professionally prepared candidates for adoption. The law entrusts this agenda to the authorities for the social and legal protection of children (§§19a et seq. of the Child Protection Act). These are the municipal authorities with extended competence, where the file documentation is collected in the first place, and the regional authorities, which carry out the actual matching and, in particular, facilitate the introduction of the child to prospective adoptive parents.

390. If the essence of a direct adoption is that the parents and the prospective adoptive parents know each other personally, trust each other, are relatives or close persons, or the child was deliberately conceived for the purpose of adoption within the framework of surrogacy, by nature no mediation is necessary, i.e., finding suitable adoptive parents for the child. Therefore, the special law also specifies by an exhaustive list when intermediation is not carried out (cf. §20 (3) of the Act on Social and Legal Protection of Children). However, the social welfare authority must be informed of the actual transfer of the child to the prospective adoptive parents (§10a(2) of the Act on Social and Legal Protection of Children), and the court must decide on the child's future fate, both in the case of immediate or pre-adoptive care and in the case of the adoption itself.

VII. Child Care Before Adoption by Prospective Adoptive Parents

391. The Civil Code regulates two types of such care, namely:

1. optional immediate care, to which the child may be transferred soon after birth, or as soon as his/her state of health permits (§§823, 824 of the Civil Code);
2. obligatory pre-adoptive care (§§826 to 829 of the Civil Code).

392. These types are distinguished from each other in particular by their purpose, conditions, duration, consequences for the child's parents, the child's family, the child itself and the person interested in adoption.

Optional Immediate Care

393. This is an innovation intended mainly for newborns (§823 of the Civil Code). The purpose is to ensure personal care of the child by an individually designated person, probably the future adoptive parent, in a situation where the child would otherwise be in an institution, collective care, in the care of a professional foster parent, etc.

394. A distinction should be made between three situations in which it is possible to transfer a child to the care of a prospective adoptive parent with his or her consent, namely:

a. immediately after both parents have given their consent to the adoption (father after the birth, mother after the sixth child; §813 of the Civil Code);
b. if the parents agree, the child may be handed over to the prospective adoptive parent for care even earlier, i.e., before the expiry of the six-week period after the birth of the child, e.g., immediately after the mother leaves the maternity hospital with the child; the parents of the child to be adopted are obliged to inform the child's social and legal protection authority of the handover to the prospective adoptive parents (§823 of the Civil Code);
c. immediately after the court concludes that there are circumstances in which the parents' consent is unlikely to be required for the adoption, e.g., in a situation where the mother 'runs away' from the maternity hospital and stays in an unknown place (§824 in conjunction with §818 of the Civil Code), but only if the child's health condition allows it.

395. Unlike mandatory pre-adoptive care, the parents of the child remain in principle the bearers of parental responsibility and have the right to exercise it in all its components except personal care of the child. They are obliged to pay maintenance to the child to the extent that the child contributes to their standard of living at the hands of the caring person. During the period of immediate custody, the caregiver has only the duty and the right to properly care for and protect the child; he or she may act in matters relating to the child's care only if it is strictly necessary (§823(2) of the Civil Code). According to the Explanatory Memorandum, if there is a substantial change in circumstances, the carer is also obliged to return the child to the institution or non-institutional institution or to the parents as soon as circumstances change, especially on the part of the parents.

396. Immediate custody can thus be temporary (until the child is returned to the parents, to an institution, to foster care, etc.), short term or medium term (during the period of the proceedings for parental neglect). It can be followed by mandatory pre-adoption care and adoption as a status change of a fundamentally permanent nature.

Obligatory Pre-adoption Care

397. In order to ensure that the adoption will be to the child's benefit, the law requires that the child be in the personal care of the prospective adoptive parent without interruption prior to the court's decision on the adoption (§§826 et seq. of the Civil Code). The purpose of mandatory pre-adoptive (temporary, pre-adoptive) care is, above all, to establish such emotional family ties between the prospective adoptive parent and the adopted child as are the rules in a healthy, natural family. If the prerequisite for adoption is a relationship between the adoptive parent and the adoptee, such as that between parent and child, or at least the foundations of such a relationship (§795 of the Civil Code), the implementation of this personal care is an essential, irreplaceable and fully justified prerequisite for adoption.

398. The law lays down the following rules for entrusting a child to pre-adoptive (temporary, pre-adoptive) care:

a. the child may not be handed over until three months have elapsed from the date on which consent to the adoption was given (§826 of the Civil Code), as the consent to the adoption could be revoked;
b. if the parents do not give consent, e.g., because of lack of interest expressed by a court order, and the guardian or custodian gives consent on their behalf, the child may not be handed over until three months have elapsed from the date on which the guardian or custodian gave consent to the adoption;
c. the court may decide on the transfer of the child only after it has made an enquiry as to the mutual suitability of the child and the adoptive parent (§827 of the Civil Code). This includes in particular an assessment of the following:
   - the personality and health of the adopter as well as his/her social environment, especially housing and home, as well as the adopter's ability to care for the child and the adopter's motives for adoption;
   - the personality and health of the child, the social environment from which the child comes and the child's rights as a parent;
   - the ethnic, religious and cultural background of the child and the adoptive parent;
   - the length of time the child has been in the care of the adoptive parent;
   - if only one spouse wishes to adopt the child, the reason why the other spouse did not join the proposal.

399. In this context, an account must also be taken of whether or not the child is already with the prospective adoptive parents. If the child is lawfully in the care of the prospective adoptive parents, the following situations in particular are relevant where the prospective adoptive parents have been entrusted with the child:

a. by the court into immediate, facultative custody (cf. §823, §824 of the Civil Code);
b. by the court into foster care, fiduciary care or into the care of a guardian;
c. by the parents or someone else.

400. If the child is not in the personal care of the persons interested in adoption, he/she may, for example, be in the care of an institution or with a foster parent for a temporary period.

401. Entrusting a child to pre-adoptive care by the court has quite significant consequences for the child's parents, the child's family of origin, the child himself and the prospective adoptive parents.

402. In the case of the child's parents, it is stipulated that:

a. after the expiration of three months from the consent to the adoption, the exercise of the rights and obligations arising from the parental responsibility of the parent shall be suspended, and the court shall appoint a guardian of the adopted child to the children's social and legal protection authority, unless the guardian has been appointed earlier (§825 of the Civil Code);

b. the previously established maintenance obligation of the parent or other person towards the child is suspended (§829 of the Civil Code). The term established means an obligation arising from the law, regardless of whether the court has decided on the maintenance obligation.

403. With regard to prospective adoptive parents, the law provides that:

a. before the adoption is decided, the child to be adopted must be in the care of the adoptive parent at the adoptive parent's expense (§829, first sentence of the Civil Code); this is not a right of the child to an equal standard of living, but only the payment of the child's basic needs;
b. the prospective adoptive parent has the duties and rights of a caring person (§829 with reference to §§953 to 957 of the Civil Code, not the broader duties and rights of a guardian); by the nature of the case, this includes in particular the duty and right to care for the child personally, to bring up the child in a narrower sense, to decide on the child's ordinary affairs, to represent the child in these matters and to administer the child's property.

404. The statutory duration of this care is quite long. However, this is related to the new concept of adoption of a minor, which consists primarily in its irrevocability as a rule and goal. Therefore, the prospective adoptive parent, albeit firmly decided and properly prepared, and the child must be given the chance to verify in real life the functioning of the newly established ties. The law provides that the adoptive parent's care of the adopted child prior to the adoption lasts for a period sufficient to establish conclusively that a relationship has been established between the adoptive parent and the child which is the purpose and aim of the adoption; this care does not end before the expiry of six months (§829(2) of the Civil Code).

405. The law expressly takes into account the situation where the prospective adoptive parent has voluntarily taken personal care of a non-adult child at a time when it was prohibited to give consent to the adoption due to the protection of the mother's six-week-old child (§813 of the Civil Code) and to apply for pre-adoptive (temporary, pre-adoptive) care. If the prospective adoptive parent has taken the child into immediate, optional care (§823, §824 of the Civil Code), the law allows for its conversion into pre-adoptive (temporary, pre-adoptive) care (§828 of the Civil Code).

VIII. Procedural Aspects

406. The Act on Special Court Proceedings regulates the proceedings in cases of adoption of a minor (§§427 et seq. of the Act on Special Court Proceedings), in which the court, in particular:

a. accepts the declaration of consent to adoption;
b. decides on the transfer of the child to pre-adoption care;
c. decides whether parental consent to adoption is required;

d. decides on an application by the parents who have consented to the adoption for the surrender of the child;
e. decides on the adoption;
f. decides on the secrecy of the adoption;
g. decides to order supervision of the success of the adoption.

407. It is an application procedure, which may be initiated only on the application of the prospective adoptive parents (§429 of the Act on Special Court Proceedings). By the nature of the case, it is an uncontested procedure, which is governed by the principle of investigation (§21 of the Civil Procedure Code). A special law provides for other prerequisites and conditions of the proceedings, local jurisdiction, the circle of parties to the proceedings, the obligation of the court to hear the child's parents at least once in principle (§437 of the Act on Special Court Proceedings), the obligation of the court to renegotiate with the child's parents (§433 of the Act on Special Court Proceedings), the declaration of the child's close relative (§442 of the Act on Special Court Proceedings), the transfer of custody of the child (§438 of the Act on Special Court Proceedings), etc.

408. The court decides on the adoption by a judgment, which is of a constitutive nature and has ex nunc effect.

IX. Legal Consequences of Adoption

409. Adoption is above all a change in status, which has implications for the entire legal order. If the law defines the adoption as complete, the child ceases to be a child and relative in the family of origin upon the legal effect of the adoption decree and becomes a child of his or her adoptive parent and a relative in the new family as if he or she had been born into that family (§§833 and 771 of the Civil Code). If the child was adopted jointly by the spouses or by the husband of his parent, he has the status of a joint child of the spouses (§832 of the Civil Code). If the adoptive parent is the spouse of one of the child's parents, the adoption does not affect the rights and obligations arising from the relationship between the adoptee and that parent and his/her relatives (§833(2) of the Civil Code).

410. Adoption has consequences both personally and financially, not only for the child but also for the adoptive parents and their relatives.

411. The adopter(s):

a. become the bearers of parental responsibility for the child, with the right to exercise all obligations and rights arising therefrom (§832(2) in conjunction with §858 of the Civil Code);
b. have an *ex lege* maintenance obligation towards the child (§910 of the Civil Code);
c. are obliged to inform the child of the fact of adoption as soon as it is appropriate, at the latest by the start of school (§836 of the Civil Code).

412. Adoption has consequences both during life and in the event of death, which is particularly evident in the context of inheritance law. Death does not extinguish kinship ties.

413. Adoption also terminates the rights and obligations of the guardian or guardian ad litem appointed to exercise the rights and obligations of the parents on their behalf (§833(1) *in fine* of the Civil Code).

414. Although the rights and obligations of the adoptee towards the original family cease (§833 of the Civil Code), the biological kinship and the barrier of marriage remain (§675 of the Civil Code).

415. Adoption *ex lege* changes the surname of the adopted child to that of the adopter. If the adoptive parents are spouses, the adopted child shall bear the surname which the spouses declared at the time of marriage to be the surname of their joint children (§835(1) of the Civil Code). However, if the adopted child, who is over 12 years of age, does not agree to the change, the court shall decide that the adopted child shall add the surname of the adopter to his/her surname. In order to avoid unwanted chaining, the law provides for clear restrictions (§835(2) *in fine* of the Civil Code). The law does not allow the child's name to be changed in adoption proceedings. However, the choice of a different or further name is allowed after the adoption decision has become final. The adoptive parents may choose another name or another name for the child by a consenting declaration before the registry office (§64 of the Civil Registry Act). The choice is limited by a time limit of six months from the legal validity of the adoption judgment. It is also stipulated that the choice may be made no later than the adoptee reaches the age of majority. If the adoptee is over 12 years of age, his consent must be attached to the declaration. Both the change of surname and, where appropriate, the choice of a new or additional name will always be entered in the birth register where the child is registered.

416. Since adoption is a change of status, the adoptive parent(s) will be registered in the registry in place of the child's parents (§797 of the Civil Code), and a new birth certificate will be issued to the child. Should only one person adopt the child, the child will have only that parent listed on the new birth certificate (§800(1), second sentence of the Civil Code). As already mentioned in connection with the child's right to know his or her origins, the adoptive parents are obliged to inform the child of the adoption (§836 of the Civil Code) and the child may consult the entry concerning his or her person in the relevant register, the birth register, after the child has reached the age of 12, or after he or she has acquired legal capacity in the case of a secret adoption (cf. §25 of the Civil Code).

417. Adoption also acquires citizenship in the Czech Republic if the child is a foreigner and at least one of the adoptive parents is a citizen of the Czech Republic (§§8 and 9 of the Act on the Citizenship in the Czech Republic No. 186/2013 Coll.).

X. Confidentiality of Adoption

418. Since 2014, it has been provided (§837 of the Civil Code) that the adoptive parent or the adoptee may propose that the court order that the adoption and its circumstances (including the blood parent and his/her consent to the adoption) be kept secret from the child's family of origin. However, the court may subsequently decide to keep them secret if a very serious situation threatening the life or health of the adopted child justifies it. As soon as the adopted child becomes legally competent, he or she has the right to know the contents of the file kept in the adoption proceedings (§838 of the Civil Code). His right to inspect the civil registry and the collection of documents when he acquires his legal capacity is regulated by a special law (§25(2) of the Civil Registry Act). In general terms, however, it should be noted that adoption is not based on anonymity in our country.

XI. Monitoring the Success of Adoption

419. Since 2014 (§839 of the Civil Code), it is possible for the court to order supervision of the adoptive parent and the adopted child for the time necessary if the circumstances of the case so justify. The supervision is usually carried out by the social and legal protection of children authority, which, even without regard to whether the supervision of the success of the adoption is ordered, provides the adoptive parents with counselling and services related to the care of the adoptee. In practice, there is talk of accompaniment, but this is mainly applied to foster care.

XII. Cancellation of Adoption

420. Adoption does not terminate either with the child's or the adoptive parents' majority or death since adoption is primarily a change of status (adoption natura imitatur). Adoption establishes a parent-child relationship between the adoptive parents and the adoptee, and the ties to the parents and the family of origin of the child cease. Therefore, the law does not speak of dissolution but only of the annulment of the adoption.

421. Adoption can only be annulled if there are compelling reasons for doing so. By laying down relatively strict conditions for adoption, the law guarantees the stability of the new family environment for the child. Nevertheless, situations may arise in which an adoption fails or is contrary to the law for various reasons, whether objective or subjective (§840 of the Civil Code). Both the adoptee and the adoptive parent may file a petition for annulment, or it is possible to join the petition. The law provides for a time limit of three years from the legal validity of the adoption judgment.

422. However, if the adoption has taken place in violation of the law, the petition can be filed at any time. This may be the case if the adoption was the result of child trafficking.

423. In the event of the annulment of the adoption, all rights and obligations between the adopter and the adoptee and other rights and obligations arising from the relationship cease. However, the property rights and obligations of the adoptee arising before the annulment of the adoption are not affected, e.g., the right to maintenance. At the same time, the previous kinship relationship is restored, and the adoptee thus legally returns to his or her family of origin (§841 of the Civil Procedure Code), including the maintenance obligation and the right of inheritance. This status change is significant from the perspective of the entire legal system.

424. The annulment of the adoption also results in the change of the adoptee's surname to the original surname, i.e., the surname the adoptee had at the time the court decided on the adoption. The adoptee may, however, declare that he/she retains the existing surname (§842 of the Civil Code).

425. If the adoption of an incapacitated minor is annulled, the situation in the original family must be investigated. If the court finds that the parents cannot properly exercise their rights and obligations arising from parental responsibility, it shall take the necessary measures, e.g., decide on another suitable educational environment for the child.

XIII. Readoption

426. Traditionally, the law provides (§§843 et seq. of the Civil Code) that an adopted child may be re-adopted, however, only if:

a. the earlier adoption has been annulled;
b. he or she is to be adopted by a later spouse of the adopter after the previous spouse who was a joint adopter has died;
c. the sole adopter or those who were joint adopters have died.

427. However, if an irrevocable adoption has taken place (*ex lege* or by court decision), this state of affairs does not prevent the adoptee from being adopted again (§845 of the Civil Code).

§3. Adoption of an Adult

I. General

428. Adoption of an adult has returned to our legal system after more than sixty years and follows the pre-1949 regulation (between 1950 and 2014, only adoption of a minor child was possible). The Civil Code regulates the adoption of an adult in Part Two together with the adoption of a minor. However, the specificity of the adoption of an adult is taken into account in a number of special provisions (§§846 to 854 of the Civil Code). However, the term adoption of a minor is not entirely precise in view of the concept of majority or self-legitimacy. It has been chosen because it is customary to speak of the adoption of an adult but not of the adoption of a person with full legal capacity.

429. Even the adoption of an adult is primarily a change in status. However, it is not a full adoption, which is typical of the adoption of minor children who have not acquired full legal capacity. Rather, the adoption of an adult is conceived as exceptional and pursues a different purpose than the adoption of a minor. In particular, the law lays down a rule of conformity with good morals (§846 of the Civil Code). Other provisions regulate the adoption of an adult, which is analogous to the adoption of a minor (§847 of the Civil Code), and the adoption of an adult, which is not analogous to the adoption of a minor (§§848 to 849 of the Civil Code). The following are the common provisions for the adoption of an adult (§§850 to 854 of the Civil Code).

430. The adoption of an adult always constitutes a change in status since the law provides that adoption means the adoption of a foreign person as one's own and that the adoption is registered in the civil registry (§794 or §797 of the Civil Code).

431. As for the adoptee, he or she must be an adult regardless of legal capacity or a minor but fully capable of legal capacity. The adoptee must not be a direct lineal relative or sibling of the adopter.

432. The adoptive parent must be an adult and have full legal capacity. As in the case of adoption of minors, only spouses or one of them may become joint adoptive parents.

433. The difference between an adoption which is similar to the adoption of a minor (§847 of the Civil Code) and an adoption which is not similar to the adoption of a minor (§848 of the Civil Code) lies in the admissibility of the adoption, i.e., in the legal prerequisites, in the degree of applicability of the legal regulation of the adoption of a minor and in the legal consequences of this form in relation to the establishment and termination of kinship relations.

434. Irrespective of the form of adoption of an adult, it is always an incomplete adoption. Incompleteness is manifested in the case of limitations in the sphere of maintenance (§853(1) of the Civil Code) and in the sphere of inheritance (§852, §853(2) of the Civil Code).

435. The regulation of the adoption of an adult applies similarly to the adoption of a minor who has been granted legal capacity (§§854 and 37 of the Civil Code). This provision must be interpreted more broadly. It also applies to persons who have acquired full legal capacity by marriage.

436. Under the adoption of the minors scheme, adults who do not have full legal capacity, i.e., persons whose legal capacity is limited by a court, may also be adopted.

437. If the marriage of the adopted person is ongoing, he/she may be adopted only with the consent of his/her spouse (§850(2) of the Civil Code). If the spouse is unable to give consent because he or she is not fully capable of exercising his or her legal capacity, or if an obstacle that is difficult to overcome prevents him or her from giving consent, the court shall separately assess whether the adoption is not contrary to the legitimate interests of the spouse or other family members.

438. The considerations of uncontroversiality and conformity with good morals, without which the minor cannot be adopted, must always be respected (§§2(3) and 846 of the Civil Code).

439. In the case of the adoption of an adult, which is similar to the adoption of a minor, it is necessary to infer the interests of the adopter's children, if the adopter is a parent, from the similar provision in the case of the adoption of a minor (§801 of the Civil Code). In the case of an adoption of an adult, which is not analogous to the adoption of a minor, special provisions apply to the children of the adopter (§852 of the Civil Code). In the case of the assessment of the interests of the adoptive parent's children, the property interests of the adoptive parent's children are not decisive, i.e., the reduction of maintenance or the reduction of their inheritance shares is not relevant. The interests of the adopter's children of whom the adopter is the parent will have to be examined by the court in the proceedings.

440. The court will always examine compliance with good morals in the proceedings ex officio and if it concludes that the adoption of the minor is not in accordance with this principle, it will reject the petition for adoption of the minor (§847(2) of the Civil Code).

II. The Purpose of the Adoption of an Adult

441. The purpose of the adoption of an adult is the adoption of a foreign adult by the adoptive parent as his/her own (§794 of the Civil Code), but not primarily the provision of a new family and family environment and care for the person of the adoptee, as is the case with minors (except for adoption under §847 of the Civil Code, where the purpose is similar to that of adoption of minors). It is also a matter of monitoring the property interests of the adoptee and the adoptive parent, particularly in terms of inheritance law and the possibility of provision.

442. In the case of the adoption of an adult, which is similar to the adoption of a minor (§847 of the Civil Code), the purpose is to straighten out the social reality in the family of the adoptee and the adoptive parent, where the adoptive parent will usually be the spouse (surviving spouse) of the adoptee's parent, former foster parent or guardian.

443. The adoption of an adult, which is not analogous to the adoption of a minor (§§848 and 849 of the Civil Code), is particularly relevant for persons who have no descendants or who have no successors in their work, whether scientific, artistic, craft or otherwise. The adopter may seek by this adoption in particular to provide for himself in old age and to bequeath his property to the adoptee, the adoptee to acquire the adopter's property.

III. Adoption of an Adult, Which Is Similar to Adoption of a Minor

444. The adoption of an adult is close in purpose to the adoption of a minor (although this may not always be the case). As regards the application of the provisions relating to the adoption of minors, including the provisions on its consequences, they apply *mutatis mutandis*, with exceptions (except for §§838 and 839, *see* §847(3) of the Civil Code). This is a command of analogy.

445. In order for the adoption of an adult by adoption analogous to the adoption of a minor to take place, at least one of the enumerated statutory conditions must be met (§847(1) CCC):

a. a natural sibling of the adopted person has been adopted by the same adoptive parent;
b. the adoptee was a minor at the time the petition for adoption was filed;
c. the adoptive parent has already cared for the adopted person as his/her own at the time of his/her minority;
d. the adoptive parent intends to adopt the child of his or her spouse.

446. In addition to the above legal conditions, other conditions must be met, including:

- the consent of the adoptee;
- the adoptive parent's affirmative expression of will;
- the consent of the adopter's spouse;
- compliance with good morals;
- the absence of an obstacle incompatible with the legitimate interest of the adoptive parent's blood parents;
- the consent of the adoptee's spouse or, where the adoptee's spouse is incapacitated and where consent cannot be obtained because it involves an obstacle that is difficult to overcome, the interests of the adoptee's spouse or, where applicable, other members of the adoptee's family;
- a reasonable age difference;
- the existence of a bond between the adoptee and the adoptive parent similar to that of a child and a parent;
- no conflict with the interests of the adoptive parent's children.

IV. Adoption of an Adult, Which Is Not Similar to Adoption of a Minor

447. Adoption, which is not analogous to the adoption of a minor, comes into consideration especially in the case of persons who have no descendants or who have no successors in their work, whether scientific, artistic, craft or other, but also in the case of those whose descendants do not provide adequate assistance in illness or old age, are unreachable, or reside in an unknown place. Similarly, there may be cases where a parent-child relationship has existed in the past between the adopter and the adopted. There may also be other situations which can be considered to be reasons of special consideration (social, health, etc.) where the new relationship is reasonably expected to be beneficial to those involved.

448. When deciding on this form of adoption of an adult, the court must consider the actual benefits of the adoption, but also whether the adoption is not abusive or detrimental to either the adopter or the adoptee and whether it is therefore appropriate to reject the application (good morals). It is not required that, prior to the adoption, the cohabitation between the adopter and the adoptee should have continued or that a relationship similar to that of parent and child should have existed between them.

449. The legislator considers this form of adoption to be complementary and exceptional to the adoption of an adult, which is similar to the adoption of a minor (§848(1) of the Civil Code).

450. The adoption has legal consequences only for the adopter and the adopted child or, where applicable, for those of the adopter's descendants who are born after the adoption or who consent to the adoption. With regard to members of the adopter's family, it shall be excluded that the adoptee acquires by adoption a legal relationship to them and derives any property rights therefrom.

451. As regards the application of the provisions relating to the adoption of minors, including the provisions on the consequences thereof, these apply *mutatis mutandis* (§848(2) of the Civil Code), i.e., more freely. As a result, those provisions on the adoption of minors which do not contradict the purpose of the adoption of minors apply, whereas the adoption of minors which is not analogous to the adoption of minors does not have its own regulation, whether in the provisions relating only to that form of adoption of minors or in the provisions common to both forms of adoption of minors.

V. Consequences of Adoption of an Adult

452. Among the common consequences are those of the adoption of an adult, regardless of the form in which the adult is adopted. These include consequences in the sphere of maintenance and inheritance and, in some cases, consequences linked to the surname of the adoptee.

453. In the case of the adoptee's maintenance obligation towards his or her ancestors and descendants, it is generally extinguished with the legal effects of the adoption. The maintenance obligation does not cease (or is renewed in the future by virtue of its flexibility) and continues only if and to the extent that there are no other persons who have a maintenance obligation or if those persons are unable to fulfil their maintenance obligation. The maintenance obligation of the adoptee thus remains only a maintenance obligation ancillary to other types of maintenance obligation and only arises for the adoptee when other persons are unable to fulfil it or have ceased to fulfil it. The adoptee is entitled to maintenance in respect of his or her ancestors or descendants only if and to the extent that the adopter is unable to fulfil his or her maintenance obligation. It can be assumed that the adoptive parent's maintenance obligation towards his children who are present at the time of the adoption and who have not consented to the adoption continues since the adoption has no legal consequences in respect of them (§852 of the Civil Code).

454. Inheritance law is significantly affected by the adoption of minors. Adoption of an adult brings the adoptee substantial advantages within the inheritance groups. The adoptee inherits from the adopter in the first legal class of heirs but does not enter into the adopter's right of succession vis-à-vis other persons (the principle of representation is excluded in the case of the adoptee's inheritance from the adopter). This means that the adoptee cannot inherit from anyone other than the adopter.

455. In principle, the adoption of an adult, unlike the adoption of minors, does not affect the adoptive parent's surname. A change of surname is not a legal consequence of adoption. It is possible for the adoptee and the adopter to express their consent to the adoptee adding the adopter's surname to his or her surname. The attachment may concern only the first surname of the adopter or the first surname of the adoptee if either of them already has a surname to be attached. If the adoptee wishes to use only the adopter's surname, i.e., to replace it with his/her existing surname, he/she may do so in accordance with the general regulations on surname changes (§72 of the Civil Registry Act).

456. In the case of an adoption which is similar to the adoption of a minor, it may be decided, on the adopter's motion, if it is in accordance with the interests of the adoptee, even before the expiry of a period of three years from the adoption decision, that the adoption is irrevocable. Otherwise, the conversion will occur *ex lege* (§840(2) of the Civil Code).

§4. Foster Care

I. General

457. If a minor child for any reason cannot be brought up in his/her own family, an artificially created substitute family is the best environment for social integration of orphaned, deserted, neglected, sick, ethnically different, older children or those with tendencies to misbehave.

Foster care is a restored institute of substitute family care. However, throughout history, it has changed significantly. In its various forms, especially in the time between the wars and shortly after World War II, it proved very successful both in theory based on paedology, a science devoted to children, and in its practical application. It was revoked in the fifties due to political and ideological reasons and replaced by collective (institutional) care. The efforts of specialists to create complete childcare, not concentrating merely on his/her physical health but also involving mental health, resulted in 1973 in a new regulation on foster care.

In many cases, it is not possible to adopt a child because the parents deny their consent even though they do not duly care for him/her, the child is placed in institutional care and the parents manifest their interest in the child only to such extent so as to bar the ruling on adoption without their consent. There are also frequent instances whereby the child is not 'suitable' for adoption due to its poor health or the child is older or undesired due to its origin. Thus, the institute of foster care ensures a family life for children who, for legal, health, psychological or social reasons, cannot be adopted. Foster care is very suitable for groups of siblings because, as a rule, they should be brought up together.

458. Removing a child from the care of parents or other relatives is always a subsidiary solution to the care of the child in the natural family, which enjoys special protection. At the same time, it is an ultima ratio solution in a situation where other instruments, such as educational measures, cannot be used to protect the best interests of the child. It must be stressed that any alternative solutions in relation to parental care are temporary. They are admissible only for the period during which the parents are unable to provide for the child themselves. They can only be used if the aim cannot be achieved by less severe means (*see* the decision of the European Court of Human Rights in *Kutzner v. Germany*, Application No. 46544/99 from 26 February 2002). Such interference must be proportionate to the aim pursued, namely, the protection of the minor child. It must also respect the rights of the child and pursue his or her best interests or welfare. Foster care institutions, which include foster care, care of a close person and personal guardianship, are special forms of care for a child at risk in a foster family or family-like environment. They have many things in common, such as their temporary nature and the fact that the parent-child family status relationship is maintained, but in practice, the mutual obligations and rights change. They also have priority in relation to collective upbringing.

459. Under contemporary law, foster care is deemed a special form of substitute care in a family or an environment resembling a family, which is mediated, managed and supervised as well as financially subsidized by the state. The main goal of foster care is to provide personal care for the child. If a child is charged in foster care, he/she does not become part of a family like through adoption. The child's parents may even remain his/her statutory representatives; principally, they may contact the child and owe duty of maintenance to the child. Bonds within the framework of a broad family, that is, siblings, grandparents, uncles and aunts, etc., remain thus unbroken, including the right to inherit.

460. The current form of foster care is short term, medium term and long term, always in relation to 'obstacles' in the personal care of the child's parents and in relation to the needs, interests, wishes of the child, etc. (§959 of the Civil Code).

461. A special form of foster care is temporary foster care, so-called professional parenting (§958(3) of the Civil Code, §27a Act on Social and Legal Protection of Children). It may only be exercised by foster parents registered in the register of persons suitable for temporary foster care maintained by the regional authority (§27a Act on Social and Legal Protection of Children). Persons registered in this register are entitled to foster care benefits, even if they do not currently have any children in their care. The selection of persons must be carried out very carefully. Applicants for temporary foster care must be prepared that their care will be short-lived and that they will usually care for the child soon after its birth.

462. The court will place the child in the care of a foster parent if:

a. neither of the parents is able to care for the child personally; this is a situation where the parents are unable to care for the child personally, whether for subjective or objective reasons, so that the care of the child is not properly secured; subjective reasons consist in particular in the parents' inability to care for the child or in their lack of interest in the child; objective reasons may be the health of the parents, the health of the child, the social and housing situation, etc.;
b. the child cannot be cared for personally by the appointed guardian;
c. the court decides on the divorce of the parents, and the child cannot be entrusted to either parent;
d. the child is cared for by a relative or close relative, and at the same time, the parent or the child's ancestor cannot be ordered to provide maintenance (§957 of the Civil Code).

II. The Personality of Foster Parents

463. A prerequisite for the establishment and functioning of foster care is the existence of a suitable foster parent, his or her consent and interest in caring for the child. This person must provide guarantees of proper care, be fully legal, be of good character and have the capacity to have a positive educational influence on the child and to provide a suitable family environment for the child. Another condition is residence in the Czech Republic (§962 of the Civil Code). Last but not least, the person must be a person whose age and state of health do not hinder the care of the child. A relative or close person takes precedence over another person, unless this is not in accordance with the interests of the child.

464. One person may be the foster parent. It is irrelevant whether he or she is married, unmarried, living alone or in partnership or in a registered partnership (cf. §13(2) RP, *see* Chapter 4).

465. Spouses or partners can be joint foster parents. Neither unmarried persons nor registered partners can be foster parents. Both spouses or partners must agree to foster care. It is not decisive whether or not the spouses have children. If they do, this must be taken into account in the preparation of foster parents and their children (§11(2) Act on Social and Legal Protection of Children) and in the mediation of foster care.

466. If a child is placed in the foster care of only one spouse or partner, the other spouse or partner must consent to this (§965(1) of the Civil Code). Exceptionally, his or her consent is not required if he or she is not fully capable of exercising his or her rights or if the measure of his or her consent involves an obstacle that is difficult to overcome (§965(2) of the Civil Code). If the spouse or partner of the person caring for the child lives in a family household with the caring spouse or partner and the child, he or she shares in the care of the child by law (§965(3) of the Civil Code).

III. Relationship of a Foster Parent and the Child

467. The duties and rights of a foster parent include:

a. obliged and entitled to care for the child personally (§966(1) of the Civil Code);
b. shall exercise the rights and duties of the parents in the upbringing of the child (§966(2) of the Civil Code);
c. obliged and entitled to decide on the child's ordinary affairs in representing the child and managing the child's property (§966(2) of the Civil Code);
d. has a duty to inform the parents of the child's essential matters (§966(2) of the Civil Code);
e. has the duty to maintain, develop and deepen the child's relationship with his or her parents, relatives and close persons, and obliged in principle to allow the parents to have contact with the child (§967 of the Civil Code).

468. If there is a disagreement between the parents and the foster parent on an essential matter concerning the child, e.g., the choice of school or profession, not only the foster parent but also the child or the parent may petition the court for a change of rights or obligations, termination of foster care or other decision (§969 of the Civil Code).

A child charged in foster care is bound to help in the foster parent's household according to his/her abilities (§968 of the Civil Code). If a child has an income arising from his/her own work or his/her estate's yield and lives in a common household with the foster parent, he/she is bound to share in covering common needs.

As a rule, a foster parent does not owe the child a duty to maintain, unless this duty arises from another family relationship, in particular, the relationship between grandparents and children.

469. In principle, the parent has the right to have personal and regular contact with the child as well as the right to information about the child (§960(2) of the Civil Code). It should be mentioned that this right is highly debated in professional circles because often the child's contact with the parents interferes with the child's development. It is therefore up to the court in disputed cases to assess whether the child's interest in the contact is not improved. The state authorities mediating foster care often consider whether it is in the child's interest to preserve bonds between the original family and the child. Children are often placed intentionally in localities as distant from their original families as possible which tends to bar the natural parents, for financial and other reasons, from contacting the child.

470. Therefore, parental consent to charge the child in foster care is not expressly required.

IV. Collective (Group) Foster Care

471. Foster care can be performed in so-called foster care facilities. These can be either flats for families with several children or, more often, municipal family houses.

In such dwellings, the foster care is carried out mostly by a married couple based on a contract binding them to perform foster care. Children are charged in their foster care, or the spouses are appointed guardians to those children.

472. In the so-called SOS Children Villages, foster care is provided predominantly by a 'fostering mother' with the help of other employees of the SOS Village. Childcare is provided mainly by so-called aunts, the women being trained to become 'fostering mothers'.

A significant role has been played by the Association of Friends of the SOS Villages. This legal entity trains prospective 'fostering mothers' for foster care performance and provides them with all kinds of help.

At present, three SOS Villages exist in the territory of our country.

V. Foster Care Financing

473. Foster care is provided by the state. A foster parent is entitled to the following allowances:[202]

a. An allowance for covering the child's needs payable by the time the child is 26 years old and is still living with the foster parent in the common household and with regard to his/her state of health, the child is not able to earn money, or if he/she is a student. The amount of the allowance varies according to the child's age, health and other criteria.
b. A foster parent is entitled to a salary for performing foster care in the amount corresponding with the number of children in his/her foster care.
c. When taking over the child in his/her care, the foster parent is entitled to a lump sum intended for purchasing not only the child's clothing but also, for example, books, a bicycle, toys and other items not ever before owned by the child (e.g., because it lived in an institutional care before).

202. §47e of the Act on Social and Legal Protection of Children.

d. A contribution for purchasing a motor vehicle if the foster parent has in his/her care at least four children.
e. Foster care allowance (repeated, for foster carers providing unmediated foster care).

As for the claims concerning health insurance regulations and the claims under labour law regulations, the child charged in foster care is regarded in the same way as one's own child even after coming of age if he/she is entitled to the allowance for covering his/her needs.

474. Parents' duty to maintain does not become extinct; the court will determine its amount. The parents do not carry out this duty towards the foster parent or the child, but the title to maintenance is passed on to the state up to the amount provided. If the parents do not duly perform their obligation to maintain the child, the relevant authority will collect the allowance up to the amount as stated for the child as a claim of the state.[203]

VI. Temporary Care (Pre-foster Care)

475. If a child is placed in institutional care upon a court decision, he/she may be temporarily placed in the care of person wishing to become a foster parent and satisfying the terms as stated even before the court rules on charging the child to foster care. Similarly, a child, who is not in institutional care, may be placed in pre-foster care upon his/her parents' consent.

The goal of pre-foster care is to avoid revoking court rulings on foster care in cases where proper contact between the child and the foster parents failed, open conflicts occur between foster parents and the child, or the child runs away, etc.

This type of care is temporary. If, within three months after the ruling on pre-foster care has become effective, a court proceeding on charging the child to foster care has not been commenced, the pre-foster care ruling will become ineffective.

Unlike adoption, a child need not be kept by his/her prospective foster parents at their own costs; on the contrary, this type of childcare is financed by the state.

476. To decide on pre-foster care is up to the relevant district authority which is obliged to advise the court on this decision within fifteen days.[204]

VII. Foster Care Extinction

477. Foster care becomes extinct upon the child's reaching the age of majority. If the child continues to live in the common household with the foster parent and is unable to provide his/her own living, the claim for financing continues to exist.

203. Civil Code §961.
204. Act No. 359/1999 Coll., Act on Social and Legal Protection of Children, §19(1).

478. The court may revoke foster care for very serious reasons only, namely, when the reasons for placing the child in foster care have become extinct, or the foster care in question did not meet its goals, etc. If the foster parent applies to the court to do so, the court is always bound to revoke it,[205] the reason being that the essential purpose of foster care is to provide childcare in a real family. If the foster parent, however, does not intend for any reason to continue in the childcare, he/she cannot be forced to do so. Revoking foster care in this case promotes proper childcare too.

§5. Entrusting a Child to the Care of Another Person

479. This form of child custody is intended in particular for cases where a relative or a person close to the child or the parents is to be the caregiver, where the child is likely to return to his/her natural family soon and where the parents or other relatives can be assigned a maintenance obligation towards the child to the extent that corresponds to the child's reasonable needs (§957 of the Civil Code). The indisputable advantage of such care is that the carer and the child know each other, they usually have a family bond with each other, and the transition of the child to foster care is not as emotionally demanding as in other forms of foster care.

480. A prerequisite for the establishment and functioning of this form of care is the existence of a suitable person and their consent to take over the care of the child. This person must provide guarantees of proper care for the child. The person must be fully self-governing, of good character, has the capacity to have a positive educational influence on the child and to provide a suitable family environment for the child.

481. The condition for entrusting the child to the care of a person is that the person must be a resident of the Czech Republic.

482. As this form of care does not involve state mediation (unlike adoption and non-relative foster care), a close or even familial relationship between the person caring for the child and the child is assumed. It also follows from the law that the court is to give preference to the relative or close relative who has taken care of the child over another (foreign) person (§954(2) of the Civil Code). However, entrusting a child to the care of a stranger is not prohibited by law. However, if it is not in the child's best interests, the court will not entrust the child to this form of care.

483. The Civil Code lays down a rule according to which the court must define the duties and rights of the caring person in the judgment (§955 of the Civil Code). The court will generally define the duties and rights of the other person so that, by exercising them, it can best ensure the care and interest of the child as determined by the individual needs.

205. Civil Code §970.

484. As of 1 January 2022, an amendment to the Act on Social and Legal Protection of Children (Act No. 336/2021 Coll.) brought foster care and custodianship closer together in the sense that a child entrusted to the care of another person is also entitled to an allowance to cover the child's needs (§47f of the Act on Social and Legal Protection of Children).

Chapter 8. Parental Responsibilities

§1. General

485. The ABGB 1811 stipulated rights and obligations of parents to children in ways distinct from those common now. The father enjoyed parental power (*patria potestas*) towards the child. The legitimate father was only entitled to decide on important matters concerning the child, and he was bound to provide for the child's maintenance in the first place. Children owed their parents respect and obedience.

The Family Law Act effective on 1 January 1950 conferred equal rights and obligations upon both parents towards the child, denoting them as parental powers.

The Family Code as effective now has not taken over this notion for the reason that all elements of power in relations of parents and children ceased to exist in the socialistic society. The notion parental power was replaced by that of rights and obligations of parents towards children.

Under family law reform of 1998, parents' rights and obligations were named parental responsibilities and also made more precise at the same time in relation to the UN Convention on the Rights of the Child.

486. In regulating parental responsibility, the Civil Code (2014) is based in particular on the Principles of European Family Law on Parental Responsibility developed by the Commission for European Family Law (CEFL). The conceptual novelty is in particular the distinction between bearing and exercising obligations and rights arising from parental responsibility, the broader content and, in particular, the consideration of the rights of the child's parents who are not fully capable of exercising their own rights.

487. The term parental responsibility is to be understood primarily in terms of partial legal and moral rules. The essence and meaning of parental responsibility lie in the value of parenthood itself, in conjunction with the value of the child's well-being. Moreover, the child is the weaker party, especially because of his or her lack of age and, as a rule, lower intellectual and volitional maturity.

488. The legal and moral conception of parental responsibility is linked to the generally recognized objective principles of justice and right from which private law springs (§3(3) of the Civil Code). This connection gives parental responsibility a valuable meaning. The legal norms governing the content of parental responsibility are also reflected in the injunction to take proper parental care of the child.

489. Parental responsibilities are defined under the law as a summary of rights and obligations involving:

a. the care of the child, including in particular the care of the child's health, physical, emotional, intellectual and moral development;
b. the protection of the child and his or her upbringing;
c. maintaining personal contact with the child;
d. ensuring his or her education;

e. determining his or her place of residence;
f. minor child's representation;
g. administration of a minor child's property.[206]

Parents' duty to maintain children is not a part of parental responsibilities. Even a parent, who was deprived of parental responsibilities, will have a duty to maintain his/her child, while the duty to maintain does not cease upon the child's full age, and on the contrary, in some cases, it may become extinct even before majority.[207] Also, the right to consent to the adoption of a child (§809 of the Civil Code) and the right to determine the child's name and surname are not a part of parental responsibilities.

490. The purpose of parental responsibility is, on the one hand, the exercise of parental responsibility by the child's parents and, on the other hand, the protection of the child's rights and legally protected interests, his or her moral and material benefit, as well as the provision of his or her upbringing and education, personal care, protection in the broadest sense of the word, the determination of his or her place of residence, the administration of his or her property, representation, etc. (§858 in conjunction with §§865 et seq. of the Civil Code).

491. The exercise of parental responsibility by both parents of a child, which is a common and desirable practice in terms of values, presupposes a parental agreement between them which binds them, albeit subject to a change in circumstances (*clausula rebus sic stantibus*), e.g., as regards the extent of personal contact with the child in relation to his age, maturity and wishes. However, in the interests of the child, many parental agreements require the approval of the court, e.g., in the matter of personal custody.

492. Parental responsibility arises *ex lege* for each parent upon the birth of the child and ceases when the child acquires full legal capacity (§30 of the Civil Code). It is irrelevant whether the child's parents are married or not, whether they live together or not, etc., although these circumstances may have a significant impact, in particular as regards the exercise of the individual obligations or rights arising therefrom.

493. The legal duration and extent of parental responsibility can only be changed by the court (§858 *in fine* of the Civil Code).

494. According to the new concept, every parent is the holder of parental responsibility, or the obligations and rights arising from it, unless he or she has been relieved of it by the court (§865 of the Civil Code). Thus, a parent who is a minor, regardless of his or her age or degree of legal capacity, and a parent whose legal capacity has been limited by a court, is also the bearer of the obligations and rights arising from parental responsibility.

---

206. *Ibid.*, §858.
207. *See* above Part II, Ch. 6, §5.

495. Not every parent has the right or obligation to exercise parental responsibility in relation to the child. With regard to the principle of the best interests of the child and his/her welfare, the law provides for the *ex lege* suspension of parental responsibility on the grounds of the immaturity or mental disorder of the parent (§868 of the Civil Code). It is thus provided that the exercise of parental responsibility:

a. of a minor incompetent parent (the parent who has not acquired full legal capacity by the earlier granting of legal capacity or by marriage) is suspended in all obligations and rights until he or she acquires full legal capacity (§868 of the Civil Code), except for the exercise of the duty and right of care and personal contact (by argument a maiori ad minus it can be inferred, that if he can personally care for the child *ex lege*, he can also have personal contact with the child); however, the court may decide, in view of the parent's personality, that the exercise of the duty and right of care is suspended until the parent acquires full legal capacity;
b. a parent whose legal capacity has been limited in this area (especially in the area of parental responsibility for a particular child) is suspended from all obligations and rights for the duration of the limitation of his/her legal capacity (§868 of the Civil Code), with no *ex lege* exception. In this case, the court may decide otherwise, i.e., the parent, in respect of his or her person, retains the exercise of the duty and right to care for and personal contact with the child.

496. When performing parental rights and obligations arising from parental responsibilities, the parents are liable to duly protect the child's interests, control his/her conduct and supervise him/her in relation to his/her age and abilities. They are entitled to apply suitable means of upbringing in such a manner that the child's dignity, health, physical, emotional, mental or moral development will not be injured.[208]

The parents' obligation to supervise must of course be considered in relation to the child's age and his/her mental level of development. A baby needs a different supervision from that exercised by parents of a child close to full age. The same is true in applying appropriate ways of upbringing.

497. The law presumes that the child's parents will agree to perform their rights and obligations. When the parents are of different opinions on some essential matter involving the child (e.g., the issues of the child's education, or who should represent the child in some particular matters, etc.,) under family law, the possible resulting parental conflict will be resolved by the court.[209]

The court will rule ex officio, and thus the matter may be instigated by either of the parents as well as by a relevant social and legal authority for the protection of children, or by a third person.

Parents exercise their rights and obligations in two ways, as implied under law. It is necessary to recognize substantial and routine matters. In routine matters, each of

208. Civil Code §884.
209. *Ibid.*, §877.

the parents exercises his/her rights and obligations individually (even though a couple living in a good relationship will probably agree on those as well) and when performing substantial matters, the parents are bound to agree on them. In cases of discord, parental agreement can be substituted by a court ruling.

The Civil Code specify what is deemed a 'substantial matter' in §877/2 of the Civil Code. Especially, these are the issues of selecting the type of school, profession, parental discord in the child's estate administration and not routine medical and similar interventions.

Another substantial issue is the question of healthcare, namely, serious surgery where the patient's consent is needed. Both parents should grant their consent on behalf of their minor child.

The issue of religious upbringing of children will probably be a substantial matter too. This is decided by the statutory representative on behalf of children below the age of 15.[210] However, it is very difficult to imagine how a court could rule in such a matter.

498. If a minor's parents do not live together and do not agree on the child's custody and maintenance, the court may rule, free from any instigation, into whose custody the child will be charged and how each of the parents will contribute to his/her maintenance.[211]

It is of no importance whether the child's parents are married or if they have never been married in the instant of the court's determination. Decisive is only the fact that the parents are not living together and cannot agree on the child's custody and care.

499. The parents cannot contractually convey their rights and obligations to another entity. They may only leave performing some partial liabilities to a third person, which, however, does not free them from their own liabilities. Thus, the parents may temporarily leave performing personal child's care to a third person (e.g., grandparents), they may apply for the child to be placed in a social care institute, etc.

Performing rights and obligations arising from parental responsibilities is resolved by law in a specific way in cases where the child has been charged to foster care or another person's care.[212]

500. The performance of parental responsibilities varies in relation to the child's age and needs. Thus, court rulings concerning minor children's care are not final (judgment estoppel, *res iudicata*, does not apply), but if the terms change, the court may alter the previous ruling even without any instigation or parents' agreement on performing their parental rights and obligations.

---

210. Act No. 3/2002 Coll., on Religious Freedom and the Status of Churches and Religious Denominations, §3.
211. Civil Code §908.
212. *See* above, Part II, Ch. 5.

501. If a parent is barred from performing his/her parental responsibilities by a serious obstacle and if the child's welfare so requires, the court may impose suspending performance of parental responsibilities.[213] Performing parental responsibilities will then be concentrated in the other parent's person, or in that of a guardian, for example, in case of one parent's long-term absence or illness, in cases when both parents must represent the child in an act in law, etc.

502. If a parent does not duly perform his/her obligations arising from his/her parental responsibility, the court will restrict his/her parental responsibilities.[214]

If a court determines restriction of parental responsibilities, the judgment rendered must contain the particulars of the restriction, that is, which rights and obligations the parent is restricted in performing. If only one of the parents will be restricted in performing parental rights and obligations by the judgment, performing these rights will be concentrated in the other parent's person. If the only living parent or both parents are restricted, the court will have to appoint a custodian who will perform these rights and duties instead of the parents.

Besides restricting parental responsibilities by a court ruling, actual restriction of parental responsibilities should also be mentioned arising from another court ruling, for example, on charging a child to foster care or on placing the child in institutional care, or the court may ban one of the parents from visiting his/her child. Actual restrictions of rights and obligations arising from parental responsibilities involve, namely, personal child's care and deciding routine matters concerning the child.

503. If a parent abuses or seriously neglects his/her parental responsibilities, he/she will be deprived of his/her parental responsibilities by the court.[215]

Neglecting obligations or abusing rights need not directly relate to facts involved in a criminal offence as provided under the Criminal Code to protect minor children; however, if an obligation was infringed or a right abused, resulting in a criminal offence, this fact must be duly considered.

Therefore, family law expressly states that if a parent committed an intentional criminal offence towards his/her minor child or used a child below 15 years of age to commit a criminal offence or acted as an instigator, aiding or assisting an offender in a crime committed by his/her child, the court will always consider whether there are reasons to commence proceedings leading to deprivation of parental responsibilities.[216]

If the only living parent or both parents are deprived of parental responsibilities, the court must appoint a guardian.

---

213. Civil Code §869.
214. *Ibid.*, §870.
215. *Ibid.*, §871.
216. *Ibid.*, §871(2).

504. Restricting or depriving parental responsibilities may involve only one of the children of one parent or all his/her children. This will depend on the circumstances of the particular case, whether the lack of interest or bad parental conduct involves all children or only some of them.

The court ruling on restricting or depriving parental responsibilities must always imply which of the parents it is concerned with in relation to which particular child. It is not possible to deprive a parent of parental responsibility 'in advance' involving the children that may be born.

§2. CHILDCARE

505. Parents, who should serve as a good example to their children by their personal life and conduct, play a decisive role in their children's care.[217]

Children's care and upbringing is the parents' right: children are entitled to parental care and upbringing. Parental rights may be restricted, and minor children may be taken away from their parents against their will only by court ruling or based on law. The parents taking care of their children are entitled to receive help from the state.[218]

506. As stated above, both parents enjoy equal rights and obligations regarding their child. If the parents do not live together as well as in relation to divorce, the court must rule on further care of the child, that is, on charging the child to one of the parent's custody or approve of the parents' agreement on alternating custody or joint custody.[219] However, the court's decision of charging the child to the custody of one of the parents does not mean any interference in the other parent's parental responsibilities but a mere decision on which of the parents will be taking care personally of the child and decide in broad extent on routine matters involving the child.

507. The child, able to create his/her own opinion and judge the impacts of the measures concerning him/her in relation to his/her age and mental development, has a right to be duly informed and to express freely his/her views on all his/her parents' decisions concerning his/her person. A child over the age of 12 is considered to be able to take in information, form his/her own opinion and express it.[220]

A child has the right to individually (without his/her parents being aware of or even against their will) apply to relevant state authorities, schools and health facilities for help involving his/her own life protection and safeguard of his/her other rights, and these authorities are bound by law to provide help for the child relevant to their powers.[221]

---

217. *Ibid.*, §884.
218. Charter of Fundamental Rights and Freedoms, Art. 32.
219. *See* above Part II, Ch. 2.
220. Civil Code §867(2) – the duty of the court to inform a child and §875(2) – the duty of parents to inform a child.
221. Act No. 359/1999 Coll., on Social and Legal Protection of Children, §8(1).

Consistent with the UN Convention on the Rights of the Child, a child can also be heard in all proceedings determining his/her substantial matters. Due attention is paid to the child's opinion as expressed, consistent with his/her mental development.[222]

508. A child living in a common household with his/her parents is obliged to help them, consistent with his/her abilities. He/she is also bound to share in the covering of common family needs in case he/she has an income of his/her own or an estate that can be used for the common needs of the family.[223]

§3. The Right to Contact the Child

509. The right to personal, direct contact stems from natural rights, from the family law status relationship between parents and children, or from parenthood in general. The maintenance of personal contact between parents and children is one of the mutual rights and obligations of parents and children when they do not live together. Without personal contact, many duties and rights would be just law in books. Parenting would not be fully realized. Therefore, the law, especially in relation to international treaties (Convention on the Rights of the Child, Convention on Contact with Children), explicitly and quite thoroughly regulates this matter as a component of parental responsibility. Recent case law indicates that 'the criteria for deciding on the custody of a child apply by analogy to the decision on access' (I. ÚS 153/16).

510. The right or obligation of parents to have contact with their own children must be distinguished from the right of third parties to have contact with the child, i.e., relatives of the child, persons close to the child (§927 of the Civil Code).

511. The different forms of contact, in particular direct and indirect contact, may be combined in the interests of the child. The rule is direct contact without the presence of other persons. Anything else is a temporary restriction on the non-custodial parent, which can only be done by law. In particular, the following rules and options may be used in the interests of the child.

512. In particular, contact is and must be understood as:

- the stay of the child for a limited period of time with a person with whom he or she does not normally live (usually the other parent, but also a person with whom the child has family ties);
- any form of communication between the child and that person;
- the provision of information to that person about the child or to the child about that person.

222. Civil Procedure Code §100(3).
223. Civil Code §886.

513. Contact can be:

- direct, with personal contact, and traditional, same time, same place, regular intervals, or non-traditional: in the form of extended holidays, e.g., in a situation where the child's parents live on different continents;
- indirect, usually narrowed down to the right to information or to interactions and communication, e.g., through correspondence, (mobile) phone or internet. This form can help to overcome initial barriers, can be a starter, can be used in the case of inter-parental contact when there is a long distance between parent and child and also when the parent is, e.g., in prison. Indirect contact can also be used when direct contact is not in the child's interest, but at the same time, it is necessary to maintain or develop the ties between parent and child and to pursue the wider dimension of the matter in the child's interest, or to leave room for both to find ways to direct standard contact in the future. The narrowest form of indirect contact is simply the right to information, which aims to inform the parents about matters concerning the child or vice versa.

514. Rules are also set for parents to each other:

- parents are obliged to communicate to each other everything essential concerning the child and his/her interests;
- the parent who has custody of the child is obliged to prepare the child properly for contact with the other parent, to facilitate the child's contact with the other parent properly and to cooperate with the other parent to the extent necessary in exercising the right of personal contact with the child;
- the custodial parent and the other parent must refrain from anything which interferes with the child's relationship with both parents or which makes it more difficult to bring up the child;
- if the custodial parent unreasonably prevents the other parent from having contact with the child on a permanent or repeated basis, such conduct shall be grounds for a new decision by the court as to which parent should have custody of the child.

§4. Upbringing of the Child

515. In particular, the law stipulates that the parents have a decisive role in the upbringing of the child and that they are to set an example to their children in every respect, especially with regard to the way of life and behaviour in the family (§884 of the Civil Code). This is a very important aspect of parental responsibility. The child is obliged to obey his or her parents and to submit to the parents' measures (§857 of the Civil Code). Until the child becomes fully autonomous, parents have the right to direct their child by educational measures as appropriate to his or her developing capacities, including restrictions aimed at protecting the morals, health and rights of the child, as well as the rights of other persons and public order (§857(2) of the Civil Code).

516. Educational measures may be used only in a form and to a degree that is appropriate to the circumstances, does not endanger the child's health or development and does not affect the child's human dignity. It must therefore be appropriate educational measures, which the law considers to be in particular such measures that parents, as holders of parental responsibility for the upbringing of the child, have the right to use in such a way that the child's dignity is not affected and the child's health, physical, emotional, intellectual and moral development is not endangered in any way (§858 of the Civil Code). Parents must always respect the dignity of their child (§883 of the Civil Code, but also many provisions of the general part, e.g., Articles, especially §§91 et seq. of the Civil Code).

517. Corporal punishment is excluded by its very nature, in view of the general rules absolutely protecting a person's personality, life and health, human dignity and mental and physical integrity. We therefore consider them to be disproportionate and unlawful in principle. It may be intentional or deliberate infliction of pain by attacking the body for a disciplinary offence, e.g., slapping, beating with the hand or with an object. Such beating on sensitive parts of the body, kicking, throwing, pinching, hitting with a book or keys on the head, pulling the hair or earlobe, etc., that marks (e.g., bruises) are usually left on the child's body should be considered physical abuse rather than punishment.

§5. Child's Education

518. The child's parents also decide on the child's education or employment in the exercise of parental responsibility. They always take into account the child's opinion in relation to his/her participation rights, his/her abilities and talents (§880(2) of the Civil Code).

519. The choice of education or employment is an important matter on which the child's parents must agree or, in the event of a disagreement, may apply to the court (expressly §877(2) of the Civil Code). It is a matter not only of the choice of primary or secondary school but also of preschool education. Although special laws often use the single number 'legal guardian', e.g., for the regulation of the registration of a child for compulsory school attendance (§36(4) of the Education Act, Act No. 561/2004 Coll.), it must be assumed that the child usually has two parents who must agree on the matter or go to court.

§6. Child's Place of Residence

520. The determination of the child's place of residence is now explicitly mentioned in the components of parental responsibility. It is thus an essential matter on which the parents of the child must agree, regardless of whether the child has been entrusted to one of them individually or to both of them in alternate or joint custody (§877(2) of the Civil Code.) If no agreement is possible, one of the parents may apply to the court, either preventively or subsequently, following exclusion from decision-making (§877 of the Civil Code). If the child is to be entrusted to a third party, this must be notified to the child welfare authority (§10a of the Act on Social and Legal Protection of Children).

521. Public registration, or the permanent residence of the child, is a matter of record only (§80 of the Civil Code).

§7. Representation of a Child

522. This is a traditional right, but also an obligation of parents belonging to parental responsibility. It follows from other provisions that parents have the duty and right to represent the child in legal actions for which the child lacks legal capacity (§§892 to 895 of the Civil Code). This is legal representation. If the child is competent, he acts alone and the legal representation by his parents does not apply.

523. Minors who are not fully capable, i.e., have partial capacity and are 'under parental responsibility', can be further divided into minors:

a. who act independently in relation to their maturity of mind and will (in particular §§31 and 32 of the Civil Code) and their capacity to work (§§34 and 35 of the Civil Code);
b. who act with the consent of a legal representative (§32 of the Civil Code);
c. who act with the consent of the legal representative and the court in the case of the operation of a commercial establishment (§33 of the Civil Code);
d. for whom their legal representative acts exclusively, i.e., usually a parent in the exercise of parental responsibility, but also, for example, a guardian.

524. If the child has both parents, they represent them jointly as legal representatives; however, either of them may act; furthermore, an analogy is provided for (§892(2) with reference to §876(3) of the Civil Code). Thus, it applies that 'if one parent acts alone in the child's affairs towards a third party who is acting in good faith, he shall be deemed to act with the consent of the other parent'.

525. The law places emphasis on parental consent. However, it provides that if the parents do not agree which parent will represent the child in legal proceedings, the court shall decide, on the parent's motion, which parent will act legally for the child and in what manner.

526. A special provision takes into account the threat of a conflict of interest (§892(3) of the Civil Code). Thus, a parent cannot represent a child if there could be a conflict of interest between him/her and the child or between children of the same parents. In practice, this provision is applied in particular in proceedings to regulate the relationship of parents to minor children for the period after divorce and in proceedings concerning the estate.

§8. Administration of the Child's Estate

527. The management of the child's assets also falls under parental responsibility. The law contains many general and specific provisions in this regard (§§896 to 905 of the Civil Code), which must always be interpreted and applied in accordance with the principle of the best interests of the child and his/her welfare or benefit. Part Three of the Civil Code, which governs absolute property rights, gives rise to a number of obligations and rights, particularly in relation to the simple management of other people's property (§§1405 et seq. of the Civil Code). These should also be taken into account. The administration of the child's property should be rather conservative. Parents should seek first and foremost to preserve the child's property, not to profit at any cost.

528. The basic principle laid down in the framework of the regulation of parental responsibility is that parents have the duty and the right to take care of the child's assets primarily as good stewards (§896 of the Civil Code). They must safely dispose of funds which may be assumed not to be needed for the payment of expenses relating to the child's assets. This also applies to the child's savings, whether generated by agreement between the parents in the context of a functioning relationship or by a court order (§917 of the Civil Code).

529. Parents act as the child's representatives in legal proceedings concerning each part of the child's property. If the parents violate their duty to take care of the child's property as good stewards, they shall jointly and severally compensate the child for the resulting damage (this is legal solidarity).

530. If it is already apparent from the circumstances during the administration of the property that the administration is considerably difficult and the parents are carrying it out properly, the court shall, on application, award them a reasonable annual or otherwise fixed remuneration for the administration of the property (§903(2) of the Civil Code).

531. In the case of the relationship between the parents, the law emphasizes the agreement of the parents; if the parents do not agree on essential matters in the care of the child's property, the court shall decide on the parent's application (§897 of the Civil Code).

532. A special provision regulates the necessity of court approval of some legal acts of the parents (§898 of the Civil Code, the list is demonstrative):

a. which concern the existing and future property of the child or individual parts of such property, unless they are ordinary matters or matters which, although exceptional, are of negligible property value;
b. by which the child:
   - acquires and disposes of the immovable property or a part thereof;
   - encumbering the property as a whole or a not insubstantial part thereof;

- acquires a gift, inheritance or bequest of not insignificant pecuniary value, or refuses such a gift, inheritance or bequest, or makes such a gift or a gift representing a not insignificant part of his property;
- enters into a contract which is binding in the long term, a credit or similar contract or a contract relating to housing, in particular a lease.

533. The sanction for non-compliance with the law is an apparent act (§§551 et seq. of the Civil Code) since the law provides that a legal act of a parent that lacks the necessary court approval is not taken into account.

534. Other provisions regulate the issue of income or profit from the child's property (§§899 to 900 of the Civil Code). The rule is that what the parents gain from the use of the child's property is acquired by the child. Income from the child's property which the parents do not use for the proper management of the child's property (profit) is first used for the maintenance of the child (even without court approval). If necessary, the parents may thereafter use the remaining profit from the child's property as a contribution to the child's own maintenance and to the maintenance of the child's minor sibling if they live in a family household with the child, unless it is necessary for important reasons to preserve it for the child for a period after the acquisition of legal capacity.

535. A different regime is provided for property. The law provides that the child's property may be used by the parents, with the approval of the court, for the maintenance of the child's own and the child's siblings only if, without the fault of the persons who have a maintenance obligation towards the child (i.e., the parents or other relatives in the direct line), a significant disproportion between the child's circumstances and those of the obliged persons would arise.

536. The child's assets include the maintenance paid in respect of the child. The general rules on the management of the child's property apply to the administration of the various amounts of maintenance. The parent into whose hands the maintenance is to be paid has the right to dispose of the maintenance in ordinary (or exceptional but negligible property value) matters. The child's property includes savings which are saved from the maintenance paid. The general rules on the management of the child's property also apply to their management.

537. Further obligations and rights are linked to the parent's obligation to hand over the child's property to the child upon the child's attainment of full legal capacity (§902 of the Civil Code). The parents shall hand over the child's assets to the child or, where appropriate, transfer their administration to them and shall, at the child's request, provide the child with an account of the administration of the assets without undue delay, but at the latest within six months of the date on which the child attains full legal capacity.

538. The parents shall also have rights in this respect. If they have incurred costs in or in connection with the administration of the child's property, they may claim compensation and, if the administration of the property has been considerably difficult, in particular because of the size or diversity of the estate, and the parents have duly administered the property, they may, after they have handed over the property administered to their child, claim a reasonable remuneration, if the yield of the property so permits.

539. It should be emphasized that, as between parents and children, the limitation period does not begin to run or run during the period of legal representation (§646 of the Civil Code).

§9. Duty to Maintain Between Parents and Children

540. Maintenance obligations of parents towards their children The duty to maintain the child arises directly from the legally existing relations between parents and children. This topic arises from the moment of the child's birth and ceases only at the moment when the child is able to support himself/herself.[224]

Ability to support himself/herself may arise even before the child comes of age (the child begins to work or receives an income from his/her own estate, enabling him/her to cover all his/her needs). Court rulings have constantly insisted that finishing compulsory school attendance does not mean that the child is able to maintain himself/herself.

541. The duty to maintain the child is owed by both parents consistent with their abilities, situation and property. A child is entitled to share his/her parents' living standard.[225] The basic rule is that the child's standard of living is to be essentially the same as that of the parents and that this consideration precedes the consideration of the child's reasonable needs (§915(1) of the Civil Code). If the child's parents do not live together and their standard of living is significantly different, the child may be deemed to have the right to share in the standard of living of the parent whose standard of living is higher (with regard to the child's welfare). The case law rightly concludes that a highly above-average income of the parent is adequate for a highly above-average level of maintenance. However, each case must be approached with regard to its specifics, and other criteria and principles must be taken into account, or values must be measured (Decision of the Constitutional Court No. IV. ÚS 650/95).

In determining the extent of the parents' maintenance obligation towards the children, account is also taken of which parent personally cares for the child and to what extent (§913(2), second sentence, Civil Code). Although the law specifies the term 'take into account', the exercise of personal care for the child can in principle be equated with the financial provision for the child's maintenance in the broadest sense. The criterion of personal care of the child applies not only to minor children of a young age but also to adult children, e.g., disabled children with special needs.

224. *Ibid.*, §911.
225. *Ibid.*, §915.

Considering particular abilities, situations and property of the parent owing due care is most decisive for the court in determining the amount of maintenance payment. The court will examine if the parent owing, for example, did not give up a good job or a property without a serious reason or whether he/she takes unreasonable risks in carrying out his/her business, etc.[226]

542. The Civil Code extends the applicability of the irrebuttable presumption of income to persons other than obligors having income from non-dependent activities, i.e., to any obligors who have not fulfilled their legal obligation to prove the relevant facts (§916 of the Civil Code). Thus, it is established that failure to prove in proceedings concerning the maintenance obligation of a parent towards a child or the maintenance obligation of another ancestor towards a minor child who has not acquired full legal capacity, the person liable for maintenance does not properly disclose his/her income to the court by submitting all documents and other supporting documents for the assessment of his/her financial circumstances and does not enable the court to ascertain other matters necessary for the decision by disclosing protected data, the average monthly income of that person shall be twenty-five times the amount of the individual subsistence minimum under another legal regulation (Act No. 110/2006 Coll., on the Minimum Subsistence Level).

543. The possibility of examining the obligor's financial circumstances enables the court to comprehensively assess his or her standard of living. The property of the obligor may consist of assets, proceeds from them, shares, real estate, while the property of the obligor may consist of movable assets, in particular, luxury cars, sports equipment. In determining the assets of the obligor, it will depend in particular on the activity of the person entitled, or the other parent, whether these facts are brought to the attention of the court, even though the proceedings in the matter of custody of minors are governed by the principle of investigation. In complicated cases, the court will order an expert report. The court assesses so-called justified (reasonable) needs on the part of the child when determining the particular amount of maintenance. These needs depend on the child's age, his/her state of health, interests, etc. Where the property situation of parents allows so, reasonable needs can also involve savings for future studying of the child.[227] The court may impose on the parent a duty to contribute monthly a certain sum of money as maintenance payment plus the duty to deposit a certain sum of money in a child's blocked bank account or impose on the parent a duty to contribute to the child's building and loan savings, life insurance, etc.

544. Besides these very general rules, there are no binding tables for stating a child's maintenance or a percentage of the parent's income prescribed under Czech law. Since spring 2010, the Czech Ministry of Justice prepared a recommended table

226. *Ibid.*, §913.
227. Civil Code §917. The option of savings in favour of the child as a portion of maintenance was allowed for only under the family law reform of 1998. Thus, the long criticized inequality of children of divorced parents when one parent contributes to the child's maintenance in an inevitable amount only was removed.

for stating a child's maintenance. This table is only to help judges and is not an act. Austrian legal regulation, which has percentage rates, was taken as a model. The table gives a rough idea of the appropriate amount of maintenance. The table serves only as a guide and does not allow us to take into account all the particularities of an individual case. However, the table may indirectly help to resolve the child's case consensually and, if possible, out of court.

We now (since 2022) use this table:

Age of the Child	*Percentage of the Income of the Liable Parent (%)*
0–5	8–14
6–10	10–16
11–15	12–18
16–and older	14–20

545. It is necessary to take into account the number of maintenance obligations of the parent in respect of all his/her children (regardless of whether and to what extent he/she may be caring for them or cohabiting with them). This means determining how many children the parent still has a maintenance obligation towards. The child whose maintenance is being calculated is also counted. Accordingly, the percentage from the table is then applied (e.g., for a 5-year-old child whose father has three other children for whom he pays maintenance, it is set as 8% of the parent's income). Any maintenance obligations towards other relatives are not taken into account.

The problem of the legal regulation, which stays the same, was that, on the one hand, this is a very general rule allowing the judge to impose support related to the particular situation of a child and his/her parents; on the other hand, it is rather difficult and demanding for judges to put in practice. Maintenance amounts for children of the same age and, basically, same needs may vary significantly not only in relation to the property situation of the parents but also, for example, in relation to the child's residence. This should also change with the new table. Now, it is easier for both parties to expect the amount of support. The court will consider the child's irregular or casual needs, but it cannot impose any payments of extraordinary expenditure.[228]

In determining support, the court will also consider other duties to support the owing parent. It is not, however, able to secure an equal living standard of all children of one parent. The court may not reduce the support right of a child in custody of a mother earning an income beyond average only because his/her living standard would be, after imposing an appropriate father's maintenance duty, higher than that of his/her father's other child born to another woman sharing with him and the child a common home.[229]

228. Published Judgment of the Court of Appeal in Hradec Kralove No. 13 Co 588/1994.
229. Published Judgment of the Court of Appeal in Prague No. 39 Co 568/1998.

546. The maintenance payment for a minor child is decided by the court ex officio. The maintenance amount may be imposed and possibly reduced or increased within three years from commencement of the proceedings. Maintenance is determined by the court in the following cases:

a. prior to the child's parents' divorce;[230]
b. when the child's parents do not share a common household (regardless of whether they are married or not) and they have not agreed on the maintenance amount;[231]
c. if the child's parents share a common household but one of them does not voluntarily fulfil his/her duty to maintain;[232]
d. upon affiliation determined by the court;[233]
e. upon the court's determination to charge the child to foster care or to another person's care;[234]
f. upon determination of claims of a pregnant woman towards the child's father;[235]
g. if terms have changed (*clausula rebus sic stantibus*), providing grounds for changing the agreement or court ruling.[236]

547. Maintenance of a child of full age will be determined by the court only upon the major child's application. The duty to maintain may be imposed only from the commencement of the court proceeding.

In determining the duty to maintain a child of age, the court will also consider whether the claim to be maintained is not against good morals.[237] The court will not support the claim to be maintained brought about by the child who, after graduation from school, does not work even though he/she could, makes his/her living through criminal activities, behaves rudely to his/her parents, etc.

548. If a parent constantly evades his/her duty to maintain, he/she may be prosecuted for neglect of due maintenance.[238] In practice, constant evading of maintenance duty means a period of more than four months. It is not decisive for commencing court proceedings whether the maintenance was determined by court ruling and to what amount.

The parent who evaded his/her maintenance duty intentionally or exposed his/her child to possible poverty by his/her failure to maintain will be punished more severely

As the interest in the maintenance owed to be reimbursed prevails over the interest to punish the parent, such parent may be enabled to express so-called effective

230. Civil Code §919.
231. *Ibid.*, §755(3).
232. *Ibid.*, §919.
233. Act on Special Court Proceedings, §422.
234. Civil Code §§956, 960.
235. *Ibid.*, §920.
236. *Ibid.*, §923, Act on Special Court Proceedings, §475.
237. Civil Code §2(3).
238. Criminal Code No. 40/2009, §§196, 197.

regret, and the prosecution will be terminated if, before the court renders its ruling, the parent owing voluntarily covers his/her debt in maintenance and his/her criminal offence has not caused permanent ill effects.

The Enforcement Code (Act No. 120/2001 Coll.) allows for enforcement by suspension of the driving licence (§71a of the Enforcement Code). An enforcement order to suspend the driving licence of the debtor can only be issued by the enforcement officer if the enforcement is to recover arrears of maintenance for a minor child, regardless of the length of the delay or the amount of the arrears. On the date of delivery of the enforcement order to the debtor, the driving licence granted under a special legal regulation shall be suspended. During the period of suspension, the holder of the driving licence may not drive motor vehicles. The bailiff shall cancel the enforcement order by suspending the driving licence:

a. if the debtor proves that he/she necessarily needs his/her driving licence to meet the basic needs of his/her life and those of persons for whom he/she has a maintenance obligation;
b. if the obligor pays the arrears of maintenance for a minor child.

Interest for Late Payment of Maintenance

549. The maintenance obligation is part of the private law system of the law of obligations. Therefore, even in the case of maintenance payments, the debtor – the obligor – may be in default (cf. §1970 of the Civil Code). The amendment to the Civil Code (Act No. 460/2016 Coll.) takes into account the fact that a maintenance debt is a 'debt' and expressly provides that a person liable for maintenance who is in default may be required by the person entitled to claim interest on the default (§921(2) of the Civil Code).

Substitute Maintenance

550. On 1 July 2021, Act No. 588/2020 Coll. on Substitute Maintenance came into force. From this time onwards, it is therefore possible to apply for a new social benefit, the so-called substitute maintenance, which is intended to provide temporary financial support to dependent children in a situation where the other parent has to pay maintenance due to a court decision, but does not (partially or not at all) fulfil his or her obligation. The state now helps single parents in a situation in which the other parent does not contribute enough to the maintenance of their child. The application for the benefit is submitted to the employment office using the prescribed form, which you can find here.

551. The beneficiary of the benefit is a dependent child for whom a legal representative (i.e., in most cases, a parent with care) can apply for the benefit. In order for the benefit to be granted, proof must be provided that enforcement proceedings have been initiated to collect the maintenance owed. The amount of the benefit is determined by the difference between the monthly maintenance amount specified in the enforcement order and the partial maintenance payment in the month in question, up to a maximum of CZK 3,000 (approx. EUR 120) per month. The benefit can be paid for up to twenty-four consecutive months. The benefits are paid monthly to the person caring for a dependent child, with the state subsequently reclaiming the amounts paid from the parent – the debtor.

Maintenance Obligations of Children Towards Their Parents

552. If the parents are in need and the children are able to earn their own living, they are bound to provide their parents with reasonable maintenance.[239]

A child is entitled to a living standard equal to that of his/her parents. However, parents are not entitled to the same living standard as their children, but in determining maintenance, the court will see that the parents will be provided with a 'decent' maintenance.

Duty to maintain the parents by their children is meant as a supportive one. A parent predominantly has a right to be maintained by his/her spouse or a divorced spouse, and only if such duty cannot be claimed, he/she may claim maintenance against his/her child.

If the parent entitled has several children, the duty to maintain will be apportioned among all of them in relation to their abilities, situation and property.[240]

The court will not support the parents' claim to be maintained if it is against good morals.[241] Thus, a parent who himself/herself did not fulfil his/her duty to maintain his/her children, evaded the duty to maintain, did not duly care for his/her children or even was deprived of his/her parental responsibilities will not be able to claim maintenance from his/her children when he/she finds himself/herself in need.

Duty of children to maintain their parents was embedded in law only as a moral duty. Regarding the general duty to work, the vast majority of citizens in totalitarian Czechoslovakia was entitled to an old-age pension; thus, courts only exceptionally imposed upon children a duty to maintain their parents. If a senior parent depended on his/her children, this rather involved personal care. Of course, if the relations between parents and children have always been good and the parents have duly fulfilled their obligations to their children, the children will provide help to them in their old age also voluntarily.

§10. International Child Abduction

553. International parental child abduction is a global problem, which affects several thousand children each year. The primary international agreement, intended to protect children from the harmful effects of their wrongful removal or retention across borders, is the Hague Convention of 25 October 1980 on the Civil Aspects of International Child Abduction.[242] This multilateral treaty, which now has eighty-two State Parties, does not seek to adjudicate on issues of custody but gives effect to the principle that an abducted child[243] should be returned promptly to his/her

239. Civil Code §915(2).
240. *Ibid.*, §914.
241. *Ibid.*, §2(3).
242. In the Czech Republic published under No. 34/1998 Coll., it became effective on 1 Mar. 1998.
243. The Convention shall cease to apply when the child attains the age of 16 years. *See* Art. 4 of the Convention.

home State. Once sent back, the child's local authorities can determine where and with whom the child should live. The 1980 Hague Child Abduction Convention is also designed to secure protection for rights of access. The Hague Convention is valid in the Czech Republic and is also directly applicable; it means that it may take priority before Czech laws. The Council Regulation (EC) No. 2201/2003 of 27 November 2003 concerning jurisdiction and the recognition and enforcement of judgments in matrimonial matters and the matters of parental responsibility is valid for the Member States of the EU.

However, Czech lawmakers also changed the procedural rules, and we now have special proceedings concerning international child parental abduction.[244] The object of these proceedings, in accordance with the Hague Convention and also the EU Regulation, is to secure the prompt return of children wrongfully removed to or retained in any Contracting State; and to ensure that rights of custody and of access under the law of one Contracting State are effectively respected in the other Contracting States. The Czech court deciding about the return of the child does not decide about his/her custody. The reason why Czech lawmakers changed the procedural rules was that, even if the Convention was directly applicable, the proceedings were longer than six weeks and also the territorial jurisdiction of the Czech court was settled in accordance with the child's stay. The courts were not able to decide in this short term. That is why the change has happened; there is only one court, the municipal court in Brno, because the central authority upon the Convention has its headquarters in the city (The Office for International Legal Protection of Children).

The court shall act rapidly in proceedings for the return of children. The decision has to be reached within six weeks from the date of commencement of the proceedings. If not, the court must give reasons for that. The parties to the case are the applicant (person claiming that a child has been removed in breach of custody rights), the person alleged to have removed the child from his/her habitual residence and the child. The return of the child cannot be prescribed automatically; the court must take the aspect of the best (superior) interest of the child into consideration. Based on the Convention and EU Regulation, the child will not be ordered to return if there is a grave risk that his/her return would expose the child to physical or psychological harm or otherwise place the child in an intolerable situation[245] or the return of the child may be refused if this would not be permitted by the fundamental principles of the requested State relating to the protection of human rights and fundamental freedom.[246] The court may also refuse to order the return of the child if it finds that the child objects to being returned and has attained an age and degree of maturity at which it is appropriate to take account of its views.

The court may also condition the return of the child on fulfilment of the adequate guarantees or outlay of so-called mirror orders[247] in the country in which the child

244. Act on Special Court Proceedings, §§478–491.
245. Article 13(b) of the Hague Convention of 25 Oct. 1980 on the Civil Aspects of International Child Abduction.
246. Article 20 of the Hague Convention of 25 Oct. 1980 on the Civil Aspects of International Child Abduction.
247. Act on Special Court Proceedings, §486, Art. 11(4) of the Council Regulation (EC) No. 2201/2003.

should return. This guarantee can, for example, help to get back to the country, safe-guarding of housing for the child and the mother, with the financial costs of the stay, maintenance and so on. It can also be a promise of the left-behind parent that he/she will not start a criminal prosecution. The problem of the guarantees is that they are only effective in the state from which the child was wrongfully removed. That is why the mirror orders can be made to let these undertakings be realized. These guarantees are valid till the court of the state where the child has returned decides about the custody of the child.

A mirror order or safe harbour order is an order made in the country where the child should return, which reflects the original order made in the country the child is staying. It is often made in circumstances where contact arrangements have been agreed and the child should return to another country. The mirror order means that the courts of the country where the child should return are aware of the original arrangements, and they give protection for the other parent in the other country.

Since 2006, we have had, in the Czech Republic, a Hague Network Judge. His challenge is to work with other network judges, to cooperate with foreign justice authorities and to inform about Czech legislation and the possibilities about mirror orders that may be executed in the Czech Republic.

Chapter 9. Guardianship and Custodianship

§1. Guardianship

I. General

554. The basic presumption for a guardian to be appointed is the fact that the child has no statutory representative.[248] In particular, these are cases when:

a. the child's parents died;
b. were deprived of their parental responsibilities;
c. performance of their parental responsibilities has been suspended;
d. the parents do not enjoy full legal capacity to perform acts in law (and for this reason, they lack performance of parental responsibilities);
e. in a situation where the parents have given their consent to the adoption and after three months have elapsed since this consent was given, as the exercise of the obligations and rights arising from parental responsibility is suspended by law and the court appoints a guardianship authority for the social and legal protection of children (§825 of the Civil Code).

A guardian is appointed ex officio by the court within the jurisdiction of which the child resides.[249]

555. Childcare may, in particular cases, be provided in other ways, for example, through institutional care as ordered earlier, foster care, or the child was charged to another person's care. However, the child's interests protection is not complete because in all the above-stated instances, the entities providing the child's care are not his/her statutory representatives, and thus they cannot decide all substantial matters involving the child.

II. Guardian's Personality

556. A guardian must of course enjoy full legal capacity to perform acts in law (in order to be able to act as the child's statutory representative). He/she must guarantee by his/her way of life that he/she will fulfil this duty consistent with the child's welfare. Thus, a person deprived of his/her own parental responsibilities will hardly be the one suitable to perform this role, similarly, like a persistent offender, an alcohol addict, a gambler, etc. The person must also agree to be appointed guardian. The court will never be able to appoint a person a guardian against his/her own will, as such a guardian would not guarantee performing his/her obligations consistent with the child's interests.

248. Civil Code §928(1).
249. *Ibid.*, §930, Act on Special Court Proceedings, §467(1).

557. A person recommended by the child's parents will be appointed guardian by the court in the first place. The parents' wish is then the basis, even though the form of parental recommendation is not expressly stipulated. It may be contained, for example, in a will (even though the genuine purpose of the will is different) or in another written document.[250] It is also possible to rely on oral statements of a parent made in the presence of, for example, a social and legal protection authority worker, a reliable witness, etc. However, the court is not absolutely bound by such a parental wish, determining predominantly on the basis of whether this recommendation is not contrary to the child's interests and on whether the person recommended guarantees to duly carry out this duty.

If nobody is thus recommended, the court will appoint as guardian a person from among the child's relatives or close persons, or another natural person.

The suitable person is selected in practice (if it is not the recommended guardian or a relative), as a rule, from the list of applicants for adoption or foster care. It may happen that although a child is, so to say, legally free, for various serious reasons (e.g., health condition or age), it is not possible to rule on adoption immediately. In such a case, one of the prospective adopters (or both spouses) may be appointed guardian (or guardians) first, and later adoption may be ruled on.

The law provides that two persons, usually spouses, may be appointed as guardians.[251] Under the law, a stranger's child may be charged either in the joint custody of a married couple or joint foster care. If a child lives in his/her guardians' family and the guardianship, besides others, plays also the role of substitute family care, it is more suitable to appoint both spouses' guardians than to leave this role to only one of them, as psychologically there is no difference between these two forms of substitute family care.

558. If a natural person may not be appointed a guardian (nobody is interested in this role, or the child has been placed in foster care or in institutional care), the court will appoint as guardian the appropriate social and legal protection authority.[252] State authorities cannot refuse the role of guardian.

With regard to increasing the protection of a minor child's interests before appointing a guardian or before he/she commences performance of his/her function, the urgent acts in law in the child's interest and representing him/her are performed by a relevant social and legal protection authority. Such situations may be, for example, when the child's parents suddenly died in a car accident and before one of the child's relatives takes the child in his/her custody and is appointed guardian by the court; for example, an orphan's annuity must be claimed on behalf of the child, covering the rent must be provided.

250. Civil Code §931.
251. *Ibid.*, §932(2).
252. *Ibid.*, §930(3).

III. Guardian's Rights and Obligations

559. The relationship between guardian and ward and its content is a private law relationship. In particular, the Civil Code provides (§928(2) of the Civil Code) that the guardian has, in principle, all the duties and rights towards the child as a parent but does not have a maintenance obligation towards the child (unless he/she is a relative in the direct line, §910 of the Civil Code). With regard to the person of the guardian or the circumstances of the child, as well as the reason why the parents do not have all the duties and rights, the court may exceptionally define the scope of the duties and rights of the guardian differently. However, the guardian is not the bearer of parental responsibility but may exercise the duties and rights belonging to it to the extent provided for by law or court decision.

560. Unlike a foster parent (§966(1) of the Civil Code), a guardian does not have to care for the child personally. The child may be placed in institutional care, in the care of a caring person or in foster care, or in temporary foster care. Personal care of the child is not the primary purpose of guardianship. However, this is often the case in practice. If the guardian has the child in his or her personal care, he or she is entitled to the same material security as the foster parent (§939 of the Civil Code, §47e of the Act on Social and Legal Protection of Children).

561. The guardian is accountable to the court for due performance of this function, and he/she exercises his/her rights and obligations towards the child under regular supervision of the court; namely, he/she is bound to inform the court of his/her ward and to present the accounts of his/her ward's estate administration.[253]

Unlike the parents, any decision concerning a substantial matter involving the ward requires the consent of the court, for example, decision on further education of the ward.

Unlike all other persons taking care of strange children, it is only the guardian who is explicitly bound to administer the ward's estate. The court may discharge the guardian of the duty to present detailed accounts of the ward's estate administration if the estate's yield is not higher than the presumed costs for the ward's care and maintenance. No later than within six months after terminating his/her guardianship, the guardian is bound to present the ward's estate administration accounts to the court. The court may relieve the guardian of this duty.

If the estate administration is especially hardy, the court may support the guardian's claim to a reasonable award payable annually or after terminating the administration.

The same rules as those for a special custodian apply to a guardian in handling a child's estate.[254]

253. *Ibid.*, §933.
254. *See* above Part II, Ch. 7, §2.

IV. Extinction of Guardianship

562. Guardianship may become extinct as follows:

a. Under law.
b. By discharging.
c. By recalling.

563. The essence of guardianship as an institute of safeguarding in relation to minor children takes for granted that guardianship ceases to exist upon full age of the ward. Guardianship also becomes extinct upon the child being adopted because adopters attain paternal responsibilities to the child and will become his/her statutory representatives.

If a guardian was appointed because the parents lack full capacity to perform acts in law, in theory, guardianship may become extinct if the court's decision on capacity restricting or incapacitating is revoked. If the guardian was appointed because the child's parent (mother) was a minor at the time when the child was born, guardianship ceases to exist upon the mother's majority or by affiliation related to a father of full age, because there will be a parent with parental responsibilities.

564. The court will always relieve a guardian of his/her guardianship upon his/her proposal.[255] No one may be forced to carry out this function. If a guardian refuses to continue to carry out this function for any subjective or objective reasons, a danger arises that the ward's interests will not be sufficiently protected.

However, an authority for social and legal protection of children may not apply for relieving of guardianship because this body is always bound to take over and duly perform this function.

As under the law, married spouses may be appointed guardians, the law must prescribe what happens if their marriage is dissolved. If one of the spouses – guardians – dies, his/her surviving spouse retains his/her function. If the guardians divorce, the guardianship does not become extinct upon divorce, but the court will always consider if it is in favour of the child's interests for both guardians to continue carrying out their functions of guardianship. Otherwise, one of the guardians will be relieved of his/her function. In this case, the court may rule on relieving the guardian of his/her function even without any proposal.

565. The court will recall a guardian who becomes incapable of carrying out his/her function or fails to fulfil his/her obligations.[256]

Incapable of carrying out is a guardian who has lost full capacity to perform acts in law or has been ill for a long time, or has been sentenced to prison, etc.

255. Civil Code §936.
256. *Ibid.*, §937.

§2. CUSTODIANSHIP

566. A custodian is appointed by the court in order to protect a minor child's interests in single cases. The court will always state the extent of the custodian's rights and duties in regard to the relevant goals for which he/she has been appointed so that the minor's protection is fully secured.[257]

567. Most often, it is a social and legal care authority (district authority) of children that is appointed custodian. In relation to foreign subjects, the International Institute of Legal Protection of Children residing in Brno is appointed custodian. In some cases, a natural person, often one of the relatives, will be appointed custodian.

568. The court may or must appoint a custodian as follows:

a. special custodian (in cases of conflicts of interest);
b. custodian in adoption proceedings;
c. custodian ad hoc;
d. custodian in cases of restricted parental responsibilities;
e. custodian for child's estate administration.

569. A special custodian is appointed if the child will not be represented by either parent. Such custodian appointed by the court will represent the child in proceedings or acts in law. No parent may represent his/her child in acts in law involving a possible conflict of interest between the parents and the child or conflict of interest between the children of the same parents.[258]

570. If consent of the parents as statutory representatives is not required in adoption, the consent to adoption is granted by a custodian appointed for this special purpose.[259] This function is always carried out by the relevant authority for social and legal protection of children.

571. A custodian may also be appointed for a child in other instances stipulated by law, only generally as necessary for other reasons consistent with the child's interests.[260] Typically, these are situations when a child has been placed in a substitute family or an institute, the parents were not deprived of their parental responsibilities, and either their residence is unknown or it is necessary to act in law on behalf of the child, and the parents are inactive.

572. A custodian is appointed to a child for a long term if both parents or the only living parent has been restricted in performing parental responsibilities.[261] The

257. *Ibid.*, §943.
258. *Ibid.*, §892(3).
259. *Ibid.*, §821(3).
260. *Ibid.*, §943.
261. *Ibid.*, §870, *see* above Part II, Ch. 7, §2.

custodian appointed takes over these rights and obligations to the extent that the parent is restricted in his/her parental responsibilities.

573. When justified, supposing the property interests of the child could be exposed to a risk, the court will appoint a custodian for the better protection of the property.[262] These may be the situations when parents are for objective reasons unable to administer the child's property (due to illness, lack of knowledge, etc.), the estate's administration itself is rather complex (e.g., copyright claims administration) and they did not opt to authorize an expert to administer the property, but also such situations when parents breach their obligations in the child's estate administration, taking risks in handling the estate or utilize it for their own needs, etc.

An estate administration custodian appointed by the court will be predominantly a natural person with sufficient expertise and abilities. It may be one of the child's relatives or a lawyer, tax consultant or other expert. If the estate is not very extensive, also an authority for social and legal protection of children may be appointed as custodian.

When appointing a child's estate administration custodian, the court will also expressly enumerate the extent of the estate to be administered by the custodian and will determine how the custodian will be or will not be allowed to handle the child's estate.

The custodian may claim petty expenses related to the estate administration as well as a reasonable reward for services from the yield of the child's estate, the amount of which is to be determined by the court.

262. Civil Code §§948–952.

Chapter 10. Kinship and Relations of Affinity

§1. Child in Relation to Other Relatives

574. The degree of consanguinity (kinship) between two persons is determined according to the number of births which separate one person from the other in the direct line of descent and, in collateral line, the number which separates both from the nearest common ancestor.[263]

575. Under family law, only the relations between ancestors and descendants and those between siblings are legally significant. Family law does not provide for relations between a child and other relatives.

Succession law relies on a broader group of relatives. Statutory heirs may also be uncles, aunts and cousins.[264]

I. Grandparents

576. Legal relations between grandparents and grandchildren arise when a child who meets one of the three legal presumptions of paternity is born either to their female child or to their male child. Although kinship between grandparents and grandchildren is very significant, it is not paid much attention to in the Code, not expressly stipulate the range of rights and obligations of grandparents and grandchildren.

577. The law provides that persons related to the child, whether close or distant, as well as persons socially close to the child, have the right to have contact with the child if the child has an emotional relationship with them that is not merely transitory and if it is clear that the lack of contact with these persons would cause harm to the child. The child also has the right to have contact with such persons if they consent to such contact (§927 of the Civil Code). As already mentioned, grandparents and grandchildren are close relatives.

578. Emphasizing the relations between grandparents and grandchildren also resulted in the possibility of a grandchild being put into his/her grandparents' custody.[265]

Very often, grandparents assume the actual personal care of their grandchildren whose parents do not want, cannot for objective or subjective reasons, or are not able to take care of their children. For this reason, the law now explicitly stipulates that in determining whether or not to place a child in the care of a person other than the parent, the court will, as a rule, prefer the child's relative. Thus, the court actually approves of the factual state.

263. *Ibid.*, §772.
264. *See* below Part IV, Ch. 1, §3.
265. Civil Code §954(2).

A grandchild may also be charged in his/her grandparents' foster care, which is not very frequent. In determining whether to place a child in his/her grandparents' custody or foster care, the social situation of the family plays an important role, that is, if the family needs to be supported financially in relation to foster care or whether the grandparents will be able to support their grandchildren within their duty to maintain.

Grandparents will also be preferred in determining who should be appointed as a child's guardian.[266]

However, the close relationship excludes the option of grandparents adopting a grandchild.[267]

579. Under the law, a mutual duty to maintain exists between grandparents and grandchildren.[268]

580. As regards the comparison of the extent of maintenance, parents have a legal obligation to provide the child with a basically equal standard of living (i.e., the highest level), but nothing is expressly provided for grandparents. In the absence of any provision to the contrary, it must be concluded, having regard to the purpose of maintenance and the best interests of the child, that grandparents are obliged to provide maintenance for their grandchildren to the extent that it can cover all the child's reasonable needs and, where appropriate, to build up savings, in so far as the ancestor's financial circumstances in relation to the minor grandchild who is not fully capable of exercising his or her rights allow it (§917 of the Civil Code).

581. If the maintenance is not paid voluntarily and if the grandchildren are minors, the court may, even without a petition, initiate proceedings in this matter and impose a maintenance obligation on each grandparent in such proportion as corresponds to the possibilities and abilities or the financial circumstances of the particular grandparent (§466 of the Civil Code). The maintenance obligation in respect of minor grandchildren may be imposed up to three years retroactively from the date of initiation of the proceedings.

582. However, if the grandchild is already an adult, proceedings for the establishment of maintenance may only be initiated on the basis of an action to which the court is bound. The procedure will be conducted in the context of contested proceedings (under the Code of Civil Procedure).

Duty to maintain is owed by all four grandparents. The court cannot determine maintenance duty of only those grandparents whose child, as a parent, is unable to fulfil his/her duty to maintain.[269]

For example, the court will not assess maintenance payments to the grandmother from the mother's side because she helps her daughter in the child's care, the grandfather has died already, the grandparents from the father's side are divorced, and the

---

266. *Ibid.*, §931.
267. *See* above Part II, Ch. 5, §2, Civil Code §804.
268. Civil Code §910.
269. *Ibid.*, §910.

grandmother receives only a disability pension while the grandfather is a businessman. The grandmother will not be assessed for maintenance as she is not able to provide any, while the grandfather will be assessed for maintenance.

583. The principle of reciprocity implies the right of grandparents to receive maintenance from their grandchildren; however, only if the grandparents are dependent on maintenance and at the same time cannot assert their rights against their spouses, former spouses or their children. Grandparents and grandchildren inherit in the first inheritance group.[270]

II. Relations among Siblings

584. Siblings are persons who have both parents in common (full siblings), or at least one parent (half-blood siblings). If a man and a woman, each having his/her own child, get married, no sibling relationship arises upon mere marriage of their parents. Only after mutual adoption of children by their parents would a relationship of siblings arise between the children adopted.

585. In connection with the divorce of the parents of minor children, or their separation, the law establishes the obligation of the court to take into account the interests of the minor children (§§906 et seq. of the Civil Code), which is interpreted by court practice as meaning that it is generally necessary for the development of at least sibling ties to entrust the minor children jointly with custody for the period after the divorce. If the children are 'separated' into different educational environments, it is also necessary to decide at the same time to regulate the parents' contact with the children so that the bonds between the siblings are strengthened or to regulate the child's contact with his or her siblings, if the best interests of the child and the family situation so require (cf. in practice, the regulation of contact between siblings occurs in particular when children are placed in different environments, or in foster care, if one of the siblings is an adult, or has a legal capacity).

586. As with grandparents, minor siblings may be charged to the custody or foster care of their adult siblings. A sibling of age may be appointed guardian of his/her minor siblings too.

587. Under Czech law, no duty to maintain arises among siblings.

588. Siblings may inherit from one another in the third inheritance group.[271]

270. *See* below Part IV, Ch. 1, §3.
271. *Ibid.*

§2. RELATIONS OF AFFINITY

589. The ABGB, as amended in 1919, prohibited marriages between persons of affinity in direct line free of any limitations, while in indirect line, it restricted only full or half-blood siblings of the other husband. This impediment involved only private law.[272]

Legally significant was the affinity of persons also after the Family Law Act of 1949 became operative. Persons in direct line of affinity could not marry. Such marriages could be permitted by local authorities for serious reasons.[273]

590. In the period 1964–2014, the law did not consider the notion of affinity.

591. Affinity is not consanguinity, as it is not based on blood ties or adoption (§771 of the Civil Code). The creation of a sister-in-law relationship is linked to the creation of a marriage and, in principle, to its existence. A sister-in-law relationship is not linked to other formal relationships (registered partnership) or de facto relationships (unmarried cohabitation).

592. The Civil Code provides that the creation of a marriage creates a relationship of in-law between one spouse and the other spouse's relatives (§774 of the Civil Code). A distinction can thus be drawn between de jure and social kinship, which does not have the legal meaning intended by the legislator in connection with the introduction of the concept of in-law into the Civil Code.

593. As regards the lines and degrees of consanguinity, the law provides that in what line and degree someone is related to one spouse, in such line and degree he is related to the other spouse (§774, second sentence, of the Civil Code).

594. In the context of the family business arrangement (§§700 et seq. of the Civil Code), affinity is relevant up to the second degree. Persons who are married are considered to be close, irrespective of other facts (§22(1) *in fine* of the Civil Code). This is a rebuttable presumption. Affinity is not an obstacle to marriage.

595. Similarly to social kinship, social affinity (i.e., beyond the law) may also be relevant. This is, for example, the fact that these persons may be close, provided that the harm suffered by one person would reasonably be regarded by the other person as his or her own harm (§22 of the Civil Code).

272. Act No. 320/1919 Coll., §25(3).
273. Family Law Act §9.

Chapter 11. Interventions of the State in Relations Between Parents and Children

§1. Introduction

596. In regard to the extent of interventions in the family system and the means used, three essential situations may be distinguished in view of the parents:

1. a state intervention in resolving a problem in a family without changing the legal status of the particular family members;
2. a state intervention may be so intensive as instigating a changed legal status of the subjects as a result; that is, the parent/parents may be suspended, limited in, or deprived of their parental responsibilities;
3. a state intervention does not change the parents' legal status, but parental responsibilities are in fact limited (e.g., imposing institutional or protective care, banning the contacts of parents and children).

597. An essential question in this respect is, namely, the question of the extent of intervention. In general, intervention or performance of power of the state in a family is relevant only if the family, for various reasons, cannot perform its duties towards the child, thus failing to provide for his/her overall protection and development. Decisive is, however, the principle of adequacy in intervening in order to act efficiently, reasonably and with regard to the child's interests and welfare and promptly in the first place. The time of a child differs from that of an adult, and efficient help must be prompt and immediate. Therefore, in the system of state protection of children, an important role is played by the state administration and self-governing authorities which are ready to help when a child is in need.

If the state does not interfere where it should, it will overestimate the right of the family to privacy, resulting in the child being deprived of its protection. However, excessively extensive intervention, where the state essentially should not act in the way it acts, may result in unlawful interference with the right to privacy and thus to raise undesirable consequences. It is an extremely sensitive issue, the resolving of which is not simple in a particular situation, not even in the developed Western European countries.

598. It is necessary to distinguish situations where the state is bound to interfere because the situation anticipated by law has occurred. Two such situations are possible:

1. the law anticipates certain particular solutions to this situation (appointing a custodian or a guardian, imposing obligatory protective care);
2. the relevant authority is bound to offer an alternative solution to the situation, which it will discuss with the parents, or with a child as well, while one of the solutions offered must be applied.

Here, it is necessary to distinguish such instances when the state is only entitled to interfere; that is, the state may (but need not) interfere and offer certain solutions at the same time. Employing these solutions as offered is, however, a matter of those to whom they are offered, that is, the parents or the child. This implies that these will be the most varied types of help to the family and the child, including consulting, social benefits.

599. An overall regulation of positive and inevitable state interference in family relations was regulated only by the Children Act, the drafting of which took a rather long time.[274]

The Act defines social and legal protection of children, namely, as:

a. protection of a child's rights to favourable development and proper upbringing;
b. protection of the rightful interests of a child, including his/her property protection;
c. acting in favour of recovery of impaired family functions.

A general definition of social and legal protection is also given by the fact that the child's protection includes an extensive set of child's rights and rightful interests provided under various regulations of family law, civil law, labour law, criminal law, but also in school attendance, healthcare regulations and others.

600. In addition to state authorities and non-governmental entities, juridical and natural persons are empowered to carry out, within a framework set by law, some activities involving social and legal protection, based on specific authorization vested in them by the Ministry of Labour and Social Affairs.

This predominantly involves the operation of various telephone lines for free aid, asylum facilities providing immediate aid to children, etc.

601. Social and legal protection is aimed at those children who need it in the first place. Therefore, the law defines the children in need of increased care. These are children whose parents died, do not perform their parental obligations, or abuse the rights arising from parental responsibilities.

Increased attention is paid to children indulging in an idle or improper way of life, namely, by avoiding compulsory school attendance, shunning work, although lacking sufficient means, consuming alcohol or drugs, earning their living with prostitution, having committed a criminal offence, or, with children under 15, by having committed an offence that would otherwise be a criminal act, by repeatedly or continuously committing misdemeanours, or otherwise posing threats to civic cohabitation, and to the children who repeatedly flee from their parents or other natural or juridical persons responsible for their care.

Social and legal protection is also provided in an increased scope to those children who have been subject to a crime posing a danger to their lives, health, human dignity or property, or there is a suspicion that such crime has been committed.

274. Act No. 359/1999 Coll., Act on Social and Legal Protection of Children.

This increased attention must be paid to children if the facts mentioned have been persistent for such a time or are of such intensity that they adversely influence the children's development.[275]

602. Just as the children with Czech citizenship are provided social and legal care, the same applies to children of foreign citizenship if they are permitted to reside in the territory of the Czech Republic permanently or long term or a proposal was filed for granting asylum.[276]

603. Within the scope given by law, social and legal care is also provided to other children regardless of their nationality if the child lacks any care or his/her life or welfare is in danger or impaired. Protection and help to such a child will comprise satisfying his/her basic needs, including accommodation, providing medical care, psychological and other necessary care.[277]

604. The first and foremost point in the social and legal protection of children, consistent with the UN Convention on the Rights of the Child, is the child's interests and welfare.[278]

605. Everybody is entitled to notify parents of defective behaviour of their children. Everyone is entitled to notify the relevant local authority of social and legal protection of children on violating the obligations or abuse of rights arising from parental responsibilities, on the fact that the parents are unable to meet the obligations arising from parental responsibilities, and on the fact that the child involved is in need of special attention. The relevant authority workers are bound to keep secret the person who notified the authority of these facts, namely, in relation to the child's parents.

606. Consistent with Article 12 of the UN Convention on the Rights of the Child the law also stipulates that the child, who is able to express his/her own attitudes and opinions, is entitled, in the view of his/her own social and legal protection, to express these attitudes and opinions while all his/her respective affairs are dealt with, even without his/her parents or other persons responsible for the child's care present. The child's attitudes and opinions as expressed must be paid reasonable attention to, consistent with the age and level of the child's mental development.[279]

607. Also, a parent or other person responsible for the child's care is entitled to apply for the help of an authority involved in social and legal child's care, state authorities or empowered persons in performing his/her rights and obligations. These authorities are bound, within their powers, to provide this help.

---

275. *Ibid.*, §6.
276. *Ibid.*, §2.
277. *Ibid.*, §§37 to 42.
278. *Ibid.*, §5.
279. *Ibid.*, §8(2).

§2. CHILDCARE ORDERS

608. Under the Civil Code, one of the opportunities of the state to interfere in a family is to impose so-called childcare orders. They are ruled on by the court or municipality and if neither of these authorities has so decided, it may be done by a district authority. All the bodies mentioned decide independently; a care order may be revoked only by the authority that imposed it.[280]

609. If an interest in proper childcare requires so, one of the aforementioned bodies may admonish the minor, his/her parents or the persons influencing adversely the child's upbringing.

A child will be admonished when at the age in which such admonition may be presumed efficient, that is, the child is able to realize his/her improper conduct or its consequences.

Parents will be admonished when having neglected or violated some of their obligations towards the child, involving not only the obligations implied in their parental responsibilities but also the duties imposed by law; for example, the parents have failed to attend a medical care centre with the child in the cases prescribed (compulsory vaccinations), the child has avoided compulsory school attendance or the parents leave the child alone without any supervision, etc.

Other persons who will be admonished under the provision stated may be relatives, entire strangers as well as those in whose care the child was placed by court decision. The reason for admonishment is their acting (or failure to act) impairing the proper upbringing of the minor.

Admonishing is mostly imposed by municipalities that tend to have the most detailed information on the necessity of such admonishment in relation to the family.

610. If admonishment fails to have any effect or the defects in the minor's or his/her parents' conduct are more serious, a supervision order over minors may be imposed. The supervision is carried out in cooperation with the school, civic associations in the place of residence or the workplace.

The supervision over minors is imposed most often by the court, for example, on finding, during divorce proceedings, that the child's care as provided is insufficient; an imposing authority may also be a district authority.

611. The relevant authority may impose a limitation over a minor in order to avoid harmful influences upon his/her upbringing, namely, visiting entertainment facilities not suitable for the particular minor.

Unlike previous care orders, this limitation is rarely imposed. It might involve, for example, a ban on attending local football matches, gambling facilities, etc. In large cities, for example, the efficiency of such limitations and the subsequent checks are rather questionable.

280. Civil Code §925.

§3. Institutional and Protective Care

612. Imposing institutional or protective care is, after depriving of parental responsibilities, the second most serious measure interfering with family relations. Under the Charter of Fundamental Rights and Freedoms (Article 32), the parents' rights may be limited, and children may be taken away from their parents against their will only upon a court ruling and under law. Institutional care is therefore relevant only if a proper family environment may not be provided for the child by his/her natural family, which no longer exists or failed to fulfil its duties. Psychologically, institutional care is relevant as a temporary solution after the child has been taken away from his/her family and before another suitable family (adoptive, foster family, etc.) has been found for him/her, or before the child is able to return to his/her original family. However, institutional care is not a good long-term solution for providing care for a child taken from his/her original family.

Before imposing institutional care, the court is always bound to examine whether the child's care cannot be provided by substitute family care, which is always to be preferred. If, after imposing institutional care the respective reasons cease to exist, or the child can be provided with substitute family care, the institutional care will be repealed by the court.[281]

613. Imposing institutional care is always ruled by a court, even without any formal instigation. In some instances, a proposal or a petition to commence proceedings is filed with the court by parents or other persons in whose custody the child was placed.

As court proceedings may take a long time and the child's protection must be provided for immediately, the civil procedure law allows a special preliminary emergency order to be issued. If a minor child finds himself/herself without any care or if his/her life or favourable development is endangered or impaired, the judge will impose, by a preliminary order, that the child be handed over to the care of a designated natural person or an institute. A preliminary order is effective for three months after being imposed. If proceedings on the merits have been opened before the expiry of that period, the court may extend the preliminary order repeatedly so that the total duration of the preliminary order does not exceed six months from its enforceability.

Such preliminary order may be imposed by a court only upon the proposal of a district authority. The proposal must be ruled on by the court without delay, no later than within twenty-four hours after it was filed.[282]

614. Institutional care is collective care of the child, the purpose of which is not to sanction, but to help the child and his or her parent in the situations regulated by law. It may fulfil various functions in relation to the reasons set out below. It is regulated by the Civil Code (§§971 et seq. of the Civil Code).

281. *Ibid.*, §971.
282. Act on Special Court Proceedings, §452.

615. The court may order institutional education if the measures taken previously have not led to a remedy (§971(1) of the Civil Code). This must be understood in the broader context of any interference by the State in the relationship between parents and child. These may be educational measures imposed under the Civil Code (§925 of the Civil Code) or under a special law (cf. §13 and 13a of the Civil Code), or other social protection measures consisting in particular of preventive and counselling activities, or judicial intervention in parental responsibility (suspension, limitation or restriction of parental responsibility or removal of parental responsibility), or decisions to restrict or prohibit personal contact between the parent and the child.

616. Placing the child in institutional care should be the last resort. It is the culmination of the intervention of the state authorities in the relationship between parents and children. Entrusting a child outside the care of his or her parents constitutes a very serious interference with parental rights. In fact, it is a restriction on the exercise of parents' duties and rights arising from parental responsibility. When considering interventions, the main focus should be on whether the means chosen is effective for the best protection of the child. It is in the best interests of the child to grow up in a functional family environment. However, if it is not possible to restore the functions of the child's own family without placing the child in another environment, the situation of the child at risk must be addressed primarily through other means, such as foster care or guardianship (cf. the dictum 'the court may order'). The court must always assess whether there are other ways of dealing with the child's particular situation (so many decisions, e.g., the European Court of Human Rights in *Couillard Maugery v. France* and of the Czech Constitutional Court No. II ÚS 838/2007). The use of other support measures is examined for all grounds for ordering institutional care.

617. In extreme cases, it is possible for the court to order institutional upbringing even without prior lesser interventions in the relationship between the parents and the child (cf.) It follows that, in exceptional cases, institutional education may be ordered without further action.

618. The court is always obliged to review at least once every six months whether the grounds for ordering institutional care continue to exist, whatever the institution (§973 of the Civil Code). Institutional care may be ordered for a maximum of three years, although it may be extended in exceptional cases (§972 of the Civil Code).

619. The grounds for ordering institutional care are that the child's upbringing, his or her physical, intellectual or mental state or his or her proper development are seriously endangered to such an extent that this state is contrary to the best interests of the child. This is a situation where the parents (or other persons and the parents are unable to prevent it) endanger the child's proper development by neglecting the child, failing to care for him or her properly, failing to supervise him or her, with the result that these actions only endanger the child and his or her proper upbringing for the time being. The endangerment of the child's upbringing must be of a certain intensity and must be socially pathological. A further reason is that the child's upbringing, his physical, mental or intellectual state or his proper development have already been seriously impaired to such an extent that it is contrary to the child's interests to remain in his current educational environment. These are situations where the conduct of the parents or other persons has already reached the intensity of the disruption of the child's upbringing, condition or proper development. The order for institutional care has a remedial function.

620. In addition, institutional care may be imposed if there are serious reasons why the parents cannot provide for the child's upbringing. Unlike the previous reasons, these are mainly objective reasons.

621. It should be emphasized that the parents' inadequate housing or financial circumstances cannot in themselves be a reason for ordering institutional care (§971(3) of the Civil Code). There may also be serious reasons on the part of the child if the parents are unable to care for the child in the home environment and do not themselves ask for assistance from the child welfare authority.

622. In such cases, institutional care has a primarily educational function.

623. The Czech Republic became the last country in the EU where it was possible to place the youngest children (under 3 years of age) in institutions. It has faced repeated criticism from the Council of Europe's European Committee of Social Rights over this. The amendment to ZSPOD No. 363/2021 amended the restrictions on the placement of the youngest children in institutional care, including precautionary measures. Placement of children under 3 years of age should be impossible after the entry into force on 1 January 2025. These children will be placed in foster care.

624. Institutional care becomes extinct upon a court ruling if the reasons for its imposing have ceased to exist. This will be in cases when the child is able to return to his/her original family or may be placed in another substitute family.

Institutional care becomes extinct no later than upon attaining majority age. If there are serious reasons, institutional care may be prolonged by a court decision to no more than one year after attaining majority age (e.g., in case of persistent problems with the child's care or the child must complete a training course in the institute after attaining majority, etc.).

625. Since 1 January 2004, there has been a new act concerning the responsibility of minors for crimes.[283] The special court with the power to rule on criminal matters concerning minors applying the Civil Procedure Code imposes protective care. Under this act, for minor crimes, protective care must be imposed in case a

---

283. Act No. 218/2003 Coll., on Responsibility of Juveniles for Crimes and on Jurisdiction in these Cases.

person, having attained the 12th year of age and is below the age of 15, has committed an offence for which the Criminal Code imposes extraordinary punishment (i.e., imprisonment of over fifteen years, up to twenty-five years). The option to impose extraordinary punishment applies to crimes like murder, terrorism, being a public menace, etc. The capability to commit criminal wrongdoings arises upon attaining the age of 15. Hereby, the child is fully responsible for committing a criminal offence yet will be judged as a juvenile delinquent.

If a child (under 15) has committed an act that would otherwise be a criminal offence, the special court may (not obligatory) impose a protective care on the child. Protective care is the most extreme penalty; the court may also impose limitation on the child (he/she may not go to the disco) or admonition with warning or placement in the therapy programme or supervision of the probation officer.[284]

Protective care will persist until required in the inmate's (the child's) interests, however, no longer than by the time he/she has attained the age of 18. If the inmate's interests require so, it may be prolonged, and in the case of institutional care, for no longer than attaining the age of 19.[285]

284. *Ibid.*, §93.
285. *Ibid.*, §22.

Part III. Matrimonial Property Law

Chapter 1. Rights and Obligations of Spouses

§1. General Principles

I. Historical Development of Matrimonial Property Law

626. The ABGB provided for a legal matrimonial regime on the principle of separate property. If persons to be married did not make a special agreement involving property, so-called marriage articles applied that their property situations did not change upon marriage. Each spouse continued to own what he/she had owned before and he/she also acquired property into his/her ownership only. If in doubt as to which of the spouses acquired the particular item or estate, a refutable presumption applied that the item or estate was acquired by the husband.[286]

The concept of separate property of married spouses had its grounds in a theory of individualism of the eighteenth century based on natural law and reflected predominantly the social position of the class of clerks and military officers of the time.

A husband was bound to care for the family funding, and therefore he was entitled, by law, to administer also the property owned by his wife (so-called *paraphernalia*) unless expressly cancelled by the wife.

The Code provided in detail for a dowry (*dos*) as well as for a widow's dowry (annuity).

The system of separate property applied as a supportive legal regime. Under marriage Articles, the spouses might agree on community property, involving either an entire property or its part, and they could agree on community property by the day of their marriage termination.

Marriage articles required a form of notarial record; however, marriage articles' registration was not provided for, with the exception of marriage articles of businessmen which were obligatorily registered in a commercial register.

627. In the period of the Family Law Act being in force (between 1 January 1950 and 31 March 1964), a subsidiary legal community property of married spouses existed.[287] This involved the property acquired by either spouse during marriage except for property acquired by gift, inheritance, items for personal use or for carrying out their profession.

---

286. ABGB §§1233 et seq.
287. Family Law Act §§22–29.

Married spouses could regulate the extent of community property differently upon contract or define its rise ending upon termination of marriage. The contract must have been made in the form of a court record. This form was applied rarely.

Upon divorce, the portion of community property belonging to a spouse responsible for the divorce could have been reduced or dispossessed of entirely.

628. Within extensive recodification in the early sixties, substantial changes were adopted in matrimonial property law. The uniform legal community property regime was replaced by a very fragmented regulation of property relations between married spouses. Besides, matrimonial property regulation was transferred to the Civil Code. The new Family Code retained only the provisions on the mutual duty to maintain between spouses and on maintenance of a divorced spouse.

629. The original regulation of a basic institute of matrimonial property law, an 'undivided co-ownership of spouses' was a legal regime, exclusively, free of any option for the spouses to agree upon a different regulation. It concerned only items that might be the subject of so-called personal property. For items pertaining to so-called private property, the regulation of the undivided co-ownership applied only as appropriate (private property was protected in a reduced measure only). The Civil Code also stipulated a special institute of personal use of the flat and site by the married spouses, which was a strange hybrid between contract law and property law. As for liabilities of married spouses, a general regime of contract law applied. Originally, very strict regulation of undivided co-ownership of spouses was slightly loosened as time passed. This type of co-ownership responded in its essence to the needs of a socialist society family with two incomes, dependent predominantly on incomes from employment or from public sources. As soon as differences between personal and private property were repealed after the Velvet Revolution and entrepreneurial activities spread rapidly, the undivided co-ownership of spouses ceased to conform to the changed economic situation. The following substantial amendments to the Civil Code[288] enabled married couples to regulate their property relations differently upon contract. Only in relation to the family law reform of 1998,[289] the Civil Code was amended concurrently, and the regime of undivided co-ownership of spouses was replaced by a substantially broader joint property of spouses.

One of the important reasons for a new regulation of matrimonial property law has been increased protection of economically weaker spouses, typically businessmen's wives.

After the adoption of the Civil Code (in force since 2014), not much has changed in the matrimonial property regime. There have only been partial modifications, which are elaborated below.

288. Act No. 509/1991 Coll., as effective on 1 Jan. 1992.
289. Act No. 91/1998 Coll., as effective on 1 Aug. 1998.

II. Contemporary Concept of Matrimonial Property Law

630. Marriage is a personal and a property community. As from 1 January 2025, all provisions relating to the matrimonial property shall also apply to same-sex partnerships entered into after 1 January 2025. Where we use the term spouses in this context, meaning also partners. Thus, matrimonial property law regulation should not lead to competition between personal and property interests of married spouses.

631. Thus, under Czech law, the following property rights may exist between married spouses:

a. a separate, exclusive property of one of the married spouses related to items acquired before marriage and to some of the items acquired during marriage;
b. exclusive obligations acquired by one of the married spouses which arose before marriage or, in some cases, also during marriage;
c. co-ownership, as among any other subjects arising before marriage or during marriage, if the gift was donated to both spouses or both spouses inherited jointly;
d. joint property of spouses:
   - to the extent as given by law;
   - to the extent as given under contract.
e. flat tenancy during marriage is stipulated separately depending on the type of flat;
f. mutual duty to maintain between spouses as given by law stipulated with no regard to the joint property of spouses;
g. common liabilities arising before marriage.

632. As for joint property of spouses being the most important institute of matrimonial property law today, married spouses can regulate its extent or administration by a contract in a modified manner. However, basically it is not possible to have joint property of spouses entirely repealed by contract or by a court decision. A special regime is stipulated in case of bankruptcy.

633. There is a new term introduced by law: items which form part of the usual equipment of common household (§698 of the Civil Code). These items always form part of common property. For now it is not, however, quite clear exactly what items should be deemed usual equipment. An interpretation prevails, arising from subjective outcomes, where the items making up the usual equipment of a common household evolve from the property situation of a particular family.

§2. The Household Expenses

634. Both spouses are bound to satisfy the family needs consistent with their abilities and property situation. Providing monetary and other means for covering the family needs may be fully or partially balanced by personal care of the common household and children.[290]

635. If one of the spouses does not perform his/her duty to share covering the expenses of the common household, the court will rule in the matter based on the petition filed by the other spouse.

Duty to cover the expenses of the common household must be distinguished from the spouses' mutual duty to maintain as well as the duty to maintain their children. These are mainly the cases when the spouses' incomes are basically equal, and thus there is no reason to rule upon mutual duty to maintain, but one of the spouses refuses to share in covering the expenses such as rent, purchasing food, cleaning and washing products for the household, etc., and considers his/her income to be his/her own 'pocket money'.

The court may not rule that such spouse is bound to contribute half of his/her income to cover the common household expenditures. In order to render the judgment to be enforceable, the court must determine a particular amount that must be paid by the spouse every month. If the common household expenses change, for example, the rent increases, it is necessary to address the court again in order to have the amount to be paid modified.[291]

The possibility to claim upon the other spouse to contribute to the common expenses of the household in court was stipulated only within the family law reform of 1998. Not too much experience was gained by applying this provision in practice, as such suits are brought about only exceptionally. If married spouses are unable to agree upon such matters, this shows that their marriage has probably broken down, and it is better to solve it by divorce.

636. The conduct of one spouse in administering common family matters binds both spouses jointly and severally.[292] A spouse may explicitly exclude such effects, but a third person must be aware of this fact.

§3. The Matrimonial Home

637. In the context of the interpretation of the personal obligations and rights of spouses, it was stated that spouses have the obligation to live together (§687 of the Civil Code). The spouses are to agree whether to live together or separately, respectively where they would both live. The obligation of the spouses to live together may not be narrowed down or identified with living in the same flat or house. Even student marriages or weekend marriages may be harmonious. After all, there are no legal models for family life. It may therefore be said that spouses may live together even if they do not live together every day because they do not want to, are not able to or do not have the financial means to set up a family household in a separate flat.

290. Civil Code §690.
291. Civil Procedure Code §154.
292. Civil Code §693.

Living in a shared flat (one room each, shared bathroom, separate kitchen) may not be considered cohabitation. However, even in this case, the spouses have the possibility to reach an agreement.

638. Private law protection of the family home is a traditional feature of European law, particularly in relation to the Recommendation of the Committee of Ministers of the Council of Europe No R (81)15 on the rights of spouses related to the occupation of the family home or flat and the use of household contents. In particular, the Recommendation protects the spouse who neither owns nor has any other direct legal right to the family household or flat and its furnishings in situations where there is a marital crisis, divorce or death.

639. The Civil Code pays special attention to this matter in the context of certain provisions on matrimonial housing (§§743 et seq. of the Civil Code).

640. First of all, it is established that the spouses have a dwelling where they have a family household (§743(1) of the Civil Code). The spouses usually agree on this matter. However, if agreement is not possible, e.g., in a pre-divorce crisis, the law provides that one of the spouses may request the other to relocate the family household for serious reasons, and the other is legally obliged to comply with it, unless the reasons for staying outweigh the reasons for the change (§743(2) of the Civil Code). The spouses may also agree on permanent separate housing, which may, however, be established in other ways, e.g., by leaving the family household, by expulsion, by deportation, by being in custody or serving a sentence.

641. A household is not defined in the law, unlike as in the case of the previous amendments. However, it may be defined, in the light of other provisions, as an economic unit consisting of people and a set of certain assets (dwelling and its furnishings). A family household may consist not only of spouses but also of registered partners, at least one parent and a child, a parent of a child, a child and a step-parent.

642. Notwithstanding the legal obligation of the spouses to live together (§687, (1) of the Civil Code), the spouses do not have to live together (they will live permanently apart according to §743(3) of the Civil Code upon agreement or upon leaving the family household by one of the spouses) and keep a family household (this is foreseen in §691 of the Civil Code). The family household of the spouses is conceptually linked to the spouses' living together. This has a significant impact, for example, in relation to meeting the needs of the family (§690 of the Civil Code), the disposition of the dwelling, i.e., a house or flat (§747 and §748 of the Civil Code), protection against domestic violence (§751 of the Civil Code) and housing after the dissolution of the marriage (§§766 et seq. of the Civil Code).

I. Individual Legal Grounds for Housing

643. If the dwelling of the spouses (house or flat) is held in community property of the spouses, the spouses' position is equal, and it is protected primarily by the legal regulation related to the community property of spouses (*see* above, §§708 et seq., in particular §713 of the Civil Code).

644. A similar conclusion may be drawn if the dwelling of the spouses is in divided co-ownership and the shares are in principle equal (§1115, §1122(3) of the Civil Code).

645. If one of the spouses has an exclusive right to the house or flat based on an obligation, in particular a lease right, the marriage gives rise to a joint lease right for both spouses reflecting the equality of rights and obligations (§745 of the Civil Code). However, it may be contractually agreed otherwise (§745(2) of the Civil Code), which is fully in line with the general principle of autonomy of will in private law. The lease of a flat in cooperative ownership of a housing cooperative is regulated by a special law (§745 of the Business Corporation Act No. 90/2012 Coll.; *see* §§739 et seq. of the Business Corporation Act for details on the joint membership of spouses in a housing cooperative).

646. The spouses may also realize their housing on the basis of other, less customary reasons for housing. These include, for example:

a. the housing is located in the dwelling of the parents or relatives of one of them (*see* §770 of the Civil Code);
b. as members of the lessor's household (§2272 of the Civil Code);
c. in a sublet (§§2274 et seq. of the Civil Code);
d. on the basis of an easement or servitude (§1297 of the Civil Code);
e. under a contract on the reserved rights of enjoyment (§§2707 et seq. of the Civil Code; *see* §2712 of the Civil Code regulating the reserved rights of enjoyment for spouses);
f. under an innominate contract.

II. Prohibition of Disposition with Family Dwelling

647. Following on from the above, the Act also provides for a prohibition of unilateral disposition of the family dwelling in a similar spirit to the prohibition of dispositions of items forming the usual furnishings of the family household (§698 of the Civil Code). The purpose of the new legislation is to protect the family as a whole, the economically weaker spouse, children and third parties in relation to European standards for the protection of the right to reside, i.e., the right to housing. Two basic situations are distinguished.

A. One of the Spouses Has the Exclusive Right to the Family Dwelling

648. If at least one of the spouses has the right to dispose of the house or flat in which the household of the spouses or family is located and the house or flat is indispensable for the living of the spouses or family, they shall refrain from anything and avoid everything that may make the living impossible or dangerous. In particular, the spouse may not, without the written consent of the other spouse, misappropriate such house or flat or establish a right to the house, i.e., part of it or the whole of it, the exercise of which is incompatible with the household of the spouses or family, unless they ensure that the spouse or family has a home similar in all respects to the existing home. If a spouse acts in violation of this rule without the consent of the other spouse, the latter may claim the invalidity of such legal act (§747 in conjunction with §586 of the Civil Code). This is a relative voidability. The limitation period does not begin or run during the marriage (§646 of the Civil Code). However, this also entails the protection of the good faith of third parties.

B. The Spouses Have a Joint Lease Right to the Family Dwelling

649. If there is a family household in the family dwelling, the prohibition of disposition or the obligation to refrain from all the above applies. It is expressly stated that the spouse may not, without written consent, terminate the lease or restrict it by a right the exercise of which is incompatible with the cohabitation of spouses or family. If a spouse acts in violation of this rule without the consent of the other spouse, the latter may claim the invalidity of such legal act (§748 in conjunction with §586 of the Civil Code).

650. The law further provides that if the disposition of the dwelling of spouses or family referred to above is to be based on agreement, whether prenuptial or between the spouses, the position of the children (hereinafter stipulated by the law) and third parties shall not be impaired unless they consent in writing (§750 of the Civil Code).

Chapter 2. The Legal Matrimonial Regime

§1. Rise of Joint Property of Spouses

651. Joint property of spouses arises upon marriage. It arises in a *matrimonium nullum* too. However, it cannot arise in *non matrimonium* or between non-marital spouses.

This specific matrimonial property community is reserved for married spouses exclusively.

§2. The Extent of the Joint Property of Spouses

652. The joint property of spouses includes:[293]

Assets acquired by one or both spouses during their marriage. The law expressly makes separate provision for two specific cases of property forming part of the matrimonial property. Specifically, these are:

- profit from what belongs exclusively to one spouse, represented by the proceeds of such property after deduction of the costs incurred to obtain the profit. Thus, not all of the proceeds of the exclusive property, but only part of them, become part of the community property. In this respect, the Civil Code has brought about a change from the previous legislation, under which the entire income was included in the community property. Profits become part of the community property at the time they are due (§711(3) of the Civil Code). This solution is new and raises a number of interpretative issues, such as determining at what point in time the profit is earned, or determining over what period of time the costs incurred on the exclusive property should be taken into account;
- the spouse's share in a company or cooperative where the spouse became a partner in the company or a member of the cooperative during the marriage. An exception to this rule is where one spouse has acquired a share in a manner which, in accordance with §709(1) of the Civil Code, gives rise to his or her sole ownership (*see* below). The acquisition of a share does not give rise to the participation of the other spouse in the company or cooperative, except in the case of housing cooperatives (§§709(3) of the Civil Code). Therefore, although a share in a cooperative or a share in a company or shares are part of the community property, the rights attached to them in relation to the legal entity (participation) are exercised only by the spouse who acquired them and thus became a shareholder in the company or a member of the cooperative.

293. *Ibid.*, §709.

653. The following assets do not form part of the community property:

a. items serving the personal needs of one of the spouses, i.e., items which each spouse uses exclusively to satisfy his/her normal needs in life (e.g., clothing, personal hygiene items, mobile phones). It is not decisive when such items were acquired or what means were used to acquire them, i.e., whether the joint means belong to the community property or to the matrimonial property. The law limits personal effects to their purpose, not their value. Often, personal effects can be very valuable, and a significant part of the community property may be used to acquire them (e.g., a special wheelchair, rehabilitation aids for one of the spouses);
b. what only one spouse has acquired by gift, inheritance or bequest; however, gifts where both spouses are on the receiving end, as well as inheritances or bequests, if acquired jointly by the spouses during the marriage, will form part of the community property. It is always up to the donor or the testator to decide what intention to express in the gift deed or in the acquisition on death;
c. what one of the spouses has acquired as compensation for non-pecuniary damage to his or her natural rights, as this compensation is of a highly personal nature and is linked only to the person of one of the spouses, in particular compensation for damage to life (e.g., compensation for the spouse as a survivor after the death of his or her parents) and health (pain and suffering or compensation for impairment of social life), or claims relating to the protection of personality (e.g., monetary compensation for defamation);
d. what has been acquired by one of the spouses through a legal transaction relating to his or her sole property; sole property is everything acquired by one of the spouses before the marriage and everything excluded from the community property under the preceding and following points. If one of the spouses legally acts and disposes of such exclusively owned property, what he or she receives for such acts does not become part of the community property (e.g., sale of exclusively owned property where the purchase price received, even if it is property acquired during the marriage, is not part of the community property);
e. what one of the spouses has acquired by way of compensation for the damage, destruction or loss of his or her reserved property, the compensation being merely another form of previous exclusive property;
f. items issued to one of the spouses pursuant to the provisions on restitution, which were already provided for in the previous legislation (*see* §143(1)(a) of the Civil Code 1964). Since the process of re-establishment has been practically completed, the Civil Code only provides for the exclusion of property acquired by one spouse from restitution in transitional provisions (cf. §3040 of the Civil Code).

654. Debts assumed (not only incurred) during the marriage also form part of the community property (§710 of the Civil Code). The acquisition of a debt by assumption requires a joint free act of the spouses or an act of one of the spouses, on a contractual basis, exceptionally also by unilateral action.

Debts Not Forming Part of the Matrimonial Property

655. Debts that have not been assumed are not part of the community property. Debts which are involuntarily incurred by one of the spouses against his or her will or without his or her will do not form part of the matrimonial property.

656. For example, debts arising from obligations incurred during the marriage by a court or other authority (fines, late payment penalties, etc.), debts arising directly from the law (e.g., taxes) or obligations arising from a legally foreseeable event (e.g., the creation of an obligation to pay maintenance as a result of the birth of a child; cf. §732 of the Civil Code).

657. Neither are all debts incurred during the marriage included in the community property. The exclusion of certain debts assumed can be found in §710 of the Civil Code. The community property does not include:

a. debts assumed by only one spouse during the marriage without the consent of the other spouse; such debts belong exclusively to the spouse who assumed them. Failure to obtain the consent of the other spouse may consist either in knowing about the assumption of the debt and not knowingly consenting to it or in not knowing about the incurrence of the debt and not having been asked for consent;

An exception to the rule just mentioned is made for debts incurred by only one spouse without the consent of the other spouse, provided that the incurrence of such debt was related to the provision of the family's daily or ordinary needs. This traditional solution does not correspond to the requirements of everyday family life. Needs which arise regularly (almost) every day in the course of the family or family household or which are otherwise common to the family must be able to be met by each spouse alone without the consent of the other spouse. The other spouse is also bound by his or her conduct and the debt incurred as a result of the conduct will form part of the community property. This includes, in particular, the purchase of goods necessary for the family's normal or ongoing consumption (purchases of food, fuel, electricity, hygiene products, etc.), costs relating to the maintenance of the joint household, the jointly occupied premises, etc.;

b. debts assumed but relating to property belonging exclusively to one spouse; such debts belong exclusively to the spouse who owns the property exclusively to the extent that they exceed the profit from that property. The community property of the spouses shall, however, include debts to the extent of the profits derived from such property. The provision follows the aforementioned rule of §709(2) of the Civil Code. If no profit is made from the exclusive property, the debt does not become part of the community property and falls entirely within the exclusive property of the spouse that is the exclusive owner.

658. Almost all assets acquired during marriage, except for the cases as mentioned above, comprise joint property of spouses. All income of spouses arising from employment and business activities, income from capital assets, intellectual property rights, social allowances belong to the joint property of spouses.

Even the profit arising from property which is not a part of the joint property of the spouses, for example, rent from real property in exclusive ownership of one of the spouses, will be part of the joint property of spouses. This fact is sometimes felt as an injustice as liabilities related to the separate property of one of the spouses are his/her liabilities only.

As for insurance contract considerations, only recovery of damages for injuries arising from insurance will not be a part of the joint property under traditional interpretation.

Preferring existence of the joint property of spouses is also manifested by express presumption that unless proved otherwise, it shall apply that assets acquired and liabilities incurred during marriage comprise the joint property of the spouses.[294]

It is not decisive here to what extent one of the spouses participated in acquiring an item or a property. For the joint property to arise, it is not decisive whether the married spouses share a common household either. Only the legal existence of their marriage is decisive. The facts, as stated, may affect settlement of the joint property after its termination.

659. Donations between married spouses are significantly limited under law. A married spouse may accept the donation, while the other spouse may donate only an item which was in his/her own exclusive ownership before, for example, acquired before marriage.

If a husband purchases a dishwasher or a TV set as a Christmas present to his wife, it is no donation as the item will remain a part of the joint property. If he presented her with a fur coat, it will be an item serving the personal need of one of the spouses and as such excluded from joint property of the spouses. However, it is not a proper 'donation' but merely an act of common property handling.

If an item is purchased, using, even partially, the means belonging to the joint property of the spouses, this item will be part of the joint property too. The means as spent will be taken into account within the joint property settlement.

660. Assets which by their nature serve the personal needs of one of the spouses are traditionally in an exclusive use of one of the spouses too. This concerns, for example, clothing and jewels. The value of this property is not decisive. However, the fact that one of the spouses owns jewels of high value may have an effect on the joint property settlement.

661. Returning the property nationalized in the fifties inevitably manifested in resolving the question of whether this property returned also comprises the joint property. Even though similar conclusions could be arrived at by interpreting the original provisions of the Civil Code 1964, under the 1991 Amendment, it was stipulated expressly that the assets which were returned to one of the spouses who

---

294. *Ibid.*, §144.

had owned them prior to marriage or were handed to this spouse as the legal successor of their original owner, based on restitution legislation, are not part of the joint property of the spouses.

§3. Administration of the Joint Property of Spouses

662. If there is joint property to the extent provided by law, either spouse has equal rights and equal liabilities as any other co-owner, co-debtor or co-creditor, implying that the rights and liabilities are performed jointly with the other spouse.

663. Both spouses use and maintain jointly assets that form part of their joint property. Routine administration of assets which are part of the joint property of the spouses may be carried out by either of them. In other matters that cannot be considered ordinary (e.g., regular transfers of immovable property):

- the spouses act jointly, i.e., both spouses are on one side of the contract together;
- one spouse acts with the consent of the other spouse, provided that the consent is given by the non-acting spouse in relation to the acting spouse and not to the third party with whom the negotiations are carried out. In order to enhance the legal certainty of the third party, it is desirable that, where he enters into a contract with only one of the spouses, he should require confirmation of the consent of the other spouse.

664. Consent may be given before the legal transaction or afterwards.

665. While the act of one spouse without the consent of the other is valid, the spouse who has not given consent is left with the possibility of invoking its invalidity. This is a case of relative nullity. If consent is given after the legal act, this leads to the healing of a possible ground of nullity.

666. The consent of the spouse to the legal act may be replaced by a court decision (§714(2) of the Civil Code). This will be the case if the spouse has refused to give consent without serious reason and contrary to the interests of the spouses, the family or the family household, or if he or she is unable to express the will, e.g., due to a temporary mental disorder.

667. Both spouses are jointly and severally liable for everything that is part of their joint property.

Both spouses are entitled and liable jointly and severally in respect of acts in law relating to their joint property.[295]

The spouses' creditors may claim full consideration, or their part, jointly from both spouses or separately from each of them. Each of the spouses is liable for the entire debt by the time the creditor is fully satisfied.

---

295. *Ibid.*, §145.

668. The regulation of the possible satisfaction of the creditor in the enforcement of a judgment (execution) from the matrimonial property sub-state is set out in §§731 and 732 of the Civil Code; procedural rules can be found in particular in §262a of the Civil Procedure Code and §42 of the Enforcement Code. The possible satisfaction from the matrimonial property will depend on the debt in question, to whom the debt belongs and at what point in time the debt was incurred. The situations in question will differ in particular as to which assets can be used to satisfy the debt and, at the same time, to what extent, if any, the matrimonial property can be used to satisfy the debt. As an overview, the following situations may be mentioned:

a. Joint debts belonging to the community of property may be satisfied out of the community property of the spouses without further delay and at the same time out of the sole property of each spouse.
b. The exclusive debts of one spouse incurred during the community of property are to be satisfied primarily from his/her exclusive property. However, it is also possible (i.e., in particular, if the exclusive property is not available or insufficient) to affect the property belonging to the community of property of the spouses.

The extent to which the community property may be affected depends on whether such a debt was incurred by only one spouse with the knowledge and in accordance with the will of the other spouse or, on the contrary, against his or her will. If the debt was incurred against the will of the other spouse and the latter expressed his/her disagreement to the creditor without undue delay after becoming aware of the debt, the community property may (according to §732 of the Civil Code) be affected only to the extent that the debtor spouse's share would have been if the community property had been dissolved and settled according to §742 of the Civil Code (settlement according to the rules of §742 of the Civil Code). This rule is intended to protect the community property from being affected too much in the event of enforcement (execution). It should be noted that the community of property is not extinguished or actually settled here (it is only a hypothetical settlement). The non-debtor spouse is only given the possibility to defend, in the context of the pending enforcement proceedings, the notional 'half' of the matrimonial property that would have accrued to him/her if the court settlement had taken place at that moment. The part of the property that would have fallen to the debtor spouse in the event of a division of the matrimonial property may be affected. The remaining part still remains in the matrimonial property. The debtor spouse still retains the same rights over it; the community of property has neither been dissolved nor reduced.

The same limitation will also apply in the case of a debt of one spouse consisting of his/her obligation to pay maintenance and a debt resulting from an unlawful act of only one spouse (§732, second sentence of the Civil Code).

Procedurally, the situation is regulated in §262b(1) of the Civil Procedure Code (similarly in §55(1) of the Enforcement Code). In the part that is not to be affected, the enforcement of the judgment should be stopped at the request of the spouse concerned.

c. Debts incurred by only one spouse before the marriage should be satisfied in priority from the sole property of the debtor spouse. However, the recovery of assets belonging to the community of property is also admissible. However, the assets belonging to the community of property may be affected only to the extent of the debtor spouse's share if the community of property had been dissolved and settled in accordance with §742 of the Civil Code.

§4. Extinction of the Joint Property of Spouses and Its Settlement

I. Extinction of the Joint Property of Spouses

A. *Dissolution of the Community Property on the Termination of the Marriage*

669. The community property of the spouses is dissolved on:

a. death of one of the spouses (*see* §764 of the Civil Code);
b. the declaration of death of one of the spouses, with the same provisions as in the case of death;
c. dissolution of the marriage, where the community property ceases to exist at the moment the judgment of dissolution of marriage becomes final;
d. a change of sex, with the proviso that the provisions on the obligations and rights of divorced spouses apply *mutatis mutandis* to the rights and obligations of former spouses in the event of the division of the community property;
e. the annulment of the marriage, in which case the provisions on the obligations and rights of divorced spouses shall apply *mutatis mutandis* to the settlement.

B. *Dissolution of the Community Property During the Marriage*

670. The community property of the spouses shall be dissolved:

a. by a court ruling in criminal proceedings imposing a penalty of forfeiture of property, if a penalty of forfeiture of property is imposed on one (or both) of the spouses during the marriage (§66 of the Criminal Code); the marriage continues, and the community of property may subsequently be restored by a court ruling (§726 of the Civil Code);
b. by a declaration of bankruptcy, where the bankruptcy of the debtor spouse's property results in the dissolution of the community property, but the marriage continues to exist (§268(1) of the Insolvency Act, Act No. 182/2006 Coll.); no new community property may be created during the duration of the effects of the declaration of bankruptcy, even if the debtor enters into a new marriage;
c. approval of a debt relief by realization of the assets if the debt relief is not granted on the basis of a joint proposal of the spouses (§408 of the Insolvency Act).

671. Furthermore, the community of property may be dissolved. In particular, the following situations:

a. dissolution of the community property by court decision (§724(1) of the Civil Code);
b. negotiation of a separate property regime (§717(1) of the Civil Code);
c. the negotiation of a regime reserving the creation of the community of property on the date of dissolution of the marriage (§717(1) of the Civil Code) if this regime is negotiated during the existence of the community of property. In such a case, the arrangement will have similar effects to the separate property regime, with the proviso that the community of property will be re-established on the date of dissolution of the marriage.

II. The Joint Property of Spouses Settlement

672. As soon as the joint property becomes extinct, either during marriage or upon dissolution of marriage, it must be settled. Partial joint property settlement occurs in case the court had ruled upon reducing the joint property as much as the items being usual equipment of a common household, or a contract was made on reducing the joint property, excluding certain items from the joint property.

A. Settlement upon the Agreement of the Spouses

673. An agreement of the spouses on their joint property settlement must be in writing. If their joint property includes real estate, the agreement becomes effective when registered in the Land Register.[296]

674. There is an exception from the principle that the joint property may be settled only after dissolution of marriage: an option to make a joint property settlement agreement and an agreement on settlement of rights and obligations of a common dwelling related to a so-called agreed divorce. However, the agreement includes a suspensive condition, and the settlement will be effective only upon the day the divorce ruling comes into force.

675. The settlement agreement may involve only parts of the assets and liabilities from the joint property as extinct. The rest of the settlement may be ruled by the court if the spouses are unable to agree upon it.[297]

296. *Ibid.*, §1105.
297. Supreme Court Decision No. 22Cdo 1622/1998.

B. Settlement upon a Court Ruling

676. If a settlement is not reached by agreement, it will be effected by the court based on a petition filed by either spouse.

It is generally observed that Czech spouses are able to agree easily on settling assets of higher value (real estate, cars, etc.). Their agreement subsequently fails on trifles (typically books, the best family coffee set, almost worthless pictures, etc.) because either spouse may have had strong emotional bonds to these items. If both spouses are not reconciled with the divorce, their quarrels on joint property settlement are often very hard, resulting in long-lasting suits.

Lawsuits in joint property settlements are time-consuming and expensive. That is, in settling joint property of a large extent, if one of the spouses has carried out a number of business activities, the settlement is very difficult to be arrived at in respect of evidence to be presented in order to show what was part of the joint property upon the dissolution of the marriage. In settlement through court proceedings, the spouses tend to 'settle' their subjective injustices and to take revenge, and thus the resulting lawsuit can be lengthy and fails to arrive at any end.

677. Unlike settlement by agreement, when the spouses, consistent with the opinion prevailing, are not strictly bound by the rules of settlement as given by law, the court is bound to settle the joint property following the rules as given below:[298]

> The law provides in §742 of the Civil Code for basic rules which are intended to enable the courts to settle the property relations of spouses or former spouses as fairly as possible. The following must be observed:
>
> a. the equal size of the shares, i.e., the shares of both spouses in the property to be settled are to be equal (§742(1)(a) of the Civil Code), the equality of the shares, i.e. parity, being the starting point from which other rules applicable to the settlement of the matrimonial property may be departed from. The settlement may therefore result in a different amount of the settlement shares, i.e. disparity;
> b. reimbursement of what has been spent from the community property on the sole property of one of the spouses, i.e., each spouse is to reimburse what has been spent from the community property on his or her sole property; this is a set-off (§742(1)(b) of the Civil Code), where the court may take this obligation into account only if this fact is established in the course of the proceedings, i.e., in particular if it is proposed by one of the parties. No expenses of any kind should be set off, but exceptional expenses, in particular in relation to the overall level of the matrimonial property. The rule for determining the value of such expenditure for the purposes of the settlement is laid down in §742(2) of the Civil Code. The basic idea is based on the assumption that a considerable period of time may elapse

298. Civil Code §742.

between the expenditure of the marital property on the community property (as well as the exclusive marital property; see next point). For the purposes of the division of the matrimonial property, the value of the marital property spent on the community property is intended to reflect the change (increase – valorisation; decrease – reduction) in the value of the part of the property on which the expenditure was incurred. Therefore, the real amount of the expenditure does not have to be taken into account;

c. reimbursement of what has been spent from the sole property of one of the spouses on the community property, with the proviso that each spouse has the right to claim reimbursement of what he or she has spent from his or her sole property on the community property; this is a contribution (§742(1)(c) of the Civil Code). The investment of funds most often results in an increase in the matrimonial property or in the fact that the funds from the matrimonial property did not have to be used, although they would otherwise have been used (savings). This is the case, for example, where the funds used to acquire (purchase) items during the marriage were partly sole funds and partly joint funds. This may also be the case where the exclusive funds are used to preserve an existing asset of the matrimonial property (investment);
d. protection of dependent children, where the court must always take into account the needs of dependent children in the settlement (§742(1)(d) of the Civil Code). The criterion of the child's support or dependency is based on the child's readiness for future gainful employment and whether the child is capable of supporting himself or herself. The interests of a joint dependent child must be taken into account, in particular in a situation where the child is entrusted to the care of one of the spouses after the dissolution of the marriage. In cases of joint custody or alternate custody, the applicability of this rule is very limited. The rule under consideration leads primarily to the determination of which part of the property goes to a particular spouse;
e. the care of the family must also be taken into account by the court in the settlement, i.e. how each spouse took care of the family, in particular how he/she took care of the children and the family household. This is a criterion of merit (§742(1)(e) of the Civil Code). At the same time, the court should also take into account the fact that one of the spouses, however, did not care for the household at all; care for the children is primarily the provision of the child's basic needs (food, health care, etc.), education, control and supervision of the child, and the provision and organisation of the child's leisure time. Care for the family household is mainly the provision of the family's daily routine (shopping, food, maintenance of the common dwelling, etc.). This is a traditional rule, historically aimed mainly at protecting housewives who cared for minor children. It must be interpreted in conjunction with the rule laid down in §742(1)(f) of the Civil Code (see (f) below). One spouse's care for the family, the children and the family household is usually (or may be) compensated by the other spouse in the form of greater merit for the acquisition and maintenance of the assets belonging to the community property (although not always);

f. merit in the acquisition and maintenance of assets belonging to the community property (§742(1)(f) of the Civil Code); if there is a disproportion in the participation in the acquisition of assets belonging to the community property between the spouses, this may lead to a change in the size of the share of both spouses in the division of the community property, provided that this rule is always to be applied in accordance with the aforementioned family care considerations.

C. Settlement upon Presumption

678. If within three years of termination of the spouses' joint property no settlement has been reached, or if within three years of the said termination no petition to the court for the joint property settlement has been filed, the movable objects handled by the spouses will be deemed to have been settled consistent with the principle of using, namely, that each spouse will be deemed an owner of such things from the joint property which he/she uses exclusively to satisfy his/her own needs or the needs of his/her family and household. Other movable and immovable property objects will be deemed part of the apportioned co-ownership, the shares (ownership interests) of each of the co-owners being equal. The same will apply as appropriate to their joint property rights, assets and liabilities.[299]

Thus, joint property of spouses is settled directly under the law. Three years after a divorce ruling has become effective, neither of the spouses may bring a suit to have the joint property settled.

D. The Joint Property of Spouses Settlement in the Succession Proceedings

679. In the settlement of the community property of the spouses that has been extinguished by the death of one of the spouses, according to the basic provisions of §§736 to 742 of the Civil Code, §§764(1), 718(2) of the Civil Code and §§162 and 163 of the Special Proceedings Act must also be taken into account. The division of the matrimonial property community takes place in the context of the proceedings concerning the estate (pursuant to §764(1) of the Civil Code). Two methods of settlement are admissible.

680. The court, or rather a notary in the capacity of a court commissioner, may approve an agreement between the surviving spouse and the heirs on the settlement of the matrimonial property. Approval of the agreement is mandatory. The court must check that the legal limits of the settlement are complied with. The freedom of the surviving spouse and the heirs to shape the content of the agreement is not unlimited. Above all, the agreement must take account of the deceased spouse's previously expressed wishes. It must therefore not contradict the instructions given by

299. *Ibid.*, §741.

the testator during his lifetime, e.g., in a contract pursuant to §718(2) of the Civil Code, in a will or in a written declaration.

681. In the absence of an agreement, the court shall determine authoritatively, in accordance with the principles set out in the Civil Code, which of the community property belongs to the estate and which belongs exclusively to the surviving spouse and, where appropriate, determine the claim necessary to settle the community property (§163(2) of the Civil Code). The settlement of the property rights and obligations of the former spouses in the context of the succession proceedings is assessed primarily according to the property regime (agreed or established by a court decision) that existed between the spouses or, where applicable, according to the instructions given by the deceased spouse during his/her lifetime regarding his/her property in the event of death.

682. A specific situation with regard to the division of the matrimonial property after the death of one of the spouses is the case where the matrimonial property of the deceased and his or her spouse has been dissolved, extinguished or reduced during the deceased's lifetime and has not yet been divided at the time of death. Pursuant to §163 of the Special Proceedings Act, the right to its settlement belongs to the estate. In such a case, as in the previous legislation, the matrimonial property is not settled in the context of the succession proceedings.

Chapter 3. Conventional Matrimonial Regimes

683. Since 1 January 1992,[300] married spouses may determine the scope of their joint property by contract to an extent modified from that given under law. Since the entry into force of the new Civil Code in 2014, the range of contractual modifications of the matrimonial property has expanded.

684. The Civil Code provides for several possibilities of contractual modifications in the context of the regulation of the contractual matrimonial property regime. These are the separate property regime, the regime reserving the creation of the community of property on the date of dissolution of the marriage and the regime of extension or reduction of the scope of the community of property under the statutory regime. The regimes are broadly defined. Within each scheme, the spouses (fiancés) are given considerable freedom to design the content of the specific modification. At the same time, it is possible to agree on more than one regime simultaneously or successively. The contract may contain a combination of different property regimes.

§1. Separate Assets Regime

685. The possibility of negotiating a separate property regime is a novelty that was only introduced by the current Civil Code. When the previous legislation was in force, such an arrangement was prevented by the mandatory inclusion of the usual common household goods in the matrimonial property, i.e., the common property could only be narrowed down to the goods constituting the usual common household goods.

686. Although this is one of the possible contractual regimes of the matrimonial property, the separation does not, in fact, extinguish the matrimonial property, or does not arise at all, if this is agreed in the premarital agreement. If the separate property regime is established during the marriage, the existing community of property must be settled. If a separate property regime has been established, each spouse may dispose of his or her property without further action or without the consent of the other spouse pursuant to §729 of the Civil Code. Actions taken in this way will be valid and effective against the other spouse. If the spouses jointly run a business under the separate property regime, each spouse may be regarded as the entrepreneur, provided that the business is carried on jointly by both of them. If one of the spouses runs the business with the help of the other spouse, they primarily share the income on the basis of an agreement which must by law be in writing. In the absence of an agreement, the spouses divide the income equally.

300. Act No. 509/1991 Coll.

§2. REGIME RESERVING THE CREATION OF COMMUNITY PROPERTY AT THE DATE OF DISSOLUTION OF THE MARRIAGE

687. A regime reserving the creation of community of property at the date of dissolution of the marriage is directed primarily at the spouses who, by such an arrangement, exclude the creation of a community of property at the time of the marriage. Such an agreement may be concluded even during the marriage. However, it will result in the dissolution of the existing community of property and its division.

688. The postponement of the creation of the community of property allows each spouse to acquire and dispose of property independently during the marriage without regard to the other spouse. Any jointly acquired property falls under community of property. Debts assumed shall also be the sole burden of each spouse. At the time of the dissolution of the marriage (death or divorce), the matrimonial property is created, albeit largely only 'notionally' and for settlement purposes only. All assets and debts acquired during the marriage which fulfil the conditions for inclusion in the matrimonial property under the statutory regime and which are still part of the matrimonial property at the time of the dissolution of the marriage become part of the community of property at that moment. A settlement shall be effected in respect of all such components. No set-off shall be made in respect of what is no longer in the sole property of either spouse because he or she has consumed, destroyed, sold, donated, etc.

§3. REGIME FOR EXTENDING THE SCOPE OF THE COMMUNITY PROPERTY

689. A contract on the extension of the matrimonial property may be concluded by the spouses during the marriage or by the spouses before the marriage. In principle, the agreement can concern any asset and any debt. The subject of the agreement can be existing assets as well as future assets or debts. Usually, the community of property is extended to include the exclusive property held by one spouse before the marriage, items otherwise excluded from the community of property, e.g., gifts, inheritances.

690. If the matrimonial property is extended by an existing asset, that asset generally becomes part of it at the same time as the change of ownership would have occurred in the case of a transfer. If the agreement between the spouses on the matrimonial property regime concerns a pre-existing asset entered in a public register, the agreement in that part takes effect against third parties upon entry in that register. If it is a prenuptial agreement, its translational effects cannot take effect until the agreement itself, i.e., at the time of the marriage, has taken effect (§720(1) of the Civil Code).

§4. Regime for Narrowing the Scope of the Community Property

691. A contract on the reduction of the matrimonial property may be concluded by both spouses and fiancés. The reduction of the community of property may concern both components which already belong to the community of property and components (assets or liabilities) which are only to become part of the community of property in the future according to the statutory rules. If the agreement is concluded during the marriage and concerns the reduction of an existing part or several parts of the community property, a settlement must be made to the extent of the reduction.

692. The agreement on the matrimonial property regime must be concluded in the form of a public document, in particular a notarial deed (§3026(1) of the Civil Code). Any other arrangement in oral, tacit or written form which does not fulfil the characteristics of a public deed will be absolutely null and void or will not give rise to the consequences of a matrimonial property regime arrangement. The invalidity cannot be remedied even by an additional addition to the form.

693. Contracts on matrimonial property regimes are registered. This is primarily for the protection of third parties and at the same time for the possibility to take account of contractual changes in any proceedings (estate, execution). The current legislation establishes two types of registers kept by the Chamber of Notaries.

I. Registration of Documents on the Matrimonial Property Regime

694. This register (§35d of the Notary Act, Act No. 358/1992 Coll.) is a continuation of the former Central Register of Marriage Contracts, kept in electronic form by the Chamber of Notaries (from 1 July 2009 to 31 December 2013), whose data it took over.

695. Entry in the register of deeds on the matrimonial property regime is mandatory by law. It is carried out ex officio by the notary who drew up the contract or agreement by remote access. The aim is to make the record and preserve the data for any post-estate proceedings.

696. The register of deeds on matrimonial property regimes is not a public list. Third parties cannot consult the register, and the entry does not have any effect on them.

II. List of Instruments Relating to Matrimonial Property Regimes

697. This list is the second type of register (*see* §35j to 35l of the Notary Act). According to §721 of the Civil Code, it is a public list. However, it is a public list of a kind since it does not fulfil some of the characteristics that are envisaged for public lists (pursuant to §§980 et seq. of the Civil Code, i.e., in particular, it is not a list of assets and rights thereto, but a list of contractual arrangements, i.e., legal acts and court decisions).

698. Both contracts on matrimonial property regimes and judgments are registered in the list of documents on matrimonial property regimes. Again, the notary who drew up the contract makes the entry. However, the entry in the List of Deeds is made by the judge (unlike in the Register of Deeds on matrimonial property regimes) only if the matrimonial property regime contract so provides, otherwise on the basis of a written request of both spouses (in accordance with §721(1) of the Civil Code and §35k(1) of the Notary Act). Registration is optional.

699. The entry of the agreement on the matrimonial property regime in the public register has, unlike the registration of deeds on the matrimonial property regime, effects in relation to third parties (*erga omnes*) and can be invoked against third parties without further delay. It is irrelevant whether or not the third parties were aware of the contents of the contract or whether they actually knew of its existence.

700. Anyone must be able to make himself or herself aware of the existence of the entry in the Register of Deeds of the matrimonial property regime. This can be done at any notary public's office or by remote access in electronic form. The actual content of the contract can be ascertained from a copy of it, which can be made by any notary on request.

701. The additional importance of the entry in the Register of Deeds of the matrimonial property regime is also manifested in the context of enforcement of judgments or execution. Pursuant to §262a of the Civil Procedure Code (similarly §42 of the Enforcement Code), before ordering the enforcement of a judgment on the matrimonial property, the court shall ascertain whether the List of Deeds on the matrimonial property regime contains a contract on the matrimonial property regime or a court decision on the dissolution of the matrimonial property, its renewal or reduction of its existing scope, or an agreement or a court decision on the modification of the contractual regime or the regime established by a court decision. In ordering enforcement, the court shall base itself on the content of such documents.

702. If the agreement is not entered in the Register of Deeds on matrimonial property regimes, the third party must be made aware of the agreement; otherwise, it will be ineffective against him.

703. Persons to be married may similarly regulate their future property relationship during their marriage by a contract made in the form of a notarial record.[301]

704. A contractual arrangement of property regimes in the event of dissolution of the marriage (§718(2) of the Civil Code), which does not fall under any of the

301. Civil Code §143a(3).

above regimes, is to a large extent a different option. The scheme of the arrangement raises some doubts as to whether it is another type of contractual arrangement or not. Although this option is not provided for in the list of contractual regimes in §717 of the Civil Code, it is certainly a different option from the above-mentioned cases, leading to different consequences. The contract may apply to any of the cases of dissolution of marriage. In particular, it may be an arrangement governing the situation in the event of divorce and in the event of death.

III. Limits to the Autonomy of the Will in the Conclusion of Marriage Contracts

705. The law gives both spouses and fiancés a wide latitude to adjust their relations freely within the framework of the envisaged contractual regimes. However, the autonomy of the will is not completely unrestricted when contracting matrimonial property regimes. Limits are set in particular in the context of the protection of third parties or, where appropriate, the protection needs of the family. Restrictions on the contractual freedom of the spouses can be found in several places in the Civil Code, but also in other regulations, such as the Insolvency Act. Exceeding the limits entails various consequences. The following basic cases can be mentioned in summary.

A. *Prohibition of Interference with the Regulation on the Usual Equipment of the Family Home*

706. A matrimonial property regime agreement pursuant to §718(3) of the Civil Code may not exclude or modify the provisions on the usual furnishings of the family home (*see* §§698 and 699 of the Civil Code).

B. *Prohibition on the Exclusion of the Husband's Ability to Provide for His Family*

707. According to §719(1) of the Civil Code, the agreement on the matrimonial property regime must not substantially affect the ability of one spouse to provide for the family. It is sufficient if the contract has such negative consequences, but not necessarily directly. In particular, the loss or limitation of the spouse's ability to provide maintenance for the members of the family in the cases and to the extent provided for by law. A contract concluded in violation of this prohibition is relatively void (§580(1) of the Civil Code). An objection may be raised by the person whom the legislation is intended to protect, i.e., in particular the other spouse (*see* §586(1) of the Civil Code). However, if other statutory conditions are met, the agreement on the matrimonial property regime may be absolutely void, i.e., if it is manifestly contrary to good morals, contrary to the law and manifestly disturbing public order (*see* §588 of the Civil Code).

708. The above rules also apply to contractual modifications of the administration of the matrimonial property (§722(1) of the Civil Code).

C. Prohibition of Retroactive Contracts

709. The prohibition of retroactive effect of a contract is one of the basic elements of the protection of third parties. Arrangements which contravene this rule are disregarded (§716(1) of the Civil Code). Such arrangements would not produce any legal effects, as they would have to be regarded as apparent legal acts (§554 of the Civil Code).

D. Prohibition of Prejudice to the Rights of Third Parties

710. A third party is any person other than the spouses (in particular, a creditor) who may be affected by the contract. The scope of such persons will vary depending on the type of contractual regime involved and also on who concludes the contract, i.e., whether spouses or fiancés.

711. The agreement on matrimonial property regimes must not affect the rights of third parties by its content or purpose. It is therefore not the violation of such rights that is required, but only the mere prejudice, i.e., for example, making it more difficult or costly to exercise them.

712. If the content or purpose of the contract affects the rights of a third party, it is relatively ineffective in relation to that party. However, it remains valid and effective in relation to the unaffected person.

713. If the contractual arrangements of spouses or fiancés were never allowed to affect the rights of third parties, the contracts would operate only between the spouses themselves. This would limit the reasonableness of entering into contractual modifications as such. From the point of view of the possible prejudice to the rights of third parties and the effects of contractual arrangements on them, two basic situations must therefore be distinguished:

1. The right of the third party concerned arose before the contractual modification. In such a case, the contractual modification is effective against the third party only if he consents to it (§719(2) of the Civil Code). The consent itself may be given before or after the conclusion of the contract. Consent after the conclusion of the contract gives rise to the effects of the contract also with respect to the consenting person. The statutory requirement of active consent leaves it to the will of the third party whether or not he voluntarily waives the protection afforded by law against the conduct of the spouses or fiancés.
   If the third party does not consent, the deal remains ineffective against him. The ineffectiveness arises directly by operation of law if the above conditions are met. If more than one-third party is affected by the contract, the effects

against them may vary according to which of them has consented to the contract and which has not. However, the contract remains valid even if the consent of the third party concerned has not been given.
Section 733 of the Civil Code further strengthens the protection of the creditor's rights. If one of the spouses undertook the commitment at a time when less than six months had elapsed between the change or exclusion of the statutory property regime by a marriage contract or a court decision, the claim of his or her creditor may be satisfied out of whatever would have been part of the community property had the marriage contract or court decision not been made. It is irrelevant whether or not the contract affects the creditor's position. If a right of a third party (in particular a creditor) is affected by a marriage contract or a court decision which has modified or excluded the legal property regime, that third party may assert his or her right on the occasion of the settlement of what was previously part of the community property, just as if the marriage contract or court decision had not occurred (§734 of the Civil Code, with §742 of the Civil Code applying).

2. The right of the third party concerned arose after the contractual modification. The consent of the third party to the conclusion of the contract of modification can realistically only be required if the relationship between the spouses and the third party already exists at the time of the contractual modification. Even if a right (claim) of a third party against the spouses, or one of them, arises after the conclusion of the matrimonial agreement on the modification of the matrimonial property, it cannot be generalized that the previously concluded agreement is always effective against such a person. The third party must know that the statutory regime has been modified. Knowledge of the conclusion of the contractual regime by the third party arises if the contract is entered in the Register of Deeds on the matrimonial property regime (its existence no longer needs to be notified to the third party) or if it concerns an existing matter entered in a public register (e.g., the Land Registry) and if the entry in such register has been made and the third party has thus had the opportunity to discover the change from the register. The last possibility is that the third party has been made aware of the existence of the contract and its contents.

714. If these conditions are met, the contractual modification is effective against the third party regardless of his consent. This concept is also the basis for the provisions of §262a of the Civil Procedure Code and §42 of the Execution Code.

Regime Based on a Court Decision

715. The court-ordered regime is the third matrimonial property regime envisaged. As in the case of the contractual regime, it will usually be only a partial modification of the pre-existing matrimonial property regime, usually statutory. The possibility of judicial modification of the community of property is based on the idea that in a long-term relationship, which the community of property undoubtedly is, it should be possible for one spouse to make changes to the relationship even against the will of the other spouse, where agreement is not possible. It is clear that the relationship between two persons who have entered into a marriage may change over time, from the ability of the spouses to communicate with each other to the ability to live together. The spouses' assets, earning capacity, as well as their approach to the disposal of assets may change considerably. A number of these factors can be potentially very dangerous for the matrimonial assets of both spouses, often with significant spill-over effects after the eventual dissolution of the marriage. Each spouse therefore has the possibility, subject to the conditions set out below, to apply to the court for an authoritative decision to change the existing matrimonial property regime.

716. Interference by the State in the matrimonial property regime is always a generally undesirable option which can only be admitted on application and can only be justified where the interest in protecting the spouse seeking judicial adjustment is greater than the interest in not disturbing purely private relations by an authoritative decision of the State (court).

717. Court proceedings for the modification of the matrimonial property are adversarial proceedings. The action may be brought by either spouse. It is usually brought by the person whose protection the modification is intended to protect. However, the law does not prohibit the application from being brought by a spouse on whose side there are compelling reasons for the modification.

718. A court decision may:

a. dissolve the community of property (analogous to the contractual regime of separate property);
b. narrow the scope of the community of property (regardless of the existence of a community of property regime);
c. restore the community of property;
d. extend the scope of the community of property;
e. amend the rules on the administration of the community property.

719. These are options which are similar to some contractual regimes. However, unlike a possible contractual modification, a court decision cannot extend the community of property to assets belonging exclusively to one of the spouses or postpone the creation of the community of property to the date of dissolution of the marriage. Neither can the court's decision, on the application of only one of the spouses, modify the matrimonial property regime in the event of the dissolution of the marriage.

Part IV. The Law of Succession

Chapter 1. Legal Succession

720. A person may become an heir on the basis of three titles of inheritance, on the basis of a contract of inheritance, a will or by law. It is possible for a person to inherit from only one of these titles, but any combination or accumulation of more than one of these titles from one testator is also possible. In these cases, however, it is not possible for an heir to inherit from one title and refuse to inherit from another.

721. Competing succession titles may arise in the following cases:

a. The will or succession contract was validly made, but the testator (the settlor) did not make it in respect of his entire estate, so that succession by operation of law takes place in respect of the remainder.
b. If a will or succession contract has been validly made, but for some reason the called heir does not inherit, then succession by operation of law takes effect. An exception to this is where the testator calls a substitute heir to the contract or testamentary heir.

722. For the determination of the share of inheritance in the case of cumulative succession, the resulting share must be determined uniformly for each heir, i.e., not separately for intestate succession and intestate succession.[302]

723. A person may inherit exclusively from a will if the testator made a valid will in which he/she included all his/her assets. A person cannot inherit exclusively from a testamentary contract; the testator must always leave ¼ of the estate free, for either testate or intestate succession.

724. Exclusive legal succession occurs in the following cases:

a. The testator has not expressed his will in either the will or the succession contract, so that succession according to the statutory classes of succession takes place.

302. Supreme Court Case No. 21 Cdo 1517/2015.

b. The testator has made his will in a will or succession contract, but these are invalid.
c. The testator has made a valid will or succession agreement, but the heirs have predeceased the testator.

725. The law in force on the date of the deceased's death shall apply to the succession.[303] If the deceased died after the date of entry into force of the Civil Code, i.e., after 1 January 2014, and if his or her death grant contradicts the law in force at the time it was made, it is deemed valid if it complies with the current Civil Code.

726. The basic source of the legal regulation of inheritance with an international element is the Private International Law Act,[304] effective from 1 January 2014. However, its importance in the area of succession law has significantly decreased as a result of the adoption of Regulation 650/2012 of the European Parliament and of the Council[305] (the 'Regulation'). The 'Regulation' applies to the succession law of persons who died after 17 August 2015. The Regulation has priority of application and direct applicability in each EU State.

727. The international element that justifies the application of the Regulation may be:

- usual residence of the deceased abroad;
- foreign nationality of the deceased;
- part or all of the deceased's estate abroad.

728. The purpose of the Regulation is to simplify cross-border succession proceedings and to make it easier for the persons concerned to deal with the legal aspects of international succession proceedings by establishing uniform rules for determining the courts competent to hear the succession and for determining the law of succession to be applied. Where the jurisdiction of a court of a Member State to rule on a succession is established, it is established for the succession as a whole and covers all the property of the deceased (whatever its nature and location). Furthermore, in most cases, the applicable law is aligned with the law of the place where the succession takes place, and decisions given in one EU Member State are automatically recognized in all other Member States under the Regulation without the need for special proceedings. It also introduces a European Certificate of Succession, allowing the status and the resulting rights and obligations of an heir, legatee, executor or administrator of the estate to be proved in another EU Member State.

729. The general threshold determinant for determining the jurisdiction of the court to deal with the succession is the *habitual residence at the time of death*. The habitual residence is as follows:

303. Civil Code §3069.
304. Act No. 91/2012 Coll.
305. Regulation No. 650/2012 of the European Parliament and of the Council.

- A place which the person concerned has designated with the intention of giving it a permanent character.
- A place which is the permanent or usual centre of the person's interests.
- The assessment of the place of habitual residence must take into account all relevant aspects, such as the length of residence, regularity of residence or the reason for staying in the territory of a State.
- For so-called cross-border workers, the country of habitual residence can always be considered to be the country of origin, where the worker has family and a centre of interests.

730. Under §22 of the Regulation, any person may choose the law governing his succession as a whole, namely the law of the State of which he is a national at the time of that choice or at the time of his death.

731. An agreement on the choice of court is only possible under the following conditions:

- The testator has chosen during his lifetime the law to govern his succession as a whole, which may be only the law of the State of which the testator was a national at the time of the choice of law or at the time of death.
- The law chosen is the law of the Member State.
- The parties concerned agree in writing that the courts of that Member State shall have jurisdiction over the succession.

732. In certain cases, so-called subsidiary or residual jurisdiction may arise when jurisdiction cannot be established on the basis of habitual residence because the person is not present in the territory of any Member State. The court of the State in which the estate is located shall then have jurisdiction to rule on the succession if:

- the deceased was a national of that Member State at the time of his death;
- the habitual residence was in the territory of that Member State, provided that, at the time the proceedings were brought, no more than five years had elapsed since the change of habitual residence.

§1. Conditions of Succession

I. Death of the Testator

733. The right of inheritance arises on the death of the testator.[306] In the context of the succession proceedings, the court only confirms (declaratively) that someone has become an heir at the time of his/her death, or approves the agreement of the heirs on the size of the shares or the renunciation of the inheritance.[307]

306. Civil Code §1479.
307. Act on Special Court Proceedings.

734. The death of a person must be determined in the prescribed manner; i.e., it must be established by a doctor after the body has been examined (or the person is declared dead) and then a death certificate issued by the registry office.[308]

II. Declaration of Death

735. If the body of a deceased person cannot be examined in the prescribed manner, the court shall declare the person dead. The court shall decide even without a petition if the person was present at such an event that his death appears certain, and in the decision it shall fix the day which shall be deemed to be the day of his death.[309]

736. If a person may reasonably be presumed to be dead, but death does not appear to be certain (it is a mere presumption), the court may, on the application of a person who has a legal interest, declare that person dead. The decision shall specify the date which shall be deemed to be the date of death. A person declared dead shall be regarded as having died.[310]

§2. CHILD

I. Eligibility to Be an Heir

737. Any legal person, i.e., a person with the capacity to have rights and obligations, is eligible to be an heir. In this respect, natural and legal persons have equal status.

738. Just like a natural person, a legal person does not need to express his or her will in any way to become an heir. Of course, in the context of the succession proceedings, the legal person must be represented by its statutory body (or other representative).

739. An unborn child (*nasciturus*) also has the capacity to be an heir.[311] For example, if a husband dies while his wife is pregnant, it is necessary to wait until the child is born alive to become an heir. If it is not born alive, it is looked upon as if it had never been. Furthermore, the condition that the inheritance must be in accordance with the interests of the nascitura must be fulfilled, otherwise it will also be disregarded.

740. The court shall appoint a guardian in the proceedings concerning the estate in special cases, namely, to an heir who is unknown, to an heir whose residence is

308. Act No. 301/2000 Coll.
309. Civil Code §26.
310. *Ibid.*, §76.
311. *Ibid.*, §25.

unknown and to an heir who has failed to be served at the known address of his residence or place of abode or at the address of his domicile.

741. If the heir is unknown or has an unknown residence, but has been notified by the court of his right to inherit by a judicial decree and has not made himself known within the time limit, he shall not be taken into account in the consideration of the succession and neither his guardian may make a declaration of acceptance or refusal of the succession on his behalf.

742. If it turns out after the court has ruled that a person has acquired the inheritance, that someone else should have been the heir, then that heir has the obligatory right to demand that the person who has acquired the inheritance return it, according to the principles of unjust enrichment.

743. The unauthorized heir is entitled to reimbursement from the authorized heir of the reasonable expenses he has incurred in the succession and also to the proceeds of the succession. However, if he knew or should have known and could have known that someone else (or someone else) was the heir, then he is only entitled to reimbursement of the necessary expenses and is obliged to give the proceeds of the inheritance to the entitled heir.[312]

744. If a legal person is to become an heir, it must legally exist at the date of the deceased's death. A legal person may inherit only by virtue of the testator's will, not by operation of law.

745. The State, which is considered a legal person for the purposes of private law, may also become an heir by virtue of the testator's will. Furthermore, the State may acquire the succession as a caduucum. Disinheritance occurs if there is no heir according to the legal succession and there is no heir by will or by contract of succession. The State has no right to refuse an inheritance or bequest. It has the status of an heir who has reserved an inventory of the estate vis-à-vis other persons.[313]

II. Doubt in the Order of Death of Multiple Heirs

746. In case of doubt as to which person died earlier and which died later, the presumption is that all these people died at the same time.[314]

747. If spouses die at the same time, their community property must first be settled so that each of them can inherit.

748. However, it is sufficient for a person to become an heir if he survives the testator, even by a very short time.

312. *Ibid.*, §1000, §1001.
313. *Ibid.*, §1634.
314. *Ibid.*, §27.

III. Incapacity to Inherit

749. Certain deliberate acts of a person – the future heir – directed against the person or property of the testator or against certain persons close to the testator, which have damaged the relationship of the future heir to those persons, result in the incapacity of the person so acting.

750. Incapacity to inherit arises by operation of law and applies to all heirs, not only to non-nominative heirs, to heirs by operation of law, by contract of succession and by will.

751. If someone commits an act in the nature of a deliberate criminal offence against the testator, his ancestor, descendant or spouse, or a reprehensible act against the testator's will, in particular by forcing or deceiving the testator to make a will, by preventing the testator from making his will or by concealing, falsifying, forging or intentionally destroying his last will, unless the testator has expressly excused him from this act, he shall be excluded from the right of succession.[315]

752. It is irrelevant whether the person committed the act as the direct perpetrator, as the person who instigated or was an accomplice, or whether or not he or she was prosecuted and convicted for the act. The aim of the legislation in §1481 of the Civil Code is to punish not only persons who have committed a criminal offence, but also those who have committed the same offence, but for which they were not criminally liable, because they committed it at a time when they were either under the age of 15 and therefore not criminally liable, or were insane at the time of the offence, or were not convicted because they died, their criminal liability was time-barred, or a pardon or amnesty was granted.

753. The deceased's spouse, who committed an act that fulfils the characteristics of domestic violence against the deceased, is also considered to be ineligible as a legal heir. The condition for this incapacity is that, at the date of the testator's death, the divorce proceedings initiated at the testator's request[316] were pending.

754. Furthermore, a parent who has been deprived of parental responsibility because he or she has abused or seriously neglected the exercise of parental responsibility through his or her own fault is also incapable of inheriting. This parent is then excluded from the legal succession to the succession of his or her child.[317]

755. Incompatibility of succession is taken into account ex officio and even the heirs cannot agree to disregard it. The court is obliged under §20(1) of the Special Proceedings Act to ascertain all facts relevant to the decision.

---

315. *Ibid.*, §1481.
316. *Ibid.*, §1482(1).
317. *Ibid.*, §1482(2).

756. It follows from the nature of the incapacity to inherit that the act giving rise to the incapacity to inherit must have occurred during the lifetime of the testator, not after his death.

757. An incapable heir does not inherit and cannot acquire a legacy. If the ineligible heir is a non-minor heir, he is not entitled to a mandatory share (§1645 of the Civil Code), but he is taken into account for the purpose of calculating the mandatory shares of the other non-minor heirs.

758. A descendant of one who is disqualified from the right of inheritance takes his place in the legal succession, even if the incapacitated heir survives the deceased. This does not apply to a descendant of a parent who is incapacitated for abuse or neglect of parental responsibility (§1482(2) of the Civil Code).

759. A substitute may take the place of an incapable heir by contract or by will if he has been called by the testator.

760. Only the testator may expressly excuse the conduct constituting incapacity for succession from the future heir.[318] A prerequisite for express remission is that the testator knew about the act. The law does not prescribe the form in which the waiver is to be made. However, a written form, signed by the testator, in which the testator states that he or she forgives the act, may be recommended as a suitable form. It is essential that the act in question be specified. This remission may also be contained in the will or in a contract by which the heir is directly called upon to inherit.

761. Incompatibility of inheritance must be distinguished from disinheritance,[319] which includes only non-nominal heirs, i.e., descendants of the testator. The essence of disinheritance is the free act of the testator who, in a situation where his descendants behave in a way which the law anticipates in the form of the so-called grounds for disinheritance, decides to deprive him of part of the right to the obligatory share.

§3. Legal Succession

I. Classes of Heirs

762. Legal (intestate) heirs are divided into six classes of inheritance, depending on the degree of kinship or the existence of a certain qualified relationship to the testator.

763. The heirs are sorted into different inheritance classes. Their entitlement to inheritance varies according to the order in which they are placed in each class.

---

318. *Ibid.*, §1481.
319. *See* Part IV, Ch. 2, §6.

A. First Hereditary Class

764. The children of the deceased and the spouse, partner or registered partner inherit in the first class of inheritance, each of them equally.

765. If one of the children does not inherit, then his/her children (grandchildren of the testator) will receive the vacant share (in case of more than one child, the children will share equally).[320]

766. A direct descendant is a child in the first degree of the descending line. It is irrelevant whether the child was born within or outside marriage. Nor is it decisive whether the child was living in the same household as the deceased at the date of his death. The child of the deceased is the child she gave birth to. In the case of a male testator, it is important that he, as testator, bears witness to one of the presumptions of paternity in respect of the child to be inherited from him and, on that basis, is registered as the father of that child.

767. A child conceived (*nasciturus*) may also be an heir if it is in accordance with its interests and if it is born alive.

768. The increment of the vacated share shall be applied in the first class of succession among the heirs if one of the heirs of that class does not inherit and his vacated share accrues to another of the heirs of that class. If the deceased's spouse does not inherit because, for example, he has refused the inheritance or has lost his capacity to inherit, the accretion of the deceased's share of the deceased's share to the deceased's children always occurs. If, however, the testator's children do not inherit, then only the right of representation in favour of their children applies to them, not the accretion of the deceased's share in favour of the spouse (or registered partner).

769. If a particular child does not inherit, his or her children will acquire this released share equally.[321] If one of these children does not inherit, his descendants shall again acquire his vacated share.

770. The reasons why a child does not inherit may be: he/she has not survived the testator (so-called predeceased), is incapable of inheriting, has refused to inherit, has renounced inheritance, has been disinherited by the testator or is not taken into account (e.g., heirs of unknown residence).

771. The descendant always represents the person of the ancestor who would otherwise have inherited, but for the facts that led to the exclusion of his inheritance. Therefore, they may not inherit more than the ancestor they represent.

---

320. Civil Code §1635(1).
321. *Ibid.*, §1635(2).

772. If the testator was not married or in partnership or in a registered partnership at the time of his death and had descendants, the descendants become universal heirs in the first class of succession. The descendants of the deceased are also non-nominal heirs (herede necesarii).

773. A prerequisite for the surviving spouse to inherit is the existence of the marriage or partnership at the time of the deceased's marriage. The spouses do not necessarily have to have lived together or shared a common household or have maintained a community of property. Conversely, if they are an unmarried couple, they cannot be heirs in the first class of succession, regardless of whether children were born to them.

774. If there were community property of the testator and his/her spouse, either in the statutory or modified extent, it must first be settled in the context of the estate proceedings.[322] The half of the community property that belongs to the deceased spouse after the settlement and the sole property of that deceased spouse (testator) will be subject to inheritance.

775. For example, an estate that was community property and the testator was survived by two children. Half of the real estate will go to the surviving spouse by way of settlement of the community property extinguished by death and the other half will be subject to inheritance. If there is no agreement between the heirs, then each child will acquire his or her own one-sixth of the property and the surviving widow will own two-thirds of the property.

776. A surviving spouse, partner or registered partner may inherit in the first class of succession only if at least one descendant of the deceased inherits. Thus, neither the spouse, partner nor the registered partner can be exclusive (universal) heirs in the first class of succession. Thus, in the first class, a spouse, partner or registered partner can inherit at most half of the estate.

B. Second Inheritance Class

777. If there are no descendants, the following shall inherit in the second class of inheritance: the testator's spouse, the testator's partner, the testator's registered partner, the testator's parents and also those who lived in the same household with the testator for at least one year before his/her death and for this reason took care of the joint household or were dependent on the testator for maintenance.[323]

778. Heirs in the second class inherit equally, but the spouse, partner or registered partner always inherits at least half of the estate.[324]

322. Act on Special Court Proceedings No. 292/2013, §§162 et seq.
323. Civil Code §1636(1).
324. *Ibid.*, §1636(2).

779. If no other person inherits, then the spouse, partner or registered partner of the deceased may acquire the entire estate in the second succession class. The testator's parents and jointly called cohabitants may inherit equally the other half of the estate. The released share of the parents or the cohabitant will accrue to the remaining person in this category, but not to the share of the surviving spouse or civil partner.

780. Only the testator's own parents are considered to be the testator's parents, not his step-parents.

781. Adoptive parents inherit in the same way as biological parents, as the adoption establishes the same legal relationship between parents and children. Conversely, the biological parents of the adopted child will not inherit, since the adoption has ended the relationship of kinship between the child and the biological parents.

782. While the relationship of kinship, marriage or partnership is not open to doubt, a relationship based on the cohabitation of the deceased for more than one year with a person who cared for him or was dependent on him for maintenance is often difficult to prove. Cohabitation is not defined by the current Civil Code. Generally, to meet this legal requirement for inheritance, it is required that the persons live together permanently, together jointly to meet the costs of their daily needs. It is completely irrelevant whether these persons are related to each other. Cohabitation is, for example, represented by living in the same apartment (dwelling), or it is not strictly necessary. The temporary residence of a person in another place, for example, during military service or while studying, does not preclude the permanence of cohabitation. The courts consider such cohabitation to be permanent if it can be inferred from objective facts that the cohabitation is permanent and not merely temporary.[325] Therefore, occasional visits, occasional overnight stays in the apartment, occasional domestic help, etc., are not sufficient to satisfy the requirement of cohabitation.

783. A prerequisite for a share in the care of a shared household must be the payment of common expenses. This is a situation where certain persons manage their joint income without discrimination. The courts have held that it is not permissible for one person in a joint household to set up another joint household.[326]

784. As regards dependence on maintenance, this does not necessarily mean the fulfilment of a maintenance obligation arising from the Civil Code, but it is the maintenance which the testator actually provided to a person.

---

325. Supreme Court of the Czech Republic, dated 2 Apr. 2020, Case No. 24 Cdo 3958/2019.
326. *Ibid.*, dated 10 Oct. 2012, Case No. 21 Cdo 678/2011.

785. The conditions for inheritance in the second class may be met, for example, by an heir who lived with the testator in a non-marital (partner) relationship – e.g., a companion, a spouse or the testator's child in foster care or the child of the testator's spouse. A sibling, uncle or niece is also not excluded, provided they meet the above conditions.

786. So-called cohabitants cannot inherit in the second inheritance class alone, if the deceased's spouse or parents do not inherit, then the cohabitants pass to the third inheritance class.

C. Third Hereditary Class

787. If the deceased's spouse or registered partner does not inherit, the deceased's parents, siblings and those who lived in the same household with the deceased for at least one year and cared for the household or were dependent on the deceased for maintenance shall inherit equally in the third class.

788. If the testator's siblings did not inherit, their children would take their place equally.[327]

789. The testator's siblings are persons who have at least one parent in common with the testator, regardless of whether these siblings were born in or out of wedlock. If one of the siblings lived in the same household with the testator, this fact shall not entitle him to two shares of the inheritance, one as a cohabitant and the other as a sibling. In this case, only one share passes to the sibling. If the testator intended to give him an advantage over the other siblings, he should have done so by means of the last acquisition.

790. The principle of accretion of the inheritance share (the so-called accretion) is also applied in the third inheritance class, which means that if one of the heirs does not inherit here, his or her empty share accrues to the other heirs. This is always the case for cohabitants; for siblings, the right of representation prevails. If, for some reason, a sibling of the testator does not inherit, for example, because he has refused the inheritance or because he has predeceased the testator, his vacant share passes equally to his children, who are nephews and nieces in relation to the testator. The law speaks here of children, not descendants. For the grandchildren of the testator's siblings are not called in the third class of succession, but only in the sixth,[328] if they do not inherit any of the heirs in the third, fourth and fifth classes of succession.

327. Civil Code §1637(2).
328. *Ibid.* §1640.

791. For example, the testator left behind a cohabitant and a brother. His sister died, leaving two children (a nephew and a niece):

Founder

Brother (1/3) Predeceased sister **Person living with (1/3)**

Nephew (1/6) + Niece of the deceased (1/6)

792. The estate should be divided as follows: a person cohabiting with the deceased in his household for one year before his death – one-third of the estate, the deceased's brother one-third of the estate, a niece one-sixth of the estate and a nephew one-third of the estate.

D. Fourth Inheritance Class

793. If none of the heirs of the third class inherit, then in the fourth class of inheritance, the grandparents of the deceased inherit equally.

794. The fourth class of inheritance was introduced into the Czech legal system in January 1983, thus expanding the statutory inheritance compared to the previous legal system. The current Civil Code has taken over the legal regulation in part, the fourth inheritance class again calls equally the grandparents of the testator, but the grandparents' children, if any, do not inherit in this class; they are called only in the sixth inheritance class (*see* sixth class of heirs). Both sets of grandparents inherit equally in the fourth class; the law does not vary the size of the inheritance share according to the party from which the grandparent is related:[329]

Founder

The father of the deceased – not inheriting here The mother of the deceased – not inheriting here

Grandfather of the testator (1/4) Grandfather of the testator (1/4)

Grandmother of the deceased (1/4) Grandmother of the deceased (1/4)

E. Fifth Inheritance Class

795. If none of the heirs in the fourth class of inheritance inherit, i.e., if none of the testator's grandparents inherit, then the grandparents of the testator's parents in

329. SVOBODA, Jiří & Ondřej KLIČKA, *Inheritance Law in Practice*, Prague, C.H. Beck 2014. Legal practice. ISBN 978-80-7400-266-3. p. 106.

the fifth class of inheritance.[330] The grandparents of the testator's father inherit half of the inheritance, and the grandparents of the testator's mother inherit the other half. Both sets of grandparents will receive an equal share of the half that accrues to them:

Founder

Father of the deceased – does not inherit here Mother of the deceased – does not inherit here

Grandfather and grandmother of the testator Grandfather and grandmother of the testator

(i.e., father's parents) – do not inherit (i.e., mother's parents) – do not inherit

Who inherits

Grandparents of the deceased's parents (great-grandparents and great-grandmothers)

Grandfather's Father (1/8) Grandfather's Father (1/8)

Grandfather's Mother (1/8) Grandfather's Mother (1/8)

Grandma's father (1/8) Grandma's father (1/8)

Grandma's mother (1/8) Grandma's mother (1/8)

If a single member of the pair does not inherit, the vacant eighth goes to the other member of the pair:[331]

Founder

Father of the deceased – does not inherit Mother of the deceased – does not inherit

Parents of the testator's father – not heirs Parents of the testator's mother – not heirs

Who inherits

Grandparents of the deceased's parents (great-grandparents and great-grandmothers)

330. Civil Code §1639(1).
331. *Ibid.*, §1639(2).

Grandfather's father died **Grandfather's father (1/8)**

Grandfather's mother (1/4) Grandfather's mother (1/8)

Grandma's father (1/8) Grandma's father (1/8)

Grandma's Mother (1/8) Grandma's Mother (1/8)

The accrual of the vacated share of one of the couples is regulated in § 1639(2) as follows: if the couple does not inherit, the vacated quarter goes to the other couple of the same party:

Founder

Father of the deceased – does not inherit Mother of the deceased – does not inherit

Parents of the father of the deceased – does not inherit Parents of the mother of the deceased – not heirs here

Who inherits

Grandparents of the deceased's parents (great-grandparents)

Grandfather's father died **Grandfather's father (1/8)**

Grandfather's mother died **Grandfather's mother (1/8)**

Grandma's father (1/4) Grandma's father (1/8)

Grandmother's mother (1/4) Grandmother's mother (1/8)

If neither of the couples on the same side inherits, then half of the inheritance accrues to the couples on the other side in the same proportion as it accrues to them directly:

Founder

Father of the deceased – does not inherit Mother of the deceased – does not inherit

Parents of the testator's father – do not inherit Parents of the testator's mother – do not inherit

Who inherits

Grandparents of the deceased's parents (great-grandparents)

Grandfather's father died **Grandfather's father (1/4)**

Grandfather's mother died **Grandfather's mother (1/4)**

Grandma's father died **Grandma's father (1/4)**

Grandmother's mother died **Grandmother's mother (1/4)**

F. Sixth Hereditary Class

796. With effect from 1 January 2014, a sixth class of heirs was added to the Czech legal system. If none of the heirs of the above-mentioned fifth inheritance class inherit, then the children of the siblings' children (i.e., grandchildren of the siblings) and the children of the testator's grandparents (i.e., uncles and aunts of the testator) are called to inherit in the sixth class, each in equal shares:[332]

Founder

the father of the deceased does not inherit the mother of the deceased does not inherit

sibling of the deceased does not inherit (3rd class) paternal grandparents (4th class)

the sibling's child does not inherit here (3rd class) nor do the maternal grandparents (4th class)

they do not inherit here

Who inherits

Child of a sibling of the testator Child of grandparents Child of grandparents

grandchild of the deceased's sibling uncle, aunt uncle, aunt

332. *Ibid.*, §1640(1).

I.e., a great-nephew or great niece of the testator on the father's side on the mother's side

If one of the grandparents' children, i.e., uncles or aunts, did not inherit, then his children would inherit:[333]

Founder

Child of a child of a sibling of the testator Child of grandparents deceased

Child of grandparents

grandchild of a sibling uncle or aunt of the deceased sibling of the mother

Testator, i.e., great-nephew, on the side of the testator's father (uncle, aunt, a great-nephew) (1/3) in his place: the testator on the part of

Four children of a grandparent's child (1/3)

The heirs, i.e., cousins of the testator's cousin, each of them (1/12)

II. Set-Off: Collation

797. Anything that the heir received from the testator free of charge during his lifetime shall be included in his share of the inheritance, except for the usual gifts. What the heir's ancestors received from the testator shall also be included in the heir's share of the inheritance.

798. The Civil Code distinguishes between set-off for the obligatory share[334] and set-off for the inheritance share.[335]

799. When set off against the obligatory share, the non-nominal heir[336] is credited with what he or she actually acquired from the estate by bequest[337] or other provision of the testator (e.g., gift on death).[338]

800. In addition, the non-nominee heir shall be credited with the obligatory share for what he has received from the testator free of charge in the last three years before his death, unless the testator has expressly ordered (in his will, contract of succession, etc.) that the credit be made for a longer period.

333. *Ibid.*, §1640(2).
334. *Ibid.*, §§1660 and 1661.
335. *Ibid.*, §1662.
336. *Ibid.*, §1492.
337. *Ibid.*, §1594.
338. *Ibid.*, §2063.

801. A non-nominee heir shall be credited with the compulsory share of what he received from the testator during his lifetime for relief relating to the costs of setting up an independent household, marital or family life or starting a business. Credit may also be given for what the testator used to pay the debts of an adult descendant. These values will be set off even if the transfer took place earlier than three years before the testator's death, unless the testator has expressed a contrary wish (in a specific death provision).

802. The set-off against the share of inheritance pursuant to §1662 of the Civil Code shall be carried out in the same way as the set-off against the obligatory share. However, the heirs (both by will and by intestacy and by operation of law) shall be set off against the share of the estate only if the testator has so ordered, by an expression of his will made in the form prescribed for a will.[339] The only exceptions are where the children of the deceased's children or their descendants inherit instead of them and where they would be unduly disadvantaged. In such cases, set-off against the share of the estate shall be made without the testator's express order.

803. For the purpose of setting off the gift against the inheritance share or obligatory share, the price of the gift is based on the price at which the gift could have been sold in the place at the time of the gift.[340] In exceptional cases, the court may take into account a different price than that which the property was worth at the time the title to it was acquired.[341]

804. Example of a credit for inheritance share. The testator left behind three children. The total value of the estate is CZK 900,000. However, he gave one of the children the sum of CZK 300,000 during his lifetime to help him start his married life. For the calculation of the credit, the value of the estate and the value of the gift are added: CZK 900,000 and CZK 300,000, which is CZK 1,200,000. This amount is divided by three, which would mean that each of the three children should have received CZK 400,000. However, the one of the children who already received CZK 300,000 during his lifetime will have that amount set off against his share and will therefore receive only CZK 100,000 (400,000–300,000), and the remaining amount will be shared equally by the other two children. Each will therefore receive CZK 400,000.

805. The same calculation would apply if one of the co-heirs had been bequeathed something extra from the estate by the testator, for example.

806. However, set-off against the share of inheritance never implies that an heir who received something from the testator during his lifetime is obliged to give anything to the other heirs after his death.

---

339. *Ibid.*, §1663.
340. Regional Court in Hradec Králové, Case No. 17 Co 57/2002 of 7.8.2009.
341. Supreme Court in Brno, Case No. 21 Cdo 1939/2013 of 13.3.2015.

III. Special Types of Succession

807. Certain rights in rem which belonged to a person are subject to a special succession regime or are subject to inheritance only after special conditions have been met. Thus, wage and salary rights,[342] a cooperative share in a housing cooperative,[343] if held in community of property, pension insurance benefits,[344] sickness insurance benefits[345] and pension savings[346] are not subject to succession. In addition, the insurance,[347] if the insured's death is the insured event, and the lease of a flat[348] also has special regulations for the transfer of rights after death.

808. The transfer of wage and salary rights of an employee (the testator) is a special case of succession. Upon the death of the employee (deceased), the wage and salary entitlements up to three times the average monthly earnings of the employee (deceased) shall pass successively to his/her spouse, children and parents if they were living in the same household at the time of death. If there are no such persons, these rights are also subject to inheritance.

809. The lease of an apartment is another special form of succession. If the tenant dies, if it is not a joint tenancy, then the tenancy passes to the members of the tenant's household who were living in the flat at the date of the tenant's death and do not own the flat. If that person is someone other than the tenant's spouse, partner, parent, sibling, son-in-law, daughter-in-law, child or grandchild, the tenancy shall only pass to that person if the landlord has agreed to the transfer of the tenancy to that person.

810. The lease of the apartment after the transfer of the lease will then expire no later than two years from the date on which the lease was transferred. The exceptions are where the person to whom the tenancy has been transferred has reached the age of 70 on the date of transfer and where the person to whom the tenancy has been transferred was under eighteen on the date of transfer (for this person the tenancy will end at the age of 20 at the latest, unless otherwise agreed with the landlord).[349]

811. If more than one person meets the conditions for the transfer of the lease, the lease passes to them jointly and severally.[350]

812. Each person to whom the lease has passed has the right to notify the landlord within one month that he or she will not continue the lease.

342. Labour Code No. 262/2006 Coll., §328 (1).
343. Civil Code §732(2).
344. Pension Insurance Act, No. 155/1995 Coll., §63.
345. Sickness Insurance Act, No. 187/2006 Coll., §51.
346. Act on Supplementary Pension Savings, No. 329/2011 Coll., §24 and §25.
347. Civil Code §2829.
348. *Ibid.*, §2279.
349. *Ibid.*, §2279(2).
350. *Ibid.*, §2279(3).

813. The tenant's descendant has the right of first refusal. If there are more than one descendant, each may separately declare that he or she does not want to continue the tenancy.[351]

814. Only if the lease does not pass to any of the above persons will it pass to the tenant's heirs. Persons living in the same household with the tenant until his death are jointly and severally liable with that heir for debts incurred before the death of the tenant.[352]

IV. Adoption

815. By adopting, the adopted child becomes a member of the adoptive family and enjoys all the rights and obligations in the same way as a biological child. The rights and obligations of the original family cease to exist absolutely as a result of an irrevocable adoption.[353] For this reason, the adopted child will also inherit from his/her adoptive parent and will have the position of an irrevocable heir after him/her. The right of the adopted child to inherit from his/her biological family shall cease as a result of the adoption. The same applies in the event of the death of the adopted child, the adoptive parents are the eventual heirs, not the biological parents.

§4. Right of the State to the Death of a Person (Bona Vacantia)

816. The State can acquire the property of the deceased in two ways. The first is that the testator makes a valid last acquisition in favour of the State. In this case, the State has exactly the same position as any other heir, with regard to §21 of the Civil Code, according to which the State is considered a legal person of private law in private law relations, unless a special regulation provides otherwise.

817. The state, or the Office of State Representation in Property Matters,[354] has the option to propose the liquidation of the estate, but only if the estate is found to be over-indebted.[355]

818. The second way in which the State acquires the estate of the deceased is when there is no contractual, testamentary or legal heir.[356] Then the inheritance goes to the State and the State is regarded as if it were the legal heir. However, it does not have the right to refuse the inheritance or the right of bequest. In relation to any

351. *Ibid.*, §2280.
352. *Ibid.*, §2282.
353. *Ibid.*, §794.
354. Act No. 201/2002 Coll., on the Office for State Representation in Property Matters.
355. Act on Special Court Proceedings, §195.
356. Civil Code §1634(1).

obligation to pay the debts of the deceased to his creditors, the State is in the position of an heir who has reserved an inventory of the estate; i.e., it will only be obliged to pay debts up to the amount of the assets listed in the inventory.[357]

819. The state, or the Office of State Representation in Property Matters,[358] has the option to propose the liquidation of the estate, but only if the estate is found to be over-indebted.[359]

820. In the liquidation of the estate, the court shall invite the creditors to submit their claims within the time limit set by the court and shall also instruct the creditors that if the debts are not settled in the liquidation, they will be extinguished. The liquidation of the estate shall be completed by the distribution of the assets among the creditors according to the order and type of their claims.

A prerequisite for ordering the liquidation of the estate is that it is over-indebted and that an order has been made determining the over-indebtedness of the estate of the deceased.[360]

357. *Ibid.,* §1634(2).
358. Act No. 201/2002 Coll., on the Office for State Representation in Property Matters.
359. Act on Special Court Proceedings (§195).
360. *Ibid.,* (§180).

Chapter 2. Testamentary Succession

§1. Capacity to Make a Will

821. The Civil Code defines a will as a revocable expression of intent by which the testator, in the event of his or her death, personally bequeaths to one or more persons at least a share in the estate or a legacy.[361]

822. A will is a truly personal legal act of the testator. It must therefore be made by the testator himself and he cannot be represented by anyone. The testator may change or revoke the will at any time during his or her lifetime.

823. The will must comply with both the general requirements of the Civil Code for the creation and validity of a legal act,[362] and the provisions on acquisition in the event of death,[363] including the legal regulation of wills.[364]

824. The reason for these stricter requirements is the fact that the will only takes effect at the time of the testator's death and is therefore no longer able to confirm whether the will contains the testator's true and genuine last will.

825. The capacity to make all last acquisitions (*see* below), including wills, is the same as the moment of acquiring full capacity. However, the Civil Code provides for the following exceptions. If a person has reached the age of 15 and has not yet acquired full legal capacity, he or she may make a last acquisition without the consent of the legal representative by means of a public deed.[365] A person who has been limited in his or her legal capacity by a court order and is not competent to make an acquisition may nevertheless make a valid acquisition in any form if he or she has recovered to the extent that he or she is able to express his or her own will.[366] The Civil Code thus places the actual state of a person's health above the court's decision, assumes that legal acts are to be viewed as valid rather than invalid[367] and the interpretation of the last acquisition is to go as far as possible towards the will of the testator.

826. A person who has been restricted may make a last acquisition, i.e., a will, but only in the form of a public deed and within his or her restrictions.[368] If the reason for the restriction was a morbid addiction to the use of alcohol, the use of psychotropic substances or similar preparations or poisons, or for a morbid addiction to the passion of gambling, he may make a will in any prescribed form within his restriction, but only for one-half of his estate. The other half, for their protection,

361. Civil Code §1494(1).
362. *Ibid.*, §§545 et seq.
363. *Ibid.*, §§1491–1493.
364. *Ibid.*, §§1494 et seq.
365. *Ibid.*, §1524.
366. *Ibid.*, §1527.
367. *Ibid.*, §574.
368. *Ibid.*, §1528(1).

shall go to the legal heirs. Only in the event of there being no legal heirs, the testator in question may then make a will for the whole of his estate.[369]

827. Problems with the assessment of full capacity usually arise for the elderly and infirm, whose mental health is often compromised by old age and mental illness. It is difficult to assess whether their expressed wishes are genuine and free and whether they have been made under duress. In the event of coercion to draw up a last will and testament during the testator's lifetime, the provision of the Civil Code could be invoked, according to which the person who has performed a legal act under duress is entitled to challenge that act.[370] However, after the death of the deceased, when the effects of the will have already taken effect, this will obviously not be possible. In the event of physical violence negating the testator's will completely, the last acquisition could be considered as apparent and therefore non-existent from the outset.[371]

828. Certain protective restrictions limit the testator's ability to make a last acquisition during the time he or she spends in a healthcare facility or in a facility that provides social services or otherwise provides such services to him or her. During this period, the testator cannot call as heir a person or legatee (*see* below reference) who manages or is employed by or otherwise acts in such a facility. The only way of breaking this restriction is by an acquisition in favour of such persons made in the form of a public deed. If the testator could easily have made an acquisition in the form of a public deed after leaving the care of such facilities, then the rule does not apply as regards the invalidity of a will or a[372] will (*see* below).

829. The testators' capacity to make the last acquisition may be partly complicated by the fact that the testator is blind or deaf. For this case, a special allographic form of will is prescribed, or the possibility is given to make a will in the form of a public deed.[373]

§2. Different Types of Wills

830. In the Czech legal system, a will always requires a written form, unless it is a so-called will with exemptions, which was introduced by the Civil Code No. 89/2012 Coll., as of 1 January 2014. The legal provisions concerning the content and form of the will are a prerequisite for the validity of the will. A will that does not comply with the formal conditions would be invalid.

831. The Civil Code has extended the autonomy of the will with regard to the obligation to include a date in the will. Previously, the will would have been invalid.

369. *Ibid.,* §1528 (2).
370. *Ibid.,* §587.
371. *Ibid.,* §551.
372. *Ibid.,* §1493.
373. *Ibid.,* §§1535 to 1536.

In the current Czech legal system, a will is only invalid in the absence of a date if the testator has made several wills which contradict each other or if the legal effects of the will otherwise depend on the time of its making.[374] The time (date) at which the will was made is important, *inter alia*, for assessing whether the testator was competent to make the will at that time.

832. The interpretation of wills is regulated by the Civil Code in §1494(2), specifically on the rules of interpretation for legal actions.[375] The will must be interpreted in such a way as to comply as far as possible with the will of the testator. The words used by the testator in the will must be interpreted according to their general meaning. However, if it is shown that the testator was accustomed to associate his own meaning with certain expressions, this special interpretation shall prevail.[376]

833. The Civil Code regulates the following four types of wills:

a. Will written in the testator's own handwriting (so-called holographic will §1533 of the Civil Code).
b. Wills not made by the testator's own hand (so-called allographic general §1534 of the Civil Code), which also includes the will of a blind testator or a testator with other sensory disabilities (so-called allographic special §§1535 and 1536 of the Civil Code).
c. Will made by a public deed (§1537 of the Civil Code), i.e., by notarial deed (§3026/2 of the Civil Code).
d. Wills with reliefs (§1542 to §1549 of the Civil Code).

I. Handwritten (Holographic) Will

834. The law requires that the will be made in the testator's own handwriting; otherwise, it will be invalid. This will must be made in full in the testator's own handwriting and signed.[377] For example, a person who normally writes with his right hand and has a broken hand may write the will with his left hand or vice versa. Even if it is not the testator's usual handwriting, it is the handwriting that he or she has made. Quite exceptional situations may also be admitted where the testator is, for example, handless and has therefore learned to write with his mouth or feet. However, no one may guide the testator's hand or otherwise physically assist him in writing. This would no longer be his distinctive handwriting, and the will would then be invalid.[378] A will can be on any surface, the most common being paper, but not excluding, for example, cloth.

374. *Ibid.*, §1494.
375. *Ibid.*, §§555 et seq.
376. *Ibid.*, §1494(2).
377. *Ibid.*, §§1534 and 1535.
378. Judgment of the Supreme Court of the Czech Republic, Case No. 21 Cdo 1744/2007, dated 3 Apr. 2008.

835. Signature is another condition for the validity of this will. The signature should include at least the surname if there is no doubt about the identity of the testator.[379] However, the words 'your father' or 'your mother' are not considered to be a signature. In accordance with §79(1) of the Civil Code, the testator may also sign the will under a pseudonym if there is no doubt as to his identity.

836. The testator may keep the handwritten will with himself or with another person, or he may deposit it with a notary. In 2001, pursuant to §35a(1) of the Notarial Code,[380] the Central Register of Wills was established, maintained by the Notary Chamber of the Czech Republic. In this register were registered wills, deeds of disinheritance and deeds of revocation of these acts, which were drawn up by notarial deed or received by a notary for safekeeping. As of 1 January 2014, this register was renamed the Register of Legal Acts in the Event of Death. Pursuant to §35b(1) and (2) of the Notarial Code,[381] in addition to wills, wills, contracts of inheritance, declarations of disinheritance and declarations that the heir entitled to the legal succession will not acquire the estate, orders for set-off against the share of inheritance, the appointment of an administrator of the estate, contracts for waiver of the right of inheritance, as well as deeds cancelling these legal acts are registered here. In the Regulation of the Chamber of Notaries on the Registration of Legal Acts in Case of Death, it is specified what the notary must write regarding the person of the deceased or the deed he either acquires or receives for safekeeping.[382] These are the name, surname and date of birth of the deceased, his/her birth number and permanent residence or other domicile. Then, the designation of the instrument, the date of its execution (if stated in the instrument), the common number of the list of deeds for legal actions in the event of death, the name, surname and address of the notary with whom the instrument is deposited.

II. Unwritten Will in the Testator's Own Handwriting (So-Called Allographic)

837. It is a will that was not written by the testator's own hand, but, e.g., on a typewriter, today probably most often on a computer, or written by a person different from the testator. The law recognizes two forms of allographic wills, namely general and special. Special is for those who have some sensory impairment.

838. In the case of a general allographic will, it must be signed by the testator in his or her own handwriting. The law prescribes that it be signed before two witnesses present at the same time, before whom the testator expressly declares that the instrument contains the expression of his last will.[383]

379. *Ibid.*, Case No. 4Cz 82/82, dated 27 Jan. 1983.
380. Act No. 358/1992 Coll.
381. *Ibid.*
382. Regulation of the Notary Chamber of the Czech Republic on the Register of Recent Acquisitions, §4(1).
383. Civil Code §1534.

839. The Civil Code does not prescribe that the witness must be familiar with the contents of the will or that he or she must read or write it. Witnesses merely certify by their signature that they were present when the testator declared that the instrument contained his will. The witnesses shall be present at the making of the will in such a way that they are able to confirm that the testator and the maker of the will are one and the same person. The witness shall sign the document and, as a general rule, add a clause indicating that he is a witness and giving details by which his identity can be ascertained.[384]

840. The law prescribes stricter conditions for persons who are unable to read or write, even if their inability is only temporary.

841. The blind person makes a will in front of three witnesses present at the same time in a document that must be read aloud by a witness who did not write the will. The will shall be read aloud by the witness who did not make the will. The testator shall certify before the witnesses that this instrument contains his last will and testament.[385]

842. If the testator is a person with a sensory disability,[386] which prevents him from reading or writing, he must make his last will and testament before three witnesses present at the same time in a document, the contents of which must be interpreted in a special mode of communication chosen by the testator by a witness who was not the writer of the will. It shall be a condition of this arrangement that all the witnesses present are familiar with the chosen mode of communication. By this chosen method, the testator shall make it clear that the instrument contains the expression of his last will.

843. In a will made by a person with a sensory disability, it is necessary to state that the testator cannot read or write, the name of the writer of the will, the reader or interpreter of the will and the manner in which the testator confirmed his will and the manner of communication chosen when making the will.[387] However, if this method of making the will was chosen by a person without sensory impairment, then the will is invalid.[388]

844. Only a person who is fully competent, who knows the language in which the last will is written or who understands the manner in which the testator communicates in the last will may be a witness. A witness may not be a person close to the testator or the heir or legatee,[389] nor an employee of the heir or legatee.[390]

---

384. *Ibid.*, §1539.
385. *Ibid.*, §1535(1).
386. Act No. 155/1998 Coll., on Communication Systems for the Deaf and Deaf-Blind (2).
387. Civil Code §1536.
388. Judgment of the Supreme Court of the Czech Republic, 21 Cdo 2230/2006, dated 24 Oct. 2006.
389. Civil Code §22.
390. *Ibid.*, §1540(1).

845. If the testator had called any of the above persons by will as heirs (or legatees), the will would need to be handwritten or witnessed by three witnesses.[391]

III. Will Made by Notarial Deed (Public Deed)

846. A will can also be made in the form of a public deed.[392] Public deed means a notarial record.[393] The notary who makes the will is obliged by law to satisfy himself that the testator's will is made with discretion, in good faith and without compulsion.[394]

847. According to the Notarial Regulations, the notarial record of the legal act of the grantor must contain the following elements:[395]

a. Place, day, month and year of legal action.
b. Name, surname of the notary and his/her seat.
c. Name, surname, residence and date of birth of the participant, witnesses, confidant and interpreter.
d. Declaration of the participant on his/her legal capacity to act within the scope of the legal act for which the notarial record is made.
e. Proof of the identity of the party, witnesses, confidant, interpreter or that the notary knows them personally.
f. Content of the legal action.
g. Indication that the notarial deed has been approved by the participant after reading.
h. Signatures of the participant, witnesses, confidant and interpreter.
i. Notary's official stamp and signature.
j. Other particulars, if provided for in the notarial rules.

848. In the following cases, the form of notarial deed for the last acquisition is compulsorily prescribed:

- In cases where the testator cannot make his own mark on the instrument.[396]
- The person has reached the age of 15 but has not yet acquired full legal capacity.[397]
- A person who has been restricted in his or her legal capacity shall acquire, within the framework of his or her restriction.[398]
- If the testator establishes a foundation by the last acquisition.[399]

---

391. *Ibid.*, §1540(2).
392. *Ibid.*, §1537.
393. *Ibid.*, §3026(2).
394. *Ibid.*, §1538.
395. Notarial Code §63(1).
396. Civil Code §563.
397. *Ibid.*, §1526.
398. *Ibid.*, §1528(1).
399. *Ibid.*, §309(1), (4).

– If the testator establishes an institution by the last acquisition.[400]
– If the last acquisition is made by illiterate persons who cannot read or write because they cannot.

IV. Will Made with Concessions (So-Called Privileged Will)

849. As of 1 January 2014, a type of will with concessions, the so-called privileged will, returned to the Czech legal system. In this extraordinary way, the testator can only make a will in case of death if he or she is in a serious situation that threatens his or her life. The concessions consist in waiving the strict formal requirements for the ordinary types of wills and, for example, for witnesses.

850. The Civil Code provides for the following forms of wills with reliefs:

– Oral last taken before three witnesses present at the same time.[401]
– The last acquisition recorded by the mayor of the village.[402]
– The last acquisition recorded by the commander of a naval vessel or aircraft.[403]
– Last acquisition recorded by the commander of a military unit of the Czech Republic.[404]

851. A testator may make a will orally before three witnesses present at the same time if he or she is in obvious and immediate danger of his or her life because of a sudden event or if he or she is in a place where social intercourse is impaired as a result of an emergency. The first situation may be caused, for example, by a sudden heart attack of the testator or a serious injury and the second by a natural event such as a tornado or flood. A condition of such a will is that the testator cannot fairly be required to make a will in any other form. Witnesses either make a record of the testator's will thus orally expressed or make a statement orally on the court record.[405]

852. If there is a reasonable apprehension that the testator will die before making a public will, the mayor of the municipality in whose territory the testator is located shall record his will. The presence of two witnesses shall be a condition. Instead of the mayor, any other person who is authorized under special regulations to exercise the powers of the mayor[406] may record the will of the testator. The municipality is obliged to deposit the testator's will so recorded with the notary without undue delay.

---

400. *Ibid.*, §418.
401. *Ibid.*, §1542.
402. *Ibid.*, §1543.
403. *Ibid.*, §1544.
404. *Ibid.*, §1545.
405. *Ibid.*, §1542(2).
406. *Ibid.*, §1543.

853. On board a sea vessel flying the flag of the Czech Republic or an aircraft registered in the Air Register of the Czech Republic, the commander of the vessel or aircraft, or their representative, may record the will of the testator, always in the presence of two witnesses. However, the law allows this possibility only if the master of the vessel or aircraft is not prevented from doing so by the safety of navigation or flight. The master of the vessel or aircraft shall record the will in the logbook and, after the completion of the voyage or flight, shall forward the will without delay to the embassy of the Czech Republic nearest to the place of landing or arrival. The representative office shall without undue delay arrange for the will to be deposited with a notary.[407]

854. In the event of the testator being involved in an armed conflict, his will may be recorded in the presence of two witnesses by a soldier of the rank of officer or above. If the will was made in this way, its validity cannot be contested. The commander shall, without undue delay, hand over the will to the Ministry of Defence of the Czech Republic, which shall again without undue delay arrange for it to be deposited with a notary.

855. In common with wills with reliefs, the following specifics apply:

- Persons who have attained the age of 15 years or persons who have limited legal capacity may also be witnesses to wills with dispensations, provided that they are able to give a reliable account of the facts relevant to the validity of the will.[408]
- A will with concessions is not invalidated if the testator or a witness did not sign the document because he or she could not write or because of some other serious impediment if the will so states.
- If the testator is alive, a will made under §1545 of the Civil Code ceases to be valid after two weeks and wills made under §§1543, 1544 and 1545 of the Civil Code after three months from the date of making (these periods do not start to run, however, if the testator cannot make a public deed).[409]

§3. Joint Will

856. Czech law does not provide for joint wills, even for spouses or partners. A will made by two testators is invalid.[410] The only valid title of inheritance made by more than one person is the contract of inheritance[411] (*see* below).

857. If several persons make a joint will, it will not be taken into account in the succession proceedings.

407. *Ibid.*, §1546.
408. *Ibid.*, §1548(1), (2).
409. *Ibid.*, §1549.
410. *Ibid.*, §1496.
411. *Ibid.*, §§1582 et seq.

§4. REVOCATION OF A WILL

858. The right to annul a will is a purely personal right of the testator which cannot be waived in advance. If the testator declares that all future acquisitions made by him in the event of his death will be void or that they will be void if not made in a particular form, then this is disregarded.[412]

859. There are two ways to revoke a will under the Civil Code:

1. By making a new will.[413]
2. By revoking the will.[414]

860. The making of a new will revokes the earlier will,[415] but only to the extent that it cannot stand alongside the later will.

861. The previous will is revoked to the extent of the previous will at the time of the making of a new will, whether or not the testator is still living at the time of death and has revoked it, revoked it by making a new will or destroyed the instrument in which the will was made.[416]

862. A new will may revoke the previous one in whole or in part. The revocation of a will may be express, where the testator expressly revokes his previous will, or tacit, where the new will does not contain such an express declaration of revocation of the previous will, but the content shows that, for example, the testator otherwise newly disposes of the same property from the previous will. If the testator makes a different disposition in the first will than in the later will, the two dispositions can then stand side by side.

863. To expressly revoke a will, the form prescribed for making a will must be followed.[417] The revocation of a will by silence is effected by the testator destroying the document on which it was made. However, it is necessary to destroy all the counterparts; the cancellation of only one of several counterparts does not render the will revoked.[418]

864. A breach of the instrument by the testator or a failure to restore the instrument in any other way, even if the testator knows that the will has been destroyed or lost, shall be deemed to invalidate the will if the intention to invalidate is clear from the circumstances.

---

412. *Ibid.*, §1581.
413. *Ibid.*, §1576.
414. *Ibid.*, §§1577 et seq.
415. *Ibid.*, §1576.
416. Decision of the Regional Court in Brno, Case No. 18 Co 385/1998, dated 26 Jul. 1998.
417. Civil Code §1577.
418. *Ibid.*, §1578.

865. A will made by the testator by a public deed shall at any time be subject to the right of the testator to have it delivered to him by a notary. The notary is only obliged to deliver it to the testator in person, and the will is therefore deemed revoked. The notary shall inform the testator of this and shall indicate the fact that the will is deemed revoked. The notary must note on the document to be issued and in his or her file that it has been issued as well as instructing the testator of the consequences of such issue.[419] If the will has been deposited in official custody, the testator also has the right to request its release. However, such release does not have the same effect as a will issued by a notary after it has been drawn up and is therefore not considered revoked.[420]

866. Since the entry into force of the Civil Code, i.e., since 1 January 2014, the rule has been applied according to which, if the testator revokes a more recent will, i.e., one made later, but preserves the earlier one, this situation is viewed as if the original will had not been revoked.[421]

867. Declarations by the testator that all his future acquisitions in the event of his death will be invalid or declarations that only acquisitions in a certain form will be valid have no legal consequences and are not taken into account.[422]

§5. Provisions in the Will and Ancillary Clauses in the Will

868. The intention contained in the last acquisition must be clear and certain. If the incomprehensibility or vagueness of the testator's will could not be eliminated, the legal act would be apparent. However, legal acts are regarded as valid rather than void and, according to §1492(2) of the Civil Code, the testator's will is to be interpreted in the will in such a way as to give effect to his will as far as possible. If only part of the will is invalid, only those parts can be severed and the remainder will be left.[423] If the nullity of a legal act is established to protect the interest of a particular person, only that person may object to the nullity.[424] Possible errors of calculation or spelling are not grounds for sanctioning a legal act if its meaning is otherwise beyond doubt.[425]

869. In the will, the testator calls (designates) the persons who are to be his heirs and may also specify the share he is to acquire from the inheritance or specify which certain things he is to acquire from his estate. The testator may specify the share as a fraction, percentage or call the heirs to specific things. If the testator calls heirs to inherit a particular thing, then that thing must exist at least at the date of his death.

419. *Ibid.*, §1579(1).
420. *Ibid.*, §1579(2).
421. *Ibid.*, §1580.
422. *Ibid.*, §1581.
423. *Ibid.*, §578.
424. *Ibid.*, §586.
425. *Ibid.*, §578.

If the property has been destroyed or transferred to another person by the time of death, the appointment ceases to have legal effect in respect of that property.[426]

870. The testator may specify an obligation to pay a certain amount of money that is not in the estate. This will is valid; the sum of money may represent a specified share of the property acquired by another heir and which must be paid to that heir as his share. This situation can also be dealt with by means of a so-called legacy, where the heir is only obliged to pay another person, the so-called legatee, a certain amount or to hand over an item[427] (*see* below).

871. If the testator calls more than one heir without specifying the shares, they inherit equally.

872. The heir's vocation must be certain. If the heir is not described by name and surname, it is sufficient if he is identified by his relationship to the testator. Therefore, the testator may call, for example, his nieces, nephews and sisters and, if he does not specify anything more, all persons who had this probate relationship to the testator at the time of his death will inherit.

873. The testator may call a substitute heir. The current legislation distinguishes two types of substitute heirs. A general substitute and a fiduciary substitute (called a successor trustee).

874. The testator may call a substitute[428] for the person he/she has called as heir in case the inheritance is not acquired for some reason (e.g., the called heir does not survive the testator). The substitute heir then assumes the legal status of the heir originally called.

875. Fiduciary succession (the so-called fideicomisary substitution), unlike trust succession, is an institution regulating the situation when the testator calls two heirs (the so-called leading heir and the subsequent heir, or the so-called leading heir and the successor in trust) and the second heir acquires the inheritance after the death of the leading heir.[429] However, trust succession can also be established in other cases, which are regulated by the following list:[430]

- The testator prohibits his/her heir from making a disposition of the property left to him/her (thereby ensuring that the legal heirs of that heir inherit).
- The testator calls someone who is not alive at the time of his death (a child, e.g., a grandchild, who is born after his death).
- The settlor calls someone and places a condition or order on them (e.g., to go to college or to look after their dog).

426. Resolution of the Regional Court in Ústí nad Labem, Case No. 5Co/1974, dated 31 Jan. 1974.
427. Civil Code §1594.
428. *Ibid.*, §1507.
429. *Ibid.*, §1512(1).
430. *Ibid.*, §1513.

– The testator calls the leading heir only for a certain period of time (the subsequent heir is to inherit up to five years after his death, for example).

876. Fiduciary succession did not exist in the Czech legal system from 1 April 1964 until 1 January 2014, when the Civil Code No. 89/2012 Coll. included it in its regulation. This expanded the autonomy of the testator's will.

877. A characteristic of fiduciary succession is the testator's attempt to think of a leading heir, but only in a limited way, and thus to establish the right of inheritance to another person. The leading heir has the status of a beneficiary of the inheritance and could only freely dispose of the inheritance if the testator had expressly allowed him to do so in the acquisition. The substitute, i.e., the trustee's successor, is not the heir of the leading heir, but the heir of the testator.[431] The appointment of an heir, both as heir apparent and successor, is a purely personal right of the testator.

878. If the testator calls more than one heir in succession, then if these successors are all alive at the time of the testator's life, their number (series) is not limited.[432] If, however, any of the called successors does not exist at the time of the testator's death (e.g., was not even conceived), this succession will cease when the first of them who was not present at the time of the testator's death acquires the estate.[433]

879. Fiduciary succession is also limited by time. It expires one hundred years after the death of the testator. The exception is where the successor trustee is to acquire the succession no later than after the death of the heir living at the time of the testator's death, then it will cease to exist when the first of the successors trustee acquires the succession.[434]

880. In contrast to the legal regulation of Civil Code 1964, where the conditions in the last acquisition according to §478 of the Civil Code 1964 did not cause any legal consequences, the conditions under the current legal regulation are a common possible content of the so-called secondary clause in the will.[435] For a condition, as well as for a time endorsement or for an order, the general rule applies that if this incidental clause in the will is only intended to cause obvious annoyance to the heir or legatee and is an expression of the testator's manifest arbitrariness, it will be disregarded.[436] The condition may be suspensive or disjunctive. If the testator calls the heir with a condition, the calling is deemed to establish a trust succession. A condition precedent shall not entitle the heir to the inheritance unless he fulfils the condition, while a condition precedent shall cause him to cease to be an heir. If a condition precedent is imposed on the heir or legatee, then it is necessary for the

431. *See* U.N. F 5520.
432. Civil Code §1514.
433. *Ibid.*, §1515(1).
434. *Ibid.*, §1515(2).
435. *Ibid.*, §1551.
436. Judgment of the Supreme Court in Brno, 24 Cdo 2864/2019, dated 5 Mar. 2020.

heir or legatee to survive the testator in order to acquire the right. If the condition imposes on the heir or legatee conduct that may be repeated, then it must be re-executed after the death of the testator, even if it has already occurred during the testator's lifetime, unless the contrary intention of the testator is expressed in the acquisition.[437] An impossible severance condition is disregarded and an impossible postponement condition is invalid.[438]

881. In addition, the testator may, in contrast to the previous legislation in force until 31 December 2013, limit someone's right of inheritance in time. The provision of time means that the heir or legatee is called for a certain period of time or only after a certain period of time has elapsed. Unlike a condition, which must always be uncertain, time is certain to occur.[439]

882. The last possible secondary clause in the will is a command (modus). Again with effect from 1 January 2014, the testator may order the heir or legatee to dispose of the property left behind in a certain way or to do something, refrain from something or to tolerate something. The order may require the heir, for example, to erect a memorial or posthumously organize an exhibition of the deceased's work or to care for a certain person or animal. The law considers an injunction to be a prohibition against alienating or encumbering the inherited property, but here there is a limitation of a reasonable time and a justification of a serious interest worthy of legal protection. In other cases, the court may, on the application of the person aggrieved, decide that the order in question shall be disregarded. It is necessary to distinguish between an order and a condition. It is a condition if the creation or extinction or modification of the right of succession is linked to it. If, however, the testator leaves something to someone with an order attached, it is treated as a condition precedent. If, therefore, the person on whom the order is imposed fails or frustrates its fulfilment, he ceases to be an heir. An order may arise not only from the will of the testator but also directly from the law. Under §1503(3) of the Civil Code, if the testator calls as heirs without specifying the poor or a specified group of persons, the municipality in whose territory the testator was last domiciled is deemed to have been called as heirs. The command is that the municipality must use the property acquired for the benefit of the designated group.

883. The settlor may establish a foundation in his or her last acquisition, both a foundation,[440] and an endowment fund.[441] For these acquisitions, the form of the public deed (notarial deed) must be observed and it must contain, in the case of a foundation, its name, purpose, the amount of the contribution and the conditions for making endowment contributions or the range of persons to whom they may be made. In the case of an endowment fund, the founder shall determine the method of appointment of the first members, the board of directors, the supervisory board and

437. Civil Code §1561.
438. *Ibid.*, §1563.
439. *Ibid.*, §§1564 et seq.
440. *Ibid.*, §§309 et seq.
441. *Ibid.*, §395.

the first members and, in the case of the first auditor. If this is not done, the executor of the will shall appoint them (*see* below). After the death of the testator, foundations and endowments require registration in the Register of Foundations and Endowments.

884. A new institute that returned to the Czech legal system on 1 January 2014 after more than sixty years is the executor of wills.[442] His task is to ensure that the will of the testator is duly executed, which, especially when it comes to setting conditions, proving time or establishing an order or bequest, can be quite necessary. It is also the executor's task to defend the validity of the will, or the validity of the disinheritance of a non-nominee heir, and he may argue against the incapacity of persons who exercise their right contrary to the will of the testator. The executor may also enforce the order,[443] issue a declaration of bequest,[444] and may be entrusted by the testator with the administration of the estate if no administrator is appointed.[445] The executor of the estate is summoned by the testator in the will and is notified by the court in the course of the probate proceedings. The executor always has the right to resign from his/her office, the effects of the resignation take effect when the notification reaches the court.[446] Unlike the administrator of the estate, his or her function may continue after the legal validity of the order on the acquisition of the estate, if this is necessary for the proper execution of the testator's will.

885. Another option of the testator, which was reintroduced into the Czech legal system back on 1 January 2014, is the establishment of a legacy. A bequest establishes the legatee's claim for the delivery of a certain thing or several things of the same kind, or the establishment of a certain right.[447] The testator calls the person of the legatee whom he intends to think in some way, but does not want to call as his heir. The legacy may be movable, immovable, a right, a claim, a pension, a scholarship. The legatee may only be a person eligible to inherit. The testator can only encumber the heirs with legacies in such a way that each is left at least a quarter of the value of the estate unencumbered by legacies.[448] If the testator bequeaths another legacy to the legatee, this is a so-called sub-legacy. The legatee is obliged to comply with it, even if the value of the sub-devise exceeds the value of the legacy. The difference between a direction and a legacy is that a direction imposes an obligation on the legatee to do or not to do something, whereas a legacy imposes an obligation on the legatee to give (perform) something. Thus, an obligatory relationship is established between the heir and the legatee by the will of the testator.

442. *Ibid.*, §1553.
443. *Ibid.*, §1571.
444. *Ibid.*, §1621(2).
445. *Ibid.*, §1554(2).
446. *Ibid.*, §1553(2).
447. *Ibid.*, §1477(1).
448. *Ibid.*, §1597(2).

§6. RESTRICTIONS

I. Heir Apparent

886. The concept of the Czech inheritance law is based on the protection of a relatively narrow circle of persons, which are referred to as non-nominative heirs and who are entitled to a mandatory share of the estate under the law. Non-nominal heirs are the children of the deceased and, if they do not inherit, then their descendants.[449] According to the legislation in force since 2014, a non-nominal heir is not entitled to a share of the estate (in contrast to the legislation under Civil Code No. 40/1964 Coll.), but only to a monetary amount equal to the value of his/her obligatory share. Another significant difference under the previous legislation[450] is the fact that a will which omits a non-nominative heir is not invalid under the current legislation.

887. A minor non-minor heir must receive at least three quarters of his legal share of the inheritance. The minor is then entitled to claim at least one quarter of his/her legal share of the inheritance.[451] The compulsory share may take the form of an inheritance share or a legacy but must be entirely unencumbered.

888. The testator may disinherit the descendant as a non-nominal heir. Disinheritance is a legal act (last acquisition) of the testator by which he deprives his descendant of the right of inheritance and of the right to the obligatory share to which he would otherwise be entitled if he were a qualified heir.[452]

889. A person who has renounced the inheritance or the mandatory share, who is incapable of inheriting or who has been disinherited by the testator shall not be entitled to the mandatory share. In calculating the compulsory shares of the other heirs, he shall be considered as if he had not been excluded from the right of succession.[453]

890. If the disinherited descendant of the testator survives, which is usually the more likely situation, then the effects of the disinheritance deed also apply to the descendants of the disinherited and they do not inherit either. However, the testator may express a contrary will in the will and these descendants of the disinherited descendants will inherit. Should the disinherited descendant die before the testator, his descendants shall inherit unless another reason applies to them for which they are separately excluded from the right of inheritance.

891. The reasons for which the testator may disinherit a descendant as a non-nominal heir under the current legislation are as follows:

---

449. *Ibid.*, §1643(1).
450. Civil Code No. 40/1964 §479.
451. Civil Code §1643(2).
452. *Ibid.*, §1642.
453. *Ibid.*, §1645.

a. he failed to provide the testator with emergency assistance;[454]
b. he showed no real interest in the testator as he should have shown;[455]
c. he has been convicted of a crime committed under circumstances indicative of his depraved character; or
d. he leads a permanently unmanaged life;
e. he is so indebted or behaves so profligately that there is a fear that he will not retain the obligatory share for his descendants (the only reason the disinheritance does not extend to the descendants of the disinherited).

892. The reason for the expulsion must be stated in the deed. If it is not stated, then that heir has the right to the obligor unless a lawful reason for the disinheritance is proved against him.[456] Although people are generally informed of the possibility of disinheriting a descendant, problems can arise when the deed itself is drawn up. In view of current practice, it is clear that the making of a disinheritance deed is a very uncertain legal step in the future and may not be intended after the death of the testator. In the case of a subsequent action for a declaration that the disinheritance deed is invalid, the weak point is proving that the disinheritance deed actually occurred, since the main witness, the testator, is no longer alive. The ability of the other heirs to prove what happened between the disinherited and the testator is very limited. In general, these are interpersonal relationships about which no one kept records, there is no way to prove whether or not anyone offered help, socialized sufficiently or did not socialize, because the testator on the other side did not seek or care to meet either. For these reasons, the only undeniable ground for disinheritance appears to be that the descendant had been convicted by a court of a crime committed in circumstances indicative of his depraved character. Although here again, under the current arrangements, there may be a debate as to what is meant by 'depraved character'. From this perspective, all other grounds for disqualification are rather vague.

893. In the case of the disinheritance ground of failure to provide emergency assistance or to show genuine interest, it must be clear beyond doubt that the testator did not refuse such assistance, according to case law.[457] The need for assistance is assessed in the context of ill health, illness or old age for which the testator was dependent on the care of another person. It will also depend on whether there was no one who could have provided assistance among the persons who shared the household with the deceased. The need for help from a descendant may also arise from other circumstances, such as natural disasters, the loss of a loved one, the threat of loss of life, health or property, etc. According to the rules of morality, a descendant is expected to assist his ancestor during these conditions, which are labelled as 'emergencies' in the law.[458]

454. Decision of the Constitutional Court No. I. ÚS 295/10, dated 7 Nov. 2012.
455. Supreme Court, Case No. 21Cdo 4512/2014, dated 11 May 2015.
456. Civil Code §1648.
457. Decision of the Constitutional Court No. I. ÚS 295/10, dated 7 Nov. 2012.
458. Judgment of the Supreme Court, Case No. 24 Cdo 2440/2021, dated 24 Nov. 2021.

894. The most questionable reasons for disinheritance are failure to show genuine interest and persistence in leading an undirected life. Even for these grounds, the conduct of the offspring in question must be examined through the yardstick of conformity with good morals. In the case of failure to show genuine interest, it is often the case that the testator divorced the mother of the offspring when the offspring was very young and that the mother and father then broke off contact with each other, i.e., that the offspring himself was not at fault.

895. The grounds for disinheritance are adopted in the current legislation, with minor exceptions, from the legislation contained in ABGB 1811.

896. The intestate heir, i.e., the descendant, will not inherit if he/she has waived his/her right of inheritance in a contract as a future heir with the future testator.[459] Whoever waives the right of inheritance also waives the right to the obligatory share and the waiver shall also operate against his descendants, unless otherwise agreed by the parties. An heir who has renounced the right of inheritance may not bring an action for the delivery of the inheritance. A future heir may also waive his right of succession in favour of a specific person. The scope of the renunciation is dispositive. The contract of renunciation requires the form of a public deed (notarial deed). The contract of revocation of the waiver may then be made in a simple written form.

459. Civil Code §1484.

Chapter 3. Inheritance Contract

897. As of 1 January 2014, the succession contract returned to the Czech legal system after more than sixty years.[460] It is the strongest legal title as it cannot be unilaterally revoked, unlike a will.

898. The succession contract is a mixed legal structure, which has elements of a will and elements of a contract. Therefore, both the law on contracts[461] and the law on acquisition on death apply to it.

899. In the contract of inheritance, the testator calls the other party or a third person as heir and the other party accepts the call. The contract of succession may be concluded by an adult testator who is fully competent. Thus, a person under 18 years of age cannot conclude a contract of succession, even if he or she has been granted full legal capacity by the court.

900. The content of the contract of succession is the call to inheritance. The contractual testator may call a contractual heir to inherit, but not more than three quarters of the entire estate. The remaining quarter must remain free, which the testator may, for example, acquire by will. This leaves him the possibility of disposing of this part until his death.

901. It is possible to add a condition to the contract of inheritance, but unlike a will, it is possible for the contracting heir to fulfil it during his or her lifetime.[462]

902. In contrast, the contracting testator may be limited in his/her legal capacity and may conclude the contract of succession with the consent of his/her guardian. This person may conclude a contract of succession to the extent that he or she has not been reduced in his or her legal capacity.

903. The other party to the contract of succession is the contracting heir, which can be either a natural or a legal person. The parties to the contract of succession may call for succession unilaterally or mutually. They may also agree in the contract to call a third party to inherit. Unless the parties to the contract agree otherwise, the party who is called as heir cannot transfer his right to another person.

904. There are specifics related to the contract of succession if the parties are spouses. In the event of a divorce, the succession contract remains valid, but either spouse may seek to have the succession contract annulled by the court. The court will only grant the application if it is directed against the spouse who caused the divorce.

---

460. *Ibid.*, §§1582 to 1593.
461. *Ibid.*, §§1721 et seq.
462. *Ibid.*, §1587.

905. During his lifetime, the contractual testator is free to dispose of the property he has included in the contract of inheritance.[463] However, if the contractual testator acquires other, competing acquisitions in the event of death or enters into a gift agreement with someone in respect of the same property, the future contractual testator may claim the relative ineffectiveness of these legal acts.

906. The testator may, in addition to a new revocation agreement, revoke the contractual profession by a subsequent will, but this needs the consent of the contractual heir, made in the form of a public deed.[464]

907. If the contract of succession does not meet the statutory prerequisites, but fulfils the requirements for a will, then the contract of succession can be converted into a will. This will be the case, for example, if the statutory form of the public deed for the succession contract is not observed or if the testator does not leave a quarter of the estate free in the contract.[465]

§1. Maintenance Provisions

908. The maintenance obligation between family members ceases upon the death of the beneficiary or obligor. A certain kind of protection is granted to the non-delegable heirs in the form of the right to payment of the obligatory share in money.[466] The Civil Code also provides for certain protection for 'certain persons' who, under the conditions laid down by law, are granted the right to provision against the heir. This provision is in fact in the form of a statutory legacy; i.e., persons may claim from the heir if they fulfil the conditions laid down by law, a certain portion of their inheritance. These persons are:[467]

- A non-probate heir who is not entitled to a compulsory share,[468] is entitled to so-called necessary maintenance from the estate, if he is not receiving it, is unable to support himself, his descendant does not inherit, nor is he called upon to make a compulsory share. This heir shall be entitled to a maximum of the amount of his obligatory share.
- The surviving spouse is entitled to reasonable maintenance from the estate for six weeks after the death of the spouse.
- A pregnant widow and the unwed mother of the testator's child are entitled to adequate maintenance until the end of the sixth week after the birth.
- A surviving spouse who has been denied or curtailed by the statutory ground has the right to the necessary provision until remarriage if he/she is unable to provide for himself/herself, if he/she is not an incapable heir, if he/she has not renounced or refused the inheritance, if he/she shared the family household with the

463. *Ibid.*, §1588.
464. *Ibid.*, §1590.
465. *Ibid.*, §1591.
466. *See* Part IV, Ch. 1, §1.
467. Civil Code §§1665 et seq.
468. *Ibid.*, §1656.

deceased (or did not share but had good reason to do so). This necessary provision may not be made if it would diminish the right of a non-minor heir.

- A surviving parent who has not been left a legal share or has been left less than one-third of his/her legal share of the inheritance is entitled to the necessary provision if he/she is not receiving such provision, is unable to support himself/herself, is not incapable of inheriting, has not renounced or refused the inheritance.
- Persons who, until the death of the deceased, received free provision in the deceased's home are entitled to the same provision for three weeks after death.

Chapter 4. Legal Actions Between the Living Related to the Estate

§1. Planning for the Future Disposal of the Estate

909. Among notaries who have been involved in probate proceedings all their lives, it is often said that a good notary dies in poverty. This is not because notarial work represents a small income, but quite the opposite. Notaries have spent much time with heirs who have been unable to agree on assets of even a small value. Protracted litigation ensued and the estate thus destroyed many family relationships.

910. In principle, considerations about the possible obligations involved in paying the fees associated with the probate procedure do not in any way force persons who are married, have descendants and a number of other relatives to entrust their property to future heirs while still alive.

911. From 1 January 2014, Act No. 340/2013 Coll. abolished the statutory tax obligation associated with the acquisition of inheritance. Since then, inheritance is among the income that is exempt from tax liability. However, it is necessary to pay a fee to the notary, which is due under the law for conducting inheritance proceedings as a court commissioner. This fee is due to him on the basis of Act No. 292/2013 Coll., on Special Court Proceedings, and its amount is regulated by the Decree.[469]

912. The notary's fee as a court commissioner under the decree in question is:

> On the first 500,000 CZK of the base 2%, on the excess amount up to 1000000 CZK of the base 0.9%, on the excess amount up to 3000000 CZK of the base 0.5%, on the excess amount up to 30000000 CZK it is 0.1%. On the excess amount up to 100 000 000,-Kč it is 0.05% and the amount above 100 000 000,-Kč of the base it is 0%.

913. The notary's fee is much higher if the liquidation of the estate is ordered.

§2. Donation on Death

914. Donation on death was reintroduced into the Czech legal system by the current Civil Code as of 1 January 2014. The testator as donor may conclude a contract with the donee, with the donation contract becoming effective only upon the death of the testator.[470] The donee accepts the gift, and the donor expressly waives his right to revoke the gift and issues a deed to the donee to that effect. Another condition of this gift is that the donee survives the donor. For greater legal certainty, the donor and donee should enter into a contract prohibiting alienation or encumbrance of the property subject to the gift. In the case of immovable property, the in

469. Decree No. 196/2001 Coll.
470. Civil Code §2063.

rem effect is then established by registration in the Land Registry. In the proceedings of the estate, the assets and liabilities of the estate include its obligations under the contract. If immovable property is the subject of the contract, then also this[471] property is then acquired by the donee on the basis of a resolution on the acquisition of inheritance, which is witnessed by the heir and in which he is obliged to deliver the subject of the gift contract to the donee, retroactively to the date of death of the testator, as donor.

§3. Insurance Contracts

915. In addition to property insurance and liability insurance, Czech law also provides insurance in case of death, bodily injury, reaching a certain age, or other events.

916. An insurance contract may also be concluded in favour of a third party.[472] The insurer may then undertake to the policyholder to provide the third party with an insurance benefit. It should be remembered that this person is called upon at the time the contract is negotiated, but the insured event may occur a long time afterwards. Therefore, the person to be insured must be identified in the insurance policy in a precise, definite and unmistakable manner, preferably by name, surname, date of birth, because if there were only a name, there could be more than one such person at the time of the insured's death. If the person to be bypassed is identified only by the name of the relationship, it is possible that all such persons (i.e., siblings, children, etc.) will be bypassed. The two ways of designating the bypassed person cannot be combined, as there could be considerable indeterminacy (e.g., if the wife is not designated by name and/or the person of that name is no longer the wife). Such a designation would be disregarded for vagueness unless it could be removed by interpretation.[473]

917. In the event of an incorrect date of birth of the insured in a life insurance policy, the insurer has the right to withdraw from the contract if it proves that it would not have concluded the contract in view of the insurance conditions in force at the time of conclusion of the contract. However, this right shall lapse if the insurer has not exercised it within two months of becoming aware of it, but at the latest, within three years of the conclusion of the contract.[474] If the insured and the survivor die at the same time or under circumstances which make it impossible to determine which of them died first, the insured shall be deemed to have survived the survivor. At that point, upon the death of the insured, his heirs would succeed to the rights under the policy, not the insured.

---

471. Judgment of the Municipal Court of Prague, 33 Ca 228/1994.
472. Civil Code §2758.
473. *Ibid.*, §553.
474. *Ibid.*, §2835.

918. If the policyholder designates his or her spouse as the assured person, and if the designation has been agreed to be irrevocable, the effects of the designation shall cease upon divorce or annulment of the marriage.[475] If the assured person designated as the assured person is an ancestor or descendant, and if the designation has been agreed to be irrevocable, the effects of the designation shall cease upon adoption by the assured person or the policyholder.

475. *Ibid.*, §2836.

Chapter 5. Distribution and Administration of the Estate

§1. Probate Proceedings

919. As already mentioned, the succession is acquired on the death of the testator, but the acquisition of the succession is confirmed by the court, which confirms it to the person whose right of succession has been established. The right to the estate, or a proportionate share of it, is already acquired by the heirs at the time of death; the court then only declaratively confirms what assets the heirs have acquired or how much of the estate they are entitled to (and this retroactively to the date of the death of the testator).

920. Since 1 January 1993, succession proceedings have been under the jurisdiction of the courts.[476] Until then, succession proceedings were under the jurisdiction of notaries. However, on the basis of Act No. 263/1992 Coll., they perform the position of the so-called Commissioner of Inheritance in the court proceedings.[477]

921. As of 1 January 2014, probate proceedings have been subject to the provisions of the Act on Special Court Proceedings.[478] Probate proceedings are initiated even without a petition, at the moment when the court learns of the death of the deceased.[479] These are so-called uncontested proceedings.

922. The purpose of the probate proceedings is to establish the circle of the testator's heirs and to determine the assets and debts of the testator (assets and liabilities of the estate).

923. For the Judicial Commissioner to establish the circle of heirs, this includes an enquiry at the Central Register of Wills.[480] In this, he or she will find out whether the deceased has left behind a contract of succession, a will, a declaration of disinheritance, a contract of renunciation of the right of inheritance or a deed revoking these legal acts.[481] In addition, the judicial commissioner ascertains information about the heirs as part of the preliminary investigation, including by ascertaining information about the heirs from lists or systems established and maintained under special regulations, which is most often the central population register.[482] Another task of the notary is to ascertain the content of the legal acts in the event of death; if the documents contain information about witnesses, then he will also question these witnesses. One of the most important procedural acts that the court commissioner does is to inform the known heirs of their right to inherit and to instruct these

476. Act No. 263/1992 Coll.
477. Act on Special Court Proceedings, §100.
478. Act on Special Court Proceedings.
479. *Ibid.*, §138/2.
480. The Central Register of Wills is a non-public list maintained since 1 Jan. 2001 in electronic form by the Notary Chamber of the Czech Republic.
481. Act on Special Court Proceedings, §140.
482. Act No. 133/2000Sb.

heirs of their right to refuse the inheritance and of their right to reserve the inventory of the estate (*see* below). It is also his duty to inform unknown heirs or heirs of unknown residence of their right to inherit by means of a decree.[483] The Judicial Commissioner also assesses the conditions of the right of succession on the basis of legal reasoning[484] or the established procedure for resolving a factual dispute.[485]

924. Finally, it issues a decree of succession, which is declaratory in nature and has retroactive effect to the date of the testator's death, in the following forms:

- Confirms the acquisition of the inheritance to the sole heir.
- Distributes the estate among the several heirs according to the testator's decree and confirms the acquisition of the estate by the several heirs according to the distribution.
- Distributes the estate among several heirs as determined by the third person appointed by the testator and confirms the acquisition of the estate by several heirs.
- Approves the agreement of the heirs on the division of the estate, which is not contrary to law, and confirms the acquisition of the inheritance by more than one heir in accordance therewith.
- Distributes the estate among several heirs at their request if the conditions laid down by law are fulfilled and shall confirm the acquisition of the estate by the several heirs according to the distribution.
- Confirms the acquisition of the succession to several heirs according to the shares of the estate, the amount of which has been determined in accordance with the law by agreement of the heirs if there has been no division of the estate.
- Confirms the acquisition of the succession to several heirs according to the legal shares of inheritance if there has been no division of the estate and no agreement of the heirs on the amount of the shares of inheritance.
- Certifies that the succession has passed to the State if no heir inherits either under the contract of succession or the will or under the legal succession.

925. Ascertaining the deceased's assets and debts is the second of the two important components of the probate process. The assets and liabilities are ascertained by the judicial commissioner from the content of the documents he/she searches in the Central Register of Deeds maintained by the Chamber of Notaries.[486] He or she also searches for information on the deceased's assets, if any, in public registers, in particular the Land Registry, the Commercial Register, the Motor Vehicle Register and the bank. It ascertains whether the testator left any property at all or, if not, whether the property is of a so-called small value,[487] which would mean that the succession proceedings would be terminated on that ground.

483. Act on Special Court Proceedings, §166.
484. *Ibid.*, §169.
485. *Ibid.*, §170.
486. *Ibid.*, §140 and §142.
487. *Ibid.*, §153 and §154.

926. An important change brought by the Civil Code as of 1 January 2014, which has been reflected procedurally in the Act on Special Court Proceedings since the same date, is the obligation of the court commissioner to instruct the heirs on the right to reserve an inventory of the estate,[488] which is more often replaced in practice by a simpler list that the administrator of the estate draws up and all heirs sign. It is also possible to replace the inventory with a joint declaration of the heirs of the estate or to draw up a list of assets and liabilities on the basis of the heirs' data. This declaration has the function of limiting the liability of the heirs for the debts of the deceased, and if this inventory (list) is made, the heirs are only obliged to pay the debts of the deceased up to the amount of the assets listed in the inventory (list).[489]

927. Another act of the court commissioner concerning the assets and debts in the estate is the invitation to creditors to submit their claims within the statute period.[490] In the case where the testator was married and had community of property, it addresses what, if any, the other spouse will inherit on settlement of the community of property extinguished by death and which part of the community of property will be subject to inheritance.[491]

928. The jurisdiction of the Czech court to hear and decide cases in the context of proceedings concerning the estate is always given, unless it falls under certain proceedings with a foreign element (*see* below). If the CR court finds that the matter does not fall within the jurisdiction of the CR court, it shall, by order, discontinue the proceedings. If the EU Regulation 650/212 applies to the succession proceedings in question, the court will declare that it has no jurisdiction.

929. Jurisdiction over the estate lies with the district courts in the first instance, the district courts in Prague and the Municipal Court in Brno.[492]

930. Local jurisdiction is called exclusive jurisdiction.[493] Under the Special Court Proceedings Act, the court with jurisdiction over the estate is the local court in whose district:

a. did the deceased have permanent residence at the time of death;
b. was the testator's last residence or place of residence;
c. is the deceased's immovable property, unless jurisdiction is established under the two above criteria;
d. the deceased has died if local jurisdiction is not available according to the above criteria.

488. *Ibid.*, §177 and §179.
489. Civil Code §1684.
490. Act on Special Court Proceedings, §174.
491. *Ibid.*, §162.
492. *Ibid.*, §3/1.
493. *Ibid.*, §98.

§2. INHERITANCE WITH AN INTERNATIONAL ELEMENT

931. If there is an international element in the inheritance, i.e., the person to be inherited or the person who is to be a party to the succession proceedings has a significant factual or legal relationship outside the Czech Republic or assets located outside the Czech Republic, then the following sources of legislation must be applied:

a. national legislation (in particular, the Civil Code and Law 292/2013Sb);
b. EU legislation;
c. international treaties.

932. The basic source of private international law in the Czech Republic since 1 January 2014 is the Private International Law Act.[494] The importance of this source in the field of inheritance law has decreased relatively. According to Regulation No. 650/2012 of the European Parliament and of the Council, this legal norm applies to the succession of persons who died after 17 August 2015. The Regulation applies to the inheritance of the estate of deceased persons, but it does not apply to tax, customs and administrative matters.

§3. ADMINISTRATION OF THE ESTATE

933. During the duration of the succession proceedings, which can be quite lengthy, care must be taken to ensure that the assets subject to the proceedings are properly administered.

934. The administration of the estate can be carried out by the following persons under the current legislation:[495]

a. the administrator called by the testator;
b. the executor of the will (unless an administrator has been appointed by the testator);
c. heir, if neither of the above two have been called;
d. in the case of multiple heirs and in the absence of an agreement between them, then all heirs;
e. an administrator appointed by the court without a petition.[496]

935. According to its basic mission, which is to carry out the so-called simple administration of the estate of the testator,[497] the administrator has the following tasks, which are, for example:

---

494. Act No. 91/2012 Coll.
495. Civil Code §1677.
496. Act on Special Court Proceedings, §157/1 to 3.
497. Civil Code §1678.

- the provision of benefits to persons who are entitled to them pursuant to §1665 et seq. of the Civil Code;
- informs referrers of their links and settles links that are due;
- ensures compliance with the reference;
- dealing with creditors who seek satisfaction of their claims against the deceased;
- proposes that, in order to locate the debts of the deceased, the court should invite the creditors to declare and prove their claims within a reasonable time;[498]
- sells, with the approval of the court, property that cannot be preserved without risk of damage or disproportionate cost;
- notify the bank with which the deceased had accounts of the deceased's death;
- notify the deceased's known creditors and debtors of the deceased's death;
- draw up a list of the estate if the court has decided that it shall replace the inventory of the estate.[499]

936. The administration shall terminate at the latest by the order confirming the succession. The administration may also be terminated earlier, e.g., when the administrator has completed the task entrusted to him. The administrator also has the right to resign from his/her office; the resignation is effective from the moment it reaches the court.[500] For serious breaches of his/her duties, the administrator (as well as the executor of the will) may be dismissed by the court, even without a petition. The office of administrator of the estate ceases on the date on which the order for the liquidation of the estate is made.[501]

937. The administrator is entitled to the usual remuneration according to the nature of the services.[502] If he was called by the testator, the latter could determine in the last acquisition whether and how the administrator should be remunerated. If the administrator was appointed by the court, he is entitled to the remuneration due to him under the Decree on the remuneration and compensation of notaries, administrators of estates and the Chamber of Notaries.[503]

498. *Ibid.*, §1711.
499. *Ibid.*, §1687(1).
500. *Ibid.*, §1559.
501. Act on Special Court Proceedings, §200.
502. Civil Code §1402(1).
503. Decree No. 196/2001SB., as amended by Decree No. 432/2013, §22 to §24.

Selected Bibliography

Civil Code Wording Effective in 2001 (Translation and Commentary in English). Prague: Trade Links, 2000.

Cepl, V. 'Bottlenecks in the Transformation of Eastern Europe'. *Journal of Law and Policy* 4, Washington University (2000).

Haderka, J. 'The Importance of Recent Changes in the Law'. *Journal of Family Law* 9, Kentucky, USA, University of Louisville (1985).

Haderka, J. *Surrogate Motherhood: Especially from the Legal Point of View*. Reports of the 7th World Congress on Medical Law, Vol. 1. Gent, Belgium, 1985.

Haderka, J. 'The Legal Regulation of Artificial Reproduction in Czechoslovak Law with Special Reference to Other European Socialist Countries'. *International Journal of the Law and the Family* 1, Oxford, UK (1987).

Haderka, J. *Czechoslovakia: Abortion and Social Security Reforms*. Annual Survey of Family Law, Vol. 11. Kentucky, USA: University of Louisville, 1988–1989.

Haderka, J. 'The Civil Law System in Czechoslovakia: Past and Present'. *Journal of the Law Society of Scotland* 34 (1989): 7.

Haderka, J. *Harmonisation du droit de la famille tchéque avec les exigences des documents internationaux touchant la situation de l'enfant*. Rapports du colloque á l'Universite jean Moulin de Lyon, 1995.

Haderka, J. *A Half-Hearted Family Law Reform in 1998*. International Survey of Family Law, 1998.

Hrusakova, M. 'Family Law in Czechoslovakia after the Revolution'. *International Journal of Law and the Family* 7, Oxford, UK (1993).

Hrusakova, M. 'Die neue Regelung der Eheschliesung in Tschechische Republik'. *Zeitschrift für das gesamte Familienrecht*, 1994, 6.

Hrusakova, M. 'Der Schutz der Familienwohnung im tschechischen Recht'. In *Der Schutz der Familenwohnung in Europäischen Rechtsordnungen*, edited by Henrich & Schwab. Gieseking – Bielfeld: BRD, 1995.

Hrusakova, M. 'Unterhaltspflichten im tschechischen Familienrecht'. In *Familiäre Solidarität. Die Begründung und die Grenzen der Unterhaltspflicht unter Verwandten*, edited by Henrich & Schwab. Gieseking – Bielfeld: BRD, 1997.

Hrusakova, M. 'Neuregelung der vermögensrechtlichen Beziehungen der Ehegatten untereinander in der Tchechischen Republik'. In *Gemeinschaft, Partnerschaft und Vermögen im europäischen Vergleich*, edited by Henrich & Schwab. Gieseking – Bielefeld: BRD, 1999.

Hrusakova, M. 'Tschechisches Gesetz über die registrierte partnerschaft'. *Zeitschrift für das gesamte Familienrecht* 18 (2006): 1337–1339.

Selected Bibliography

Hurdik, J. 'Die Konzeption und das System der juristischen Personen in der Tschechischen'. Republik, in *Entwicklung des Zivilrechts in Osteuropa* 5. Dresden: Band, 1998.

Knapp, V. 'Il Diritto Comparato e il Crollo del Comunismo'. *Rivista di diritto civile*, 1996.

Müller, W. 'Zur Diskussion um die systematische Einordnung des Familienrechts'. *Rabels Zeitschrift*, 1973.

Radvanova, S. 'L'évolution de la réglementation juridique du placement des enfants en famille nourricieres. République Tcheque'. In *L'enfant et les familles nourricieres en droit comparé*. Presses de l'Université des sciences sociales de Toulouse, 1997.

Westphalová, L. *Rechtliche Aspekte zum Thema Beendigung einer Ehe in der Tschechischen Republik, ZfRV (Zeitschrift für Rechtsvergleichung, Internationales Privatrecht und Europarecht)*, č. 3, MANZ, Wien 2006, 93–98, ISSN 0514-275X.

Zuklinova, M. *Problemi in materie di rapporti matrimoniali e sociale in Europa,* edited by Milano: di Communita, 1999.

Zuklinova, M. *Marriage Report – Czech Republic*. Milano: Dott. A. Giuffré Editore, 1998.

Selected Bibliography in Czech (Textbooks, Commentaries and Monographs)

Elias, K. & M. Zuklinova. *Principy a vychodiska noveho kodexu soukromeho prava (Principles of New Private Law Codex)*. Prague: Linde, 2001.

Fiala, J., et al. *Obcanske pravo (Civil Law)*. Textbook, 3rd edn. Masarykova: Universita Brno, 2002.

Haderka, J. *Uzavirani manzelstvi z hlediska pravniho (Conclusion of Marriage)*. Prague: Academia, 1977.

Holub, M. & H. Nova. *Zakon o rodine a predpisy souvisici (Family Code)*. Prague: Linde 2000.

Hrusakova, M. *Dite, rodina, stat (Child, Family, State)*. Masarykova: Universita Brno, 1994.

Hrusakova, M. & Z. Kralickova. *Ceske rodinne pravo (Czech Family Law)*. Textbook, 3rd edn. Masarykova: Universita Brno, 2006.

Hrusakova, M., et al. *Family Code Commentary*. 4th edn. Prague: C.H. Beck, 2009.

Hurdik, J., J. Fiala & M. Hrusakova. *Uvod do soukromeho prava (Introduction in Private Law)*. Masarykova: Universita Brno, 1997.

Jehlicka, J., et al. *Civil Code Commentary*. 8th edn. Prague: C.H. Beck, 2001.

Knappova, M. & J. Svestka (eds). *Obcanske pravo hmotne I., II., III. (Civil Substantial Law)*. Textbook. Prague: ASPI, 2005.

Kralíčková, Z., M. Hrušáková & L. Westphalová. *Civil Code Commentary*. 2nd edn. Prague. C.H. Beck, 2020.

Křáĺíčková, Z., M. Hrušáková & L. Westphalová. *Family Law*. 3rd edn. Prague: C.H. Beck, 2022.

Kucera, R. *Dedictvi (Inheritance)*. Prague: Linde, 2001.

Mikes, J. *Dedicke pravo (Law of Succession)*. Prague: Informatorium, 1993.

Radvanova, S. & M. Zuklinova. *Instituty rodinneho prava (Institutes of Family Law)*. Prague: C.H. Beck, 1999.

Radvanova, S. *O rodine, manzelstvi a detech (About the Family, Marriage and Children)*. Prague, 1978.

Tezka, O. & H. Nova. *Vyzivovaci povinnost (Maintenance Duty)*. Prague: Linde, 1995.

Selected Journals Publishing Family Law and Successional Law Articles

Ad notam (Specialized for notaries).
Bulletin advokacie (Specialized for barristers).
Pravni praxe (Legal Practice, for all branches of law).
Pravni radce (Legal Adviser, for all branches of law).
Pravni rozhledy (Legal Review, for all branches of law).
Pravnik (Lawyer, theory of law).
Pravo a rodina (Law and Family).
Soudce (Judge).
Soudni rozhledy (Specialized in court practice).

Index

The numbers here refer to paragraph numbers.

Index

Index

www.ingramcontent.com/pod-product-compliance
Ingram Content Group UK Ltd.
Pitfield, Milton Keynes, MK11 3LW, UK
UKHW020136290926
15471UKWH00003B/512